Sir Vivian

Sir Vivian

The Definitive Autobiography

VIV RICHARDS

with Bob Harris

MICHAEL JOSEPH

LONDON

To my Mother and Father

MICHAEL JOSEPH
Published by the Penguin Group
Penguin Books Ltd, 27 Wrights Lane, London w8 5tz, England
Penguin Putnam Inc., 375 Hudson Street, New York, New York 10014, USA
Penguin Books Australia Ltd, Ringwood, Victoria, Australia
Penguin Books Canada Ltd, 10 Alcorn Avenue, Toronto, Ontario, Canada m4v 3b2
Penguin Books (NZ) Ltd, Private Bag 102902, NSMC, Auckland, New Zealand

Penguin Books Ltd, Registered Offices: Harmondsworth, Middlesex, England

First published 2000

5

Copyright © Vivian Richards, 2000
The moral right of the author has been asserted

The publishers wish to thank the following copyright holders for use of their photographs:
Patrick Eager: 4, 5, 6, 7, 8, 9, 10, 11, 12, 13, 14, 15, 16, 17, 18, 21, 22, 25, 26, 27, 29, 30, 31, 32, 33, 37;
Camera Press: 19; Allsport: 20, 23, 24, 28, 34, 35, 38, 39; Melanie J. Etherington: 36.

Set in 12/14.75 pt Monotype Bembo
Typeset by Rowland Phototypesetting Ltd,
Bury St Edmunds, Suffolk
Printed in England by Clays Ltd, St Ives plc

A CIP catalogue record for this book is available from the British Library

ISBN 0-718-14434-1

Contents

Acknowledgments

Viv Richards and Bob Harris would like to thank their editor Rowland White for his enthusiasm, effort and professionalism; Jonathan Harris and Jane Morgan; Paul Clarke and Virgin Airways.

Prologue

My eyelids flick open as the roar of the crowd outside the dressing-room signals the fall of the first West Indies wicket and gives me my usual alarm call.

The clock is running and officially I have two minutes to make my way from the comfort and sanctuary of the physiotherapist's massage table to the middle. But there is no rush. This is a long tried and tested routine. After all, it is my livelihood, how I earn my money and how I fulfil the dreams of a boy from a little Caribbean island called Antigua and Barbuda.

I check the most important pieces of equipment again: pads are fastened, the essential box is in place and bootlaces are tied. It's hot – but then, apart from those first few weeks of an English season, it usually is, for cricket is essentially a warm-weather sport. Having been born under the sun, I prefer it this way. But, despite my upbringing, I sweat a lot, and I splash some cold water on to my face from the sink in the corner both to cool me down and to wash any sleep from my eyes. I select the number one bat from my current collection of five. I always have four or five bats with me, including my best and most trustworthy. Every bat is categorized and numbered from one to five. I give each of them marks out of ten. There is always one with a little more beef than the others, and another one that comes down with a little less weight for a quicker bowler. The reasoning is that if I am going to take up the challenge of a real pacey man, I want a bat I can fan around, not something so heavy that by the time you get it up around your head the ball is already in the wicket-keeper's gloves. No, if that happens you are already defeated. I then pick up my batting gloves, pop a piece of chewing gum in my mouth and put another couple of sticks in my pocket. Finally, my treasured West Indian cap. I wouldn't want to go out to bat without it, for it is my symbol. I am proud of that maroon cap and proud to wear it. Helmet? Forget it. I tried one once in a dressing-room and felt trapped. I like to be free, to live on my nerves and be able to react in a fraction of a second against the bully at the other end who is trying to rip off my head. From the length of my sleep in the dressing-room it is fairly obvious that the fast bowlers are still in action and the ball is still hard and new, encouraging the slips and short legs to crowd round the wicket for the new batsman. With everything in order, I make my way through the dressing-room into the harsh light of day and out towards the wicket.

It is a long familiar walk, and on the way I have a routine that helps me to keep focused. I tap my bat on the ground as I walk purposefully towards the wicket. This action, like my so-called swagger, is perceived in some quarters as arrogance. It is far more basic than that, because I am assuring myself that the rubber grip on my bat handle has not ridden up. But if the opposition see my walk and my actions as intimidating, then I am not going to disillusion them. I want them to know that I am confident and that I am not going to allow them to gain any early psychological advantage over me. Little or nothing is said as I pass my outgoing team mate. He probably wishes me luck, but I don't hear either him or the crowd. My mind is set, and the last thing I need to hear either from him or from the not-out batsman is how well the bowler is bowling or how badly the wicket is playing. My mind is clear of gremlins because I did not see the last wicket fall and, apart from the first couple of balls bowled, I have seen none of the cricket. This is now my war. Me and my chewing gum against the world – well, at least eleven men who want to see me back in the pavilion or on the way to hospital. Particularly the one with the ball in his hand in the far distance, the one pawing the ground like an enraged bull, his tail up after claiming a victim with his previous delivery. He is a bully. Most fast bowlers are by their very nature. It is up to me to tame him, both for the sake of my team and probably my continued good health.

Gloves on, I ask the umpire for guard: leg stump. Once at the crease, I first tap my thigh guard then make sure that my body and arms are adequately protected, and that I am wearing a box covering my most tender area. That is one place you don't want to be hit without the protection of armour. I have seen more than one of my colleagues rush back to the pavilion when they have realized their omission.

I take in the field at a glance, pat my bat once again and finally look up at my mortal enemy as he picks up pace at the far end of the ground. In a quick mental snapshot I want to see how he is holding the ball and his body language, to see beyond his eyes into his soul, to find out everything I can about this man who is hell-bent on my destruction. My face is set and my eyes, I know, are cold and fixed. I am ready to take up the challenge again. The comments from the close fielders and the roar of the crowd merge into a blur of background noise as I lift my favourite bat and focus on the hard piece of red leather with its razor-sharp seam hurtling towards me at almost a hundred miles an hour . . .

The build-up to the most memorable innings of my cricket career scarcely gave a hint of what was to come. What is more, it is not a score that anyone will easily find by scanning the history books. I have no doubt that when my best innings are discussed, most people would think that I would go for one of the World Cup Finals or the fastest hundred against England, or that my century in St John's in the first test match on my home island would be the one. But this one was special for lots of reasons. There was little to suggest that this game, in February 1983, would be anything out of the ordinary and, indeed, it raised only a passing stir of interest outside the two competing countries, West Indies and India. In fact, if anything, I was pretty down at the time. I had broken my right thumb playing for the Leeward Islands against Guyana in Antigua when the ball was hurled in from the outfield and busted my hand as I took it behind the stumps. The injury made me very doubtful for the first test against India. There was no question of having a net as I could not even hold a bat, so I couldn't practise and all I could do was to keep myself physically fit. The situation was becoming more than a little frustrating. What is more, the game was to be played at Sabina Park in Jamaica and that set me in my mind turning back the scorebook pages to previous innings – or, rather, the lack of them – at one of my favourite grounds. It was amazing because I have always felt that I had incredible support in Jamaica. The crowd were always loud, raucous and very knowledgeable. I have always felt close to them and they have given me tremendous support over the years. Because of the mixtures of races we have on some of the other islands, for example Guyana and Trinidad, when India are the visitors sometimes those with Asian backgrounds find it hard to make up their mind who to support. But the grounds in Jamaica, along with those in Barbados, were always where I found my best support – at least until St John's became a cricket venue in my native Antigua. Jamaica in particular created the same sort of sporting atmosphere I had experienced when I watched England play football at Wembley or Liverpool at Anfield. I always felt their love for me, and for years I tried hard – maybe too hard – to thank them for their support and to fulfil what they felt about me. They knew what I could do, having listened on their radios, as all West Indians do wherever they are and wherever the cricket is being played in the world, and some of them had watched my better innings on their televisions. But I wanted to show them Viv Richards at full flow in the flesh.

But today, thoughts of a fifty – never mind a big century – seemed a lot to ask. The routines are set in stone, however you feel. Every cricketer goes through his own little side-show and I was no different; in fact was probably worse than most, though with less gear to take to games, what with having no helmet and only minimal protection. I suppose the routines – checking my gear, chewing my gum – helped me to focus, but the injury took its toll. In order to protect my thumb, I couldn't even field in the slips, and I took just the one catch in the outfield off Andy Roberts to send back Dilip Vengsarkar. I batted first wicket down and felt very rusty and dull as I scraped together 29 before giving a catch to Venkat off Ravi Shastri. It was hardly the sort of display I wanted to give those colourful Jamaican fans. The entire match seemed to have taken on a slightly unreal atmosphere; there was no urgency, particularly among the Indian batsmen when we were bowling in the second innings. Everything was dead, totally flat, the game was gently petering out to a draw and the stadium was becoming emptier and emptier as people left, convinced that there would be no result, a tame draw – and West Indian people loathe that sort of cricket. However, it didn't work out that way, as my Antiguan countryman Andy Roberts came in with a demanding spell and broke the back of the innings, finishing with five for 39. They lost their last four wickets for 6 runs. But although India, as a result, was bowled out for 174, it still left us needing 172 to win with just half an hour plus 20 overs in which to score them. The game still looked to be heading inevitably for a draw, especially with bowlers like Kapil Dev, Singh Sandhu, Venkataraghavan and Mohinder Amarnath defending an admittedly low total but with so little time. This was no one-day match with restricted fielding and there couldn't have been anyone outside our dressing-room who thought this would be anything other than a stalemate. Even I thought that we would just go and bat it out.

But our captain, Clive Lloyd, thought differently. He decided to give it the charge, telling us to go out and fire on all cylinders, take a chance and give it the gun, at least until we had lost six wickets or so. When he gave these instructions, my adrenalin began to flow and suddenly there was no need for preparing for a particular match or a particular innings. This sort of thing was unheard of in a test match, a huge challenge. I felt I had been given the licence to go for it. There were others in the team who thought we might be committing suicide, but Clive won them over despite the empty ground and unreal atmosphere.

We went for it!

I watched the first couple of deliveries because we were approaching something unusual. I was curious to find out what sort of start we were going to have. Then, as I saw things were going quietly, and with Clive promoting himself to number three (quite rightly in the circumstances), I began to relax. I was helped in my preparations knowing that when the skipper gives you the licence to be free it is the greatest feeling of all for a batsman of my nature. Normally the skipper is annoyed when batsmen play certain shots and get themselves out with a soft dismissal, and it can be quite confusing. But here I was, told that I could fire on all cylinders. We boasted two of the best opening bats in the world in Gordon Greenidge and Desmond Haynes, and on this day they set about building us later batsmen a platform. They put bat to ball but did nothing silly and we moved steadily onwards. Satisfied with what I saw, I did what I always did before an innings: I went to sleep! It didn't matter what the circumstances were, if there was a place where I could get my head down, I did just that. I didn't need a wake-up call when we were playing away from home because the roar of the home crowd – especially if it was in Australia or India – would always tell me when a wicket had fallen, with the firecrackers an added racket in India just to tell me it was time to get up and go into the lions' den. Then the wickets began to fall as Kapil Dev bowled Desmond for 34 and had our captain caught by Amarnath for 3, and suddenly it was like the first day of the test instead of the last. As the excitement began to build, so did the crowd. Being the last day of the first test, there was little crowd control and the gatemen had long since lost interest. I began to go through the old familiar routine. I splashed a little water on my face, popped some gum in my mouth, put my cap on and strode out to bat.

As usual, the supporters had heard what was happening either on their transistors or by word of mouth, and they came streaming back through the unguarded turnstiles. When I went out we were two wickets down for 65 and any result was still on the cards. Because I had not had much match practice courtesy of the broken thumb, I just went out relishing the freedom Clive had given me, looking for a feast on the back of my natural instinct to attack. I took my regular guard of leg stump. Venkat bowled his off-spinners to me and I went after him from the start, going berserk, hitting fours and sixes, and before I knew it we were right up with the run rate. I was feeling a real buzz and when I looked up suddenly the stadium was full, with fans clamping their transistors to their ears, jumping off the wall, falling off the stands and, at the finish, pouring over the boundary walls to pat me on the back. How the

Jamaicans love their cricket, especially when the batsman is putting bat to ball the way we did that day. I was in for only 36 balls for my 61, with the ball going sweetly right from the start. Every time I hit a boundary (I hit 4 sixes and 5 fours) it sounded more like a crowd at a boxing match as they grunted rather than cheered as bat hit ball. I was swinging my arms so freely but, because of my problems with my right hand, I favoured my left – and it conked out in that innings. I had to have pain-killing pills and spray as my right thumb was throbbing, and my arm just collapsed. Just holding the bat became a problem as there was no feeling in the arm, and it was a trial and a tribulation to accomplish what we did. This to me was what it was all about, not doing it just for you but for the team and for the cause. To be there. It could not have been better.

We won in the last over.

1. My Island in the Sun

I have often been accused of being single-minded and obstinate. I plead guilty to both charges and, indeed, my failings almost cost me my career in cricket before it had even begun. I was banned from all representative cricket by my native Antigua for two years – not that my cricket world extended much beyond the Leeward Islands in those days. Not just any two years but, perhaps, the most important 24 months of greatest development. I was just seventeen and had broken into the Antigua side when I set the unwanted record in a two-innings game of being out three times without scoring a run and I caused a near riot by my actions.

Although I was still only a kid I had already built up quite a following on my island and when I played for Antigua in the Leeward Islands tournament at the Recreation Ground in St John's my fan club were present and in full voice, supported by the local schools, who had been given a half-day's holiday to watch.

It was my first game for Antigua and everyone was talking about this young flash-in-the-pan, the new guy who was going to do this and do that. All my neighbours and school friends were telling everyone who would listen what Vivi was going to do against these little teams from places like St Kitts. I didn't tell them any different. So the expectations were very high for a teenager in his first big game, but short leg caught me off my pads off the first ball I received. There was no wood on the ball, but I knew that I was in trouble from the moment the umpire joined the bowler in his appeal – and then gave me out. I think that was what hurt most, and because of it I stamped my feet like a petulant child, smashed my bat against my pads and then on the ground and lingered in the middle as I aimed a few choice phrases in the direction of what I considered to be a biased and unfair umpire. Before I knew it, spectators were tumbling over the fences, holding up hastily scribbled placards and bringing play to a halt, saying 'No Vivi, no match'. Play was suspended and there was a hasty discussion before it was decided, quite wrongly, that I should be reinstated and should go out and bat again. That was the worst possible decision, and the worst thing I could have done was to agree. It helped put the spectators back on the right side of the fence and the game was resumed, but I was in no frame of mind to play and had no thought of the consequences. The result was predictable in every way: I was stumped without scoring. In the second innings – my third – I was out for a duck once more as I gently wafted one towards the covers. A world record. Three ducks in one match. It was all very humiliating because all those who had shouted 'No Vivi, no match' were the same ones who turned against me, shouting at me that I couldn't bat and worse. This was something that lasted through the two years of my suspension. The very people who had sent me out to bat again were now sitting in judgement against me. I had done wrong, having nearly caused a riot and brought the game into disrepute, but they were the ones who told me to bat again and they were the ones who then banned me for doing so. The word 'hypocrites' comes instantly to mind.

I heard of my ban, to begin from the end of the season, on the local radio station, with the story quickly picked up by the local newspapers, even making the front page in this cricket-crazy community. From being the golden boy, I was now in disgrace. People shouted abuse as they walked past my parents' house in Drake Street. It was very scary and, for the rest of that season before my ban came into effect, my cricket went to pieces, further fuelling the anger and derision against me. I was very disappointed and started to play lots more soccer and, for a while, I might well have opted permanently for football instead of cricket. But deep within me I was determined to succeed and show everyone that they were wrong about me. It had been my first match of any real importance and I had wanted so much to do well. I was cheated out and, not having the experience of playing before such a big crowd and being the new kid on the block, I made the wrong decisions with the help of adults who should have known better and who should have helped me through my first crisis. All these things were a factor. I was wrong and deserved punishment, but I felt that the two-year ban was a long time. I was still able to play for my neighbourhood, practise with the team and play in park games but I had to watch my peers making progress, leaving me distraught and frustrated. Perhaps, in retrospect, it was a good thing that it happened early because at least it gave me a chance to reassess my attitude, to realize that certain things aren't on, such as disputing umpires' decisions. It opened my eyes and, fortunately, I was a good learner.

From a very early age cricket dominated my life. My schoolwork suffered a hell of a lot and I used to have problems with my homework, which is why I now have my son Mali work as hard at his lessons as he does at his cricket and tennis.

I had a headmaster who was lenient, and I now regret that I let my schoolwork slip. When you are involved in two major sports as I was, it was all the year round and I missed a lot of lessons. My maths, apart from counting my runs, was not good and I should have worked harder; but one thing I am proud of is my knowledge of history and geography. I knew all about my own island and the West Indies and about the history of Britain. Had I not played cricket, I might well have been a historian – or maybe a priest! With all the church I went to I couldn't avoid learning about the wider aspects of religion. Maybe I would have been another Reverend David Sheppard, combining the cloth with cricket. I certainly had no trouble passing my Religious Instruction exams. But I never seriously contemplated going into the church. I really couldn't see anything beyond cricket. I always wanted to be a cricketer. My father was so strict that we didn't hang around the street corners much, and when we did we got disciplined for it. Knowing that your father was respected in the local area, you couldn't even swear without it getting back to him.

Antigua is a small island and a tight-knit community and I wasn't that exposed to too many things, other than the sports pavilions, the steel band house and the neighbourhood. I was never around the gangsters, always around solid people. If you are brought up

into a good life, go to church and have Bible lessons, it is pretty
hard to get into serious trouble and I was pretty fortunate to be
involved in that environment. The same attitude isn't there as much
now, but it certainly helped me become a much more rounded
individual.

Carnival is very important in the Caribbean, and it is important
to me too. I missed a lot because English county cricket kept me
away in July. It made me sick to miss it because it had been such
a big part of my life. I grew up for the summer festival, looking
forward to it as a little boy. The pleasure was as much in the
preparing as in the participation, with such crucial things as making
sure you had the right jeans and the right shoes to 'jump up' in
when you were getting ready for the kiddies' carnival and then
later growing up around a band called Brute Force. All my friends
played, and during the weeks leading up to the carnival it became
the focal point of our life, revolving around the yards where we
held our rehearsals. It was more than just the music, as we would
play cards and dominoes or simply sit down and relax; sometimes
the guys would cook. It was just as Bob Marley sang about it in
French Town. We all had a whip-round for the money to buy the
food and drinks. As we matured, we joined in all the various events
around carnival and it became the highlight of the year – and
still is!

My two favourite shows in the carnival were the steel band and
the calypso competitions. The steel band produced great rivalry all
round the island and we would clash with steel bands from the
Point area. When two bands get close, they just beat hell out of
the home-made instruments, trying to outdo each other in terms
of volume. You have never heard anything like it.

In Antigua there is the opening of carnival, the kiddies' shows,
the teen shows and in the evenings there are teenage pageants, the
local queen show and the Caribbean show, which is popular because
of the interest from other islands, and the calypso show. In my
view carnival can never be carnival without the steel band; steel
band is the rhythm that created carnival. Suddenly we found out
there was an easier way to do the same thing with the introduction

of all the electronic stuff produced by popular groups like the Burnin' Flames, but we must preserve the steel band because it is part of the culture and the history.

The steel band competition seems to have gone, and I weep for that. I remember the famous names on Panorama night; it was the big, big night on our small island. Hell's Gate, Brute Force, Red Star, Halcyon and Super Star from Point. Every area had a band and one or two of us would sneak away and listen to how each of them was sounding and afterwards we would go back and say, 'There is work to do.' That spirit is dead. I cannot forgive the people who claim to have our culture at heart but who have made no effort to look after the carnival. I will do my best to revive it.

The Notting Hill Carnival came to prominence while I was playing my cricket in England and I went to see it in order to compare it with my beloved Antiguan festival. It was tremendous, with the camaraderie, the revelry and everyone having fun and coming out to party, West Indian style. What I was delighted to see was the serious integration. I saw little black, white and Indian kids jumping up in the same troupe and the same dance group. That, for me, was the greatest sight I could ever see in England. It was building bridges and helping understanding of others' cultures. It was lovely to see white folk jumping up with black folks. Who says white men can't jump? In my view that's a load of rubbish, you couldn't distinguish one from the other. All you need is the rhythm. Embrace it and enjoy it. I became a regular. But it was different. In Antigua the celebration went on for days, with each day having its special meaning and tradition. In London you cannot stop the world for the carnival. In Antigua you can.

While I was still at school, aged around fourteen and upwards, I earned some pocket money by serving in a bar called Darcy's in St John's. Darcy Williams was a local character who was enthusiastic about cricket and was chairman of a local cricket club. He took an interest in me and looked after me so that when I finished school I would play for his team and work in his bar and restaurant.

My job was always there in the holidays whenever I wanted it. I was paid $30 Eastern Caribbean, and with tips I could more than double that to $EC70, which was around £17, a great deal of money at the time. It was a big place and that meant I was very active, going from table to table with food and drinks. The support of Darcy was good for me and he was as keen as I was for me to progress. He used to buy my pads and bats and there was nothing I wanted in terms of cricket gear. I was very sad when he died, and I was one of the last people to see him. When he passed away it was a great loss in my life.

I was no great scholar and I regretted not getting my pass in maths and generally not working harder. I enjoyed history, geography and religious instruction; history, particularly our local history, was most important to me, along with geography. I soaked it up; anything about my island and the West Indies captivated me and the broader interest helped me when eventually I travelled the globe. I am still interested and keep in regular touch through the excellent Discovery Channel on satellite television. I also enjoy writing and I used to write a lot of poems, short stories and the lyrics for some calypso singers. I still do that, writing about things that are happening in my environment and from my view of politics.

After leaving school I worked briefly for the inter-island airline LIAT (cruelly known by some people as Luggage In Another Town) on the reservations side. Again, it was through my contacts in cricket that I landed this comfortable job, but I was spending so much time away playing representative cricket that there were problems from my employers. I grew up in an area called the Ovals and was ruled over by a very dominant father, Malcolm, a prison officer. My cricket prowess came from my father, who represented Antigua and Barbuda. He was an all-rounder for the island and a prominent name when it came to cricket in the region. As a little boy I took my lead from my father. He used to bring home his cricket gear and he would bowl to my younger brother Mervyn and me in our backyard. While he liked sport, he was a very strict disciplinarian; influenced by his job, being in the prison service, he brought that discipline back to the family home. Like all growing young men, there were times when I would test this stern man and argue with him, feeling that I was so right and he was so wrong. Eventually there comes a moment in every young person's life when you stop and listen, remembering those things that were said in the past.

I may have thought that he was harsh at the time but, in many ways, I have taken after him and if there are things I want to get off my chest I tend to be honest and straightforward and I try to deal with things as honestly and purely as I can without hurting anyone. I may be a little blunt (like him) at times, but I am proud of the way I have turned out and he deserves the credit if there is any due.

It would have been easy to drift off in the wrong direction; but even when I went to England, my parents made sure I packed my Bible. They gave me certain scriptures and psalms to read which they said would help me in whatever trials and tribulations I might go through. Having that sort of upbringing was a help.

Whatever the church a person attends, it brings a certain together-ness. When I was a little boy and in the choir, I was attending church three times every Sunday. Only sickness would keep me away from two sessions of Sunday school and evening mass. It wasn't great at the time, as I would much rather have spent the day playing football or cricket, but now I appreciate it. A religious background gives you that solidness and the opportunity to choose, and sometimes you choose the right thing because of that back-ground.

Black magic and witchcraft were also strong in the Caribbean and particularly in Antigua and, as kids, we were always in mortal dread of the Jumbies, the devil's disciples. Half a dozen houses from my parents' home there lived a guy who was known as the local witchcraft man. When you are kids you are, of course, susceptible to stories of such a nature, and subsequently everything that happens takes on a particular meaning.

Whenever he passed he always had a wooden club in his hand and, for no apparent reason, he attracted all the dogs in the area.

They sensed when he was around and the domestic dogs would start barking in their backyards, while the strays would follow him around, yapping at his heels. You could tell when he was around from streets away. Doctor Night, as he was known, looked filthy and evil and would often dress up in shorts with no shoes or shirt, carrying his club in one hand and a bucket or a sack in the other. The word was that he used to club selected dogs and stuff them in the bag and take them home, although no one ever actually saw him do it. As far as we were concerned he was the devil man and, when I came into contact with him, goose bumps would suddenly appear and the hairs on the back of my neck would stand up.

He was also illiterate and he would often call us kids to fill in his Vernon's and Littlewood's football coupons. We would dread it and when he would shout, 'Hello, sonny, come here, Vivi,' I would shake and want to run, but my legs would be frozen to the ground. He was quite polite and would say, 'Will you fill in my coupon, please.' I wanted to flee, but I knew from the stories that if I did he would get me some day. It was the most nerve-racking time of my life. Here I was with Doctor Night filling out his pools coupon with slow hands and fingers, willing myself to hurry but unable to. He would always say, 'Thank you.' In truth, all he was was an odd-ball. He was always polite and never hurt any child that I heard of. But I was in my pre-teens and very impressionable – especially when it was the adults, who should have known better, who whispered the stories about him and his strange ways.

Despite our childish fantasies about Doctor Night, we could always rely on the strength of our faith in God. I don't believe it is the same nowadays and I admit that I hardly go to church myself any more, although I always try to be there on special occasions like Christmas Eve and other celebratory days. I am sure that the discipline helped as I became older. There were plenty of kids I knew who went the wrong way. Some of those whom we looked up to as being streetwise and full of knowledge went in the wrong direction, and some ended up in prison, both at home and in America.

Others, who had that solid upbringing like myself, prospered.

Tooko Benjamin was a very close friend and he went off to America to better himself, setting up his own business and establishing himself. I could tell, watching him growing, that he was smart and wise even though he didn't go to Grammar School. He was blessed and sometimes you cannot teach that. He comes home every year for Carnival and I feel proud whenever I see him. Another of my fellow Ovals Boys was Roy 'Exile' Gums, who also succeeded in business. Then there are the others who you are not so proud of, like Eugene Carbon who's been in and out of prison. Yet he was part of a close household and would protect us younger boys. We all had our rough times when we were young and there is always a debt to certain of our oldest friends who helped prepare me for the competitive world. There were some really wicked nicknames and, apart from Tooko, Exile and Tohijo Carbon, there was Becket Michael and the wonderfully named Monkey Lettuce. I was Yagga, named after my favourite cricketer, Lawrence Rowe.

Needless to say, we all played cricket and this was where our competitive edge was at its strongest, even with my brother Mervyn. To make sure the scorer was paying attention, when he and I used to bat together, I developed the habit of shouting to the scorer: 'One to IR' or 'Six to IR' so that the scorer wouldn't get confused between Isaac Vivian Alexander Richards and Mervyn Richards. My brother also caught the habit and he would call out, 'One to MR.' We were so keen and competitive that neither of us wanted to be deprived of a run. We would even keep count in our heads. I would shout to the scorer, 'Hey, Billy, how many I got, man?'

'Seven.'

'How can you say seven, man? Did you forget the one I took to mid on?'

Tooko and myself formed a partnership and we would take on anyone at either football or cricket. We must have been slightly crazy, for we would play two against two on a full-size pitch in the full heat of the day. We were both of a very competitive nature, and when we ran out of opponents we would play one against one. We even played one against one at cricket where you had only a wicket-keeper to help and you had to run to fetch every ball. The only way you could get your opponent out was by hitting the stumps or by a very fortunate caught-and-bowled. I am sure that this helped me to develop my competitive instincts. I was never surrounded by negative attitudes and it helped to prepare me for the big world when I came face to face with it.

A big bone of contention for my brother Mervyn and me was that we weren't allowed to play football or cricket on a Sunday. Our father would say that we had six other days in the week to do what we wanted, but the seventh day was for worship. The family would eat together and go to church together: church in the morning, a sleep in the afternoon before going to Sunday school and then to church again in the evening. The recreation ground was only just down the road from where we lived and our mates would tease us about not being able to play on Sunday. It was the one afternoon when everyone else seemed to gather in the park and play sport. It was a big problem for us as both Mervyn, a couple of years younger than me, and I played for the Ovals cricket and football teams and most of our big games were played on Sundays when everyone was supposed to be available.

As we grew older our team began to rely more and more on the Richards brothers; they felt better when we were playing and missed us when we were not around, and especially on Sunday. It all came to a head one day when the man who ran the team came and told us we had an important game and was there any way we could make ourselves available. We conferred and came up with the momentous decision that we would skip church and play. The game was away and we plotted to give our cricket gear to our team mates and dress up in our Sunday school clothes and pretend that everything was normal.

Everything went to plan and we skipped away, changed and took our places in the team. But my father had developed a keen ear and a good sense for wrongdoing in his years at the prison and I should have realized that all was not as it seemed. I was out in the middle, batting and feeling pretty good, when the wicket-keeper suddenly said to me, 'That looks like your father over there, Viv man.' I wondered whether this could be my first experience of sledging. In a small community like ours all the opposition knew that the Richards boys were not supposed to be playing on a Sunday. I thought he was trying to make me lose concentration. But he persisted and said, 'Yeah man, that sure look like your father out there.'

I wanted to look, but it was a while before I was brave enough. There he stood. For a moment I was rooted to the spot. Then the fear factor came into play and I was on the point of dropping the bat and running. It must have been pretty obvious that I was about to make a break for it, when he shouted out, 'No, no need for that now, there's lots of time to deal with you later.'

He must have been standing there for a long time and maybe he was pleased with the way I was batting, but I still knew that I was in for it that night when I got home. The match finished, we won and everyone was happy . . . except Merv and me. We were decidedly unhappy and the last thing we wanted to do was to go home and face the wrath of our father.

We eventually reached our house and he laid into the pair of us. But our mother stood up for us and eventually we reached a compromise that, providing we went to church, we could play our cricket. Church had never been sweeter after that.

My father was as hard a cricketer as he was a person and was very keen for me to do well. He was also passionate about the statistical side of it. If I scored 150 he would be pleased but would ask why I hadn't gone on to score 200. He would tell me I should be going on and that, the way I was batting, the only way the bowlers would get me out was with a prayer book and by praying for divine intervention.

He was very positive about what he wanted me to achieve. But cricket to him was very much a sport and not a proper job. I had some problems with him to begin with. He wanted me to go to America where his mother had come from and where most of his family lived. He had arranged for a place in a college over there for me and for a part-time job to pay for my further education. The last thing he had in mind was for me making a living by holding a cricket bat or ball. He played and gave a lot to the game, but he never got anything out of it in return and he couldn't see why anyone should be paid for what he considered a pastime and not a job.

Mervyn wasn't just my brother. He was the closest person to me on earth, my best friend. We lived under the same roof and shared the same father and mother. Everyone tells me that Mervyn could have made it as a cricketer; but he was much more switched on by the fun side of the game, whereas he was an outstanding footballer and, had he been given the chance in England in that sport the way I had been with cricket, I am sure he would have made it big. But, at that time, the big clubs weren't interested in any soccer talent there might be in the West Indies. In that respect he was born before his time. I played with him at school, for a club team and in our national team and, providing he could focus, he would have made it all the way. But the closest he came was having trials with the American side, Washington Diplomats.

However, there was always a doubt about his commitment. I was finally convinced that he wasn't that serious about his sport when he played for Antigua in a game on Nevis. His music group, the Mindreachers, was performing the same night and he decided to fly back from Nevis to Antigua, sing and then go back again! It is inevitable that sport has to suffer in a situation such as that. However, if someone had the same insight with him that Graham Taylor had when he spotted and signed Dwight Yorke for Aston Villa, Merv could have hit the big time.

I had to make up my mind between the two sports when a cricket tour clashed with a football tour; everyone was saying that I had to play for the Antigua National Football team. I looked at both games, and cricket had a much more organized structure while football was more of a rebel sport. Cricket offered a proper route to the top, and that persuaded me to choose the cricket tour.

My father had two other boys, Donald and David, who had different mothers. I was pleased when I got to know my other brothers. Donald was at Antigua Grammar School and used to play a serious part in my life. Donald played cricket and football for Antigua and also represented the Leeward Islands at cricket, as did my father, Mervyn and myself. It must have been something in our genes – or in the water! I became so close to him that I used to watch him play football and I would wash his car down on Friday, pay day, and he would reward my work with pocket money. He would also give me matinee money when it was hard to come by.

I wasn't that close to David at the time because for quite a long period of time he went to America to live with his mother. When he came back I fortunately came to know him better and became close to his children, Donna and David Junior, and even became like a father figure to them. My mother is still very much in touch with David, who gets on very well with the rest of the family and whenever he is in town he goes there to eat a meal and brings presents from the States for her. There is a whole lot of love between them and he was embraced by her as our brother. She is so mild and loving that she never had any problems with having David as one of her own.

When I found out about Donald and David I was proud to suddenly discover that I had two older brothers. I would go to the recreation ground and carry Donald's boots, and when I became a little older he passed on his old boots and cricket bats to me when he had finished with them. But there will always be something special between Mervyn and me. We grew up together, we fought together and we played cricket and football against each other in the backyard. That is where a lot of my toughness came from because we were so aggressive.

Another distraction for Mervyn at the time was the fact that he was also a drama artist at one of the local drama schools. He was a singer, a poet and a writer, and to do all these at any one time was difficult and that is why he never really excelled at any one sport. But he was blessed. He was good at almost everything he tried his hand at.

I loved us being able to walk out on the football or cricket field together, and if someone tackled my brother too hard I used to feel it and it would hurt me. He was a ball player and it was me who protected him. I would tell his marker that I would be after him if he kicked my brother again. There are some awful people around who hate ball players and feel they have to kick them to pieces. But they knew that if they kicked Mervyn they had to kick me as well. It was a simple method. I used to jump in and say, 'Not today – try it some other time.' Perhaps that is why I became known as Bull on the football field.

I was more than a little sad when Mervyn moved to America with his wife Patsy and his daughter Elissa. There was so much in Antigua and I was worried for the safety of him and his family in such a rough environment as New York. I stayed with them a few times there and reassured myself – but I was very happy when he and his family moved back. It was like the old days again, and he now works in the government sports department.

While Mervyn made his trip to the States, my preference had always been for England. I was not overawed at the prospect. I had played against England spinner Derek Underwood and other county players and it wasn't really a cocky statement when, looking at these professionals, I compared myself to them and said, 'Hey, Viv, man, if you get an opportunity like this you must take it on. You are as good as these guys!'

I always combined cricket and football. They were my favourite sports and I was picked to play both for my school team. I was a centre half at soccer, but I wasn't a dirty player; maybe I'd give the odd tug on an opponent's jersey, but I despised those who went in over the ball. To me, timing was everything and a tackle could have just as great an impact as clogging if you timed it just as he was about to kick the ball; it was better than going over the top, and you didn't get punished.

We had a super football team at Antigua Grammar School, where we were considered so talented that we were the only school team allowed to play in the senior Antigua Premier League. It meant that I was pretty hardened from an early age. Here we were, still at school, and playing against grown men at both cricket and football. What's more, men who didn't like to be made to look silly by a bunch of schoolboys! I was lucky that my headmaster, Loydstone Jacobs, was a sports fanatic. He not only encouraged those of us who played but he would also involve the entire school, and if we had a big match he would give everyone the day off to watch. He was a very caring individual and if we had a game at 4.30 he would let the players go home after the morning sessions of 8 a.m. to noon so that we could have a little rest. The ground would then be full of screaming kids and adults who would support the golden boys of the island. We weren't as physically developed as our opponents, but I am sure it helped me mature at an early age and stood me in good stead as my cricket career progressed.

At cricket we played against all the top players, including Andy Roberts, who played for a different school and for a club called Rising Sun. Ours was a good school for developing top sportsmen and top politicians, with many going on to scholarships in America. It was a great launching pad for the future, and past pupils were held up to us as mentors and we were expected to follow their example. Both individually and as teams we won a lot of trophies, they were small but treasured. There were prizes and awards for the top players at the end of a series and all sorts of other incentives, while supporters would also give rewards. One of the stores in town might offer a trip to a neighbouring island if you scored 100 or took five wickets, and it was encouragement like this that gave youngsters added incentive to get out and play.

Charlie Henry, one of the local businessmen, introduced me to the thrills of test cricket when he took a group of us young cricketers to Bridgetown in Barbados to watch the West Indies play New Zealand. Imagine the impact it had on me when I watched the great Garfield Sobers hit one century and another came from Charlie Davis. To cap an unforgettable visit, I was then introduced to Sir Garfield in the dressing-rooms after the day's play. Even better was when Lawrence Rowe, one of my great heroes, gave me a pair of his gloves as a keepsake. I didn't tell him at the time that I had his nickname 'Yagga' sprayed on our backyard fence or that I was also known by the same *nom de guerre* because of my respect for him. To me he was a great player with a lot of time to play, while another player I appreciated a lot was Seymour Nurse. Other heroes were, of course, the three Ws, Sir Clyde Walcott, Sir Frank Worrell and Sir Everton Weekes. I also loved fast bowler Wes Hall with his macho style, the way he rushed in, shirt open, gold chain flashing in the Caribbean sun.

Other than West Indians, I liked Greg Chappell for the way he approached his innings; his brother Ian, with his rough, tough attitude to performing, was strong both mentally and physically and with a win-at-all-costs attitude. Of the English players I liked Ken Barrington, in my view one of the better players, a man who was brave, had lots of guts and a very good technique when facing Wes Hall and Charlie Griffith. He was simply a very strong, dogged man, who used to hit the ball so sweetly. I admired him more than all the other English batsmen of the time. I wanted to be like Seymour Nurse when I was a kid, playing those delicate little shots. But early on I realized that I had to be myself and that I could not live Seymour Nurse through Viv Richards.

It took a while because I was all of twenty before I took these things fully on board. Before that, one day I would want to bat one way and another day I would bat like someone else. What I was forgetting was how Viv wanted to bat. No, I told myself, I have to do it my way and feel proud about the way I am doing it. I could still gather my strength and inspiration from what others were doing, learn the good things and add them to my library. This is what I tried to do, quietly and without much confusion.

While there was little real coaching to be had, my father was my greatest inspiration. He made me aware that bowlers can have their days too. More important than coaching was practice. I practised a lot when I was young. Whatever limited space was available, we would use it to improve our performance. It was not just batting or bowling, I would practise my fielding, picking the ball up, whipping it in over the stumps, getting my arm strong with the help of the school wicket-keeper, someone from the local club or even just a bunch of friends. The other way of improving the throwing was pure Caribbean: skimming flat stones across the blue water, making them slide and skip, with contests of who can make them bounce the most number of times.

Then there were the mangoes. We used to throw stones up at

these tropical fruit, aiming for the stem so that we wouldn't damage the edible part, and then hurl ourselves forward to catch the falling fruit so that it did not hit the ground and break.

As for batting, if I wasn't physically hitting the ball I would stand in front of a full-length mirror to practise my shots. I took the idea from the great boxer Muhammad Ali. I used to shadow-bat a lot, playing all the shots, tightening the defence, feeling the pick-up of the bat, how the grip felt. The mirror gave me the full picture and was my old-fashioned version of the modern video. When I went on tour with the Under-16s, while the others were in bed asleep, I would be up, tapping the bat in the night and early in the morning. It was my ritual.

Improvisation had to be the key because of the lack of facilities in the region, somewhat compensated for by nature. In place of a net there is the sun, sand and sea to provide the basic ingredients for beach cricket. There is nothing quite like being involved in beach cricket, and it is such a part of a Caribbean Sunday that, quite often, we would rush from our proper, organized game of cricket to start again on the beach. It is a ritual that goes back for years, especially during the close season. We would play football in the morning then run to the beach and have fun until we saw each other again on the Monday.

There is an art and a skill all its own in beach cricket, playing just on the water line where the Caribbean washes the sand nice and flat. The bowler won't bowl when it's dry, he will wait until there is a little water and then the ball skims off the wet surface at a frightening pace. Even with the best eyes in the world you can get seriously hurt, especially when you play with a tennis ball. Who can get hurt by a tennis ball, you ask. This is different. The tennis ball is put on the stove to burn off the fluff and that makes it hard so that when it hits the slick surface the ball rears up. If it hits you on your bare chest it is like taking an uppercut from Mike Tyson and if it hits you elsewhere you will be screaming like a baby. If you are a smart enough batsman you slow things down and take your guard as you see the water running away so that the soft sand absorbs the bounce.

It was a lot simpler to play on the beach than having to prepare a wicket yourself for a proper game. We would have to find a field and, providing we had a little patch cut out, we would water and roll it and water and roll it. We were our own groundsmen and could spend a week helping to get a pitch ready and then be out first ball for a duck. We used to be seriously fed up with that situation. The roller was, of course, improvised, using old rollers filled with concrete. There was always one about. We would find a field, cut open a spot, make it level and then water, roll, water, roll, until it was flat. The most important thing was to get it level. It might well be used for all sorts of things in the week but, come Friday, we would work on it and put thorn branches around it to stop people, the goats and the cows going on it. The last thing we wanted was a cow's hoof marks on a length. We had no affiliation with organized grounds; we just had to find somewhere clear enough and vacant enough to play on.

Even our test ground, the Recreation Ground, is more than a cricket pitch and is used for all sorts of events. It's a vibrant place and it has borne the brunt of the load of fixtures over the years, with test matches, carnival, and church seminars. It is the Carnegie Hall of Antigua. Visitors to the carnival cannot believe what they are seeing when great low-loader lorries trundle round the outfield and stages are put up and activities take place where the square should be. You certainly couldn't imagine it happening at the Oval or Lord's – but then neither could it be imagined, a few weeks later, when Brian Lara scored 375 off England's attack, as he did in 1994. But whatever happens on it, they always seem to come up with a good batting wicket. It is supposed to be a dead track. Certainly it used to be quicker, but if you put something in you can usually get something out.

Cricket is a religion in Antigua, dominating everyday life. But back in my youth it was not considered a proper profession. No one made a living out of cricket, as my father always pointed out so forcibly. As far as my father was concerned sport was sport, but he was as strict about participation as he was about my work and when I was suspended from the game he was very angry. He declared that out was out, but he also agreed that the officials were as much in the wrong as I was by sending me back out to bat again.

During my two-year suspension from cricket I used all the unreleased energy caused by my frustration to do other things. The football season was fine, but I began boxing as well and I went to the gym in New Street. I needed other things to do in order to keep my mind and body fit.

Sam, a Trinidadian, helped me with my boxing. The fights were mainly neighbourhood bouts, where one group would back their man against another. It was all totally unpredictable because you never knew the weight or the style of your opponent; if you had time to find out, it would have been a lot easier. As it was, we faced each other with little knowledge of whether the opponent was a big puncher or a skilful defensive boxer. The usual venue was the Squeeze Inn, where they erected a makeshift ring. It was all great fun, but the boxing also helped me develop my physical side and especially my reactions. Blocking and slipping punches was not far removed from the skills required when facing a fast bowler and a series of bouncers. This was no amateur stuff and there were definitely no helmets! But I did wear a gum-shield. Money was put up, we would get in the ring and would proceed to have a go at each other. The winner took all.

I found myself fighting guys who were much older and often bigger. This was catch-weight; there was no weigh-in. The opponents from neighbouring Grace Farm were not only older but also meaner and were invariably possessed of a wicked mentality and little knowledge of the Queensberry Rules. I wouldn't have liked to fight them in the street, but in the ring it was different: there was a referee and some measure of control, even though it was far removed from the Amateur Boxing Association in the United Kingdom.

Sam rated me and wanted me to go further, but I was playing football, practising my cricket and starting to dabble with a little basketball as well. I boxed when a fight came along but I didn't have the passion for the sport that I had for cricket or even for football, and training just for boxing was not an option. Fighting was hard but not as hard as facing Dennis Lillee and Jeff Thomson.

I have always felt that when you are growing up you need a discipline. It is a hard world out there. When I was in England I would hear about kids having problems with school bullies, so bad that in extreme cases it sometimes ended in suicide. I discovered that the best way to sort out the bully was to fight back, and often I would finish up bullying the bully.

For all the other sports and the pleasure they gave me, I seriously missed my cricket; despite the severity of the punishment there was no appeal against the ban. My father said I was wrong and had to take my punishment, and he washed his hands of the entire thing.

Thankfully the people of Antigua forgave me eventually and, indeed, I have a great deal to thank them for as, in 1972, Andy Roberts and I were sent to England to the Alf Gover Cricket School to help us further our skills. This was organized not by the Antiguan Cricket Association who had banned me but by a group who called themselves the Antigua Voluntary Coaching Committee. They raised the money with barbecues, dances and second-hand sales. Had it been left to the cricket authorities, I guess I would have stayed where I was or, worse, followed my father's instructions and gone to America to pursue a career outside the game. There were still those on the island who thought I was a bad boy and not worth the investment, even though I had served my time and had come back to score lots of runs.

Andy Roberts and I were close but not that close. He was and still is a quiet and laid-back individual. He was slightly older than I was, but we had played against each other as children and eventually we played together for the Leeward Islands. In comparison to Andy I suppose I was brash in what I wanted from life, but to counter that I had a lot of respect for my elders and I was also a good individual who was keen to learn as quickly as I could.

We didn't need the money just for the flights and the coaching but, because money was tight at home, for spending money and warm winter clothes to wear when we were in England. It may have sounded a trivial matter but, to someone who was used to wearing shorts and a T-shirt, neither of us had the clothes to combat a grey, cold, miserable, English winter. It was November when we arrived, bleak and cold to a youngster who had known nothing but sunshine all his life.

It was a nightmare – and, to make matters worse, I lost my spending money. One moment it was in the back pocket of my jeans and the next it was gone. What I had left was spent on feeding the electric meter to make sure we could have the electric fire on all the time. I was baffled as to why we had to pay to keep warm on top of the board and lodging money for our digs in Putney.

I felt miserable, ill and very homesick; but I decided that if I was going to succeed in life I would have to get stuck in and fight back. Sure enough, things improved, particularly when we moved to Hackney to stay with Andy's sister, where we were warm and comfortable and were reunited with local food and mixed once more with Caribbean folks. I was also introduced to the English pub culture and settled on drinking Guinness because the adverts told me it was good for me! That was how gullible I was at the time.

Even the cricket was alien to me and I was staggered to discover just how much I still had to learn about this game I loved so much. Alf Gover quickly saw that my stance was too open and he helped me tighten up my defence; but generally I was surprised to be told how little I knew. When we both went for a trial at the Surrey indoor nets which turned out to be abortive, the depression returned. They did not think we were good enough even to further our cricket education. But the coaching still helped me enormously. Having been an attacking, aggressive player, it helped me to tighten up on my defence and to realize the importance of this. My natural instinct was to hit the ball but I learned that a good bowler would exploit any gap I left and I had to be a bit more respectful to the bowler.

With little money to spend, our social life was limited to the occasional visit to a pub or cinema. The highlight of the entire visit was a trip to Highbury to watch Arsenal play Leeds United, but more often than not it was a night in front of the television set to keep out of the cold. It was so bad that one day Andy didn't get out of bed at all and, when I was asked where he was and why, I had to tell Mr Gover: 'It's the cold, man, it's the cold.'

After our scheduled six weeks we returned home. I decided that I would take from the experience what I thought my game needed but I would still retain my own natural instincts. The trip, however, did nothing to convince my father that I should concentrate on cricket rather than going to college and to work in New York. His theory was that cricket was a sport and that you couldn't feed a family on cricket balls.

Despite the experience of the coaching at the Alf Gover School, England still remained the place to be if you wanted to be a professional cricketer, and my dreams were of those lazy summer days rather than misty, damp November evenings. I thought that my prospects of playing county cricket in England had disappeared, but my hopes were resurrected thanks to the visit of a wandering English side.

In fact, a small cutting from the *Cricketer* magazine had more effect on my career than those six weeks with Alf Gover. Colin Cowdrey had been with Kent on a pre-season tour and he played in a game which earned the following brief mention: 'The locals made a fight of it mainly due to 23-year-old Vivian Richards, a batsman of sound technique and bold method. Cowdrey felt he would play for the West Indies soon.'

This prediction had been picked up by the Somerset Vice-Chairman, Len Creed, who arrived in Antigua with a touring side called the Mendip Acorns and who promptly asked the taxi driver who drove him from the airport whether he had heard of me and, if he had, where could he get hold of me. Like most cab drivers on the island, this one, Willie, was cricket mad and he immediately set off looking for me. Not surprisingly I was playing cricket, and Willie could scarcely wait for me to finish my innings to drag me away, saying that I had to come straight away to meet the Somerset chairman (*sic*), who had come all the way from England just to see me. Willie was prone to a little exaggeration.

Willie drove me straight to the Blue Waters Hotel, where I met up with Mr Creed. He told me that he was looking for an overseas cricketer. He explained that they already had a West Indian, Hallam Moseley from Barbados, and wondered whether I would like to come back with him for a trial with a view to becoming a Somerset player. I wasn't that naïve and I knew that I was a long way off achieving what most West Indian cricketers dreamed of – playing in an English county side as a professional. I knew that the upcoming game against the Mendip Acorns was going to be a fairly significant factor in my future one way or the other.

Had that in fact been so, I would probably have blown my chances. Word had quickly sped around the island grapevine and everyone at the ground knew what was on for me, and I was a quivering wreck by the time I went out to bat. I was soon beaten by a turning ball from the Kent and England bowler, Derek Underwood, and was comfortably stumped – only for the local umpire, Nookie, to shake his head and give me not out, much to the disgust of the English players. But even with that reprieve I limped to 24 before being run out by so far that even I would have been embarrassed had I been given not out again.

All I could do now was field as well as I could, and I threw myself into a task I enjoyed anyway. Fortunately, all those hours of throwing rocks at mango stems and skimming flat stones across the smooth blue waters of the Caribbean came to my rescue, and Len was so impressed with my fielding that he invited me back anyway.

It was not what my father wanted. He had tried his utmost to put me on what he believed to be the right road and create a career for myself outside cricket. We fell out quite seriously when I was given the opportunity to travel to England at the same time as he had made plans for me to go to New York. I totally ignored his wishes and said I was going to test the waters in England to see whether or not I could make it. I felt I owed it to myself to find out.

He himself moved back to the States and I began to send him some clippings from the English papers, and finally he began to see it was a serious business and he gained some satisfaction. It dawned on him that his son was a professional sportsman who was playing regularly, appearing on television, while he was gaining some notoriety of his own being interviewed as the father of Viv Richards. Suddenly he was full of himself and was always available for quotes when the newspapers rang him from England; gradually he became a little more flexible and, eventually, a very proud father – once I had proved myself in his eyes.

2. Cider with Rosie

My arrival in England in 1973 for the start of my professional cricket career was a near disaster, and it came close to ending right in the Customs and Excise lounge at Heathrow Airport. It looked as though I was going to be shipped straight back to the Caribbean on the next flight to Antigua.

My sponsor, Len Creed, was a well-meaning man who was fired with enthusiasm but who was sometimes lacking in the knowledge and background to see his ideas through. This was unfortunately the case when I touched down in London, and it quickly became evident that he didn't know the first thing about bringing cricketers into the country to play for their living. He simply hadn't thought it out and had not even applied for a work permit for me. When I told Customs and Immigration who I was and what I was doing, they weren't at all impressed. They wanted to see documentation and authorization. Quite understandably, they neither knew nor cared who this young West Indian was. I told them I intended to play cricket for a team in Bath called Lansdown but I wasn't able to tell them how much or even whether I was being paid at all; this left them in a very suspicious frame of mind. Indeed they were all for sending me back home straight away.

I was sat on a bench, my head in my hands, feeling thoroughly humiliated and in a distraught frame of mind. I was asked if I could give the official the name of the man who was sponsoring me. At least that was something I *was* in possession of, and he had promised me that he would be waiting at the airport to take me down to Bath. They kindly offered to tannoy him and when he arrived he was looking almost as relieved to see me as I was to see him after spending a couple of hours in limbo.

There was a great deal of discussion before I was finally released into his custody with my passport suitably stamped. I was told that

I could stay for three weeks while my work permit was being sorted out – and not a day longer.

As we motored west I asked Mr Creed what the problem was and how he had managed to solve what looked to be an intractable puzzle. He gave me a lot of waffle and told me I would never know. As it happened, I did find out when I was the subject of 'This Is Your Life', during which the host, Eamonn Andrews, introduced me to the man who had helped me into the country on that fateful day. It was the Chief Immigration Officer from Heathrow . . . who just happened to be a senior freemason along with guess who? Dear old Len Creed.

A work permit was scarcely relevant as I had no job and Somerset were not only not paying me, they weren't even specially interested in a young batsman brought over by the over-enthusiastic Vice-Chairman at his own expense. I was being totally sponsored by the generous Mr Creed, who had paid not only for my air fare but also my accommodation and living expenses. Somerset obviously didn't rate Mr Creed's knowledge of cricket too highly or his validity as a scout for players. The players were of much the same opinion when I turned up to play for the Under-25 team.

Even though I had already experienced London in November, England was still a rude awakening. That was winter. This was summer. There hardly seemed to be any difference, as it was still cold and damp.

There were a lot of things going on in my mind. I was totally confused. Summer? There weren't even any leaves on the trees! But I wanted to play cricket in England so much that I was prepared to go through all the rituals to make it work. This was an opportunity I was not going to let go by. County cricket had been a dream, along with opening the little white gate at headquarters and walking out to bat at Lord's. It would have been the easiest thing in the world to have packed my gear and gone straight back home. I was determined that I would stay.

Clothes were once again a problem – or, rather, the lack of them. My idea of an English summer and reality were miles apart.

Open-neck shirts and shorts weren't going to be particularly useful. Fortunately there was a friend of mine who was studying law in England and he had a little overcoat, which he kindly gave to me. I wore it everywhere. I remember there were no pockets, but it remained my most useful and most used item of clothing.

It was also then that I started to wear hats for the first time in my life but, even so, I had problems with the blood circulation in my extremities, fingers and feet. I found that a difficult problem to overcome and my favourite place was in front of the fireplace rather than going out, and whatever money I had I kept for the meter, something I had learnt from my previous visit.

The mornings looked like night time, and I would wake up in the dark and turn over and go back to sleep again. This often made me late for training and it took me time to become fully adjusted. Somerset were good to me at the time and overlooked my tardiness, probably because they could see that I was so keen to learn and develop. But first of all I had to prove myself, and that meant showing what I could do in Mr Creed's local club, Lansdown, in the beautiful city of Bath.

Thanks to a late withdrawal, I was able to play that first Saturday in the seaside town of Weston-super-Mare and duly made my English cricket debut on 26 April 1973 on a real pudding of a pitch. We bowled them out for under 100 and, after a long hard look at this unusual surface, I cut loose and finished the game off with a couple of sixes and a nice little half-century.

I began by living with Mr Creed, but obviously that could not go on indefinitely and I went looking for digs. The first night away from my sponsor, I was booked in to the local YMCA, but after a night out with the Lansdown lads I found all the doors locked and bolted and had to stay at one of the chaps' houses.

I enjoyed my cricket at the Lansdown Club and appreciated the help of people like Shandy Perera, a player from Sri Lanka who helped me understand the English wickets. It must have worked because the runs began to come, especially against local rivals Trowbridge, where I hit a century in 76 minutes and then scored

146 at home, with my last seven scoring shots all going for six!

I needed to make an impression if I was to have an opportunity with Somerset and I had to make the most of my chances for the Under-25s. A big score against local rivals Gloucestershire did me no harm at all, especially when they expressed an interest in signing me on. I think it was that, more than anything else, that stirred Somerset into action. I still harboured my own doubts as I earned my £1 a day as assistant groundsman at Lansdown but, at the end of the season, I was offered a two-year contract. I worked it out that it would net me around £2,000 providing I picked up some bonuses.

But money was the last thing on my mind. It had been difficult living on so little money, but it helped that I would have my ploughman's lunch at the club and help myself to a free beer from over the bar. They didn't always get much work out of me in the afternoon; it only took a couple to make me a menace when I was put in charge of the heavy roller. Looking after the ground and the square helped pass the time, but I lived for the practice nights and the games at weekends.

I was welcomed into the community and especially by the players and supporters at Lansdown. I spent a lot of time at the house of the Jenkins family. There were four boys in the house and they all played cricket for the club. I would also watch one of the brothers play rugby for Bath.

When they heard that I had dabbled with football in Antigua, they tried me out with a little touch rugby, but Bath weren't the club they are now and they didn't have the structure to make them an attractive proposition. Anyway, football had always been my second preferred sport and I was much more interested in the trial I had with Bath City football club. It took me by surprise because the game was so physical; I was knackered before I touched the ball. I honestly believe that I could have made it at football, but it would have needed total commitment on my part. My love for cricket and my freezing feet quickly persuaded me that I was not destined to be a professional footballer. I couldn't tackle properly because I couldn't feel my feet.

I love football, and most of all the kind of English football that I fell in love with in those first years in the country. Liverpool were the side that took my fancy, I liked their style and their successful record. I watched them once and was bowled over by their players like Tommy Smith, Phil Thompson, Steve Heighway, John Tosh-ack, Kevin Keegan and Emlyn Hughes. That was some team. Even though there have been some disappointments recently, I still support them – although I am hardly aware of who is playing for them as foreign players come and go with alarming rapidity. I really like the skills of Michael Owen, Jamie Redknapp and Robbie Fowler. The club seem to be getting their passion back under the watchful eye of Gerard Houllier. They still have a lot to sort out, but they remain the team whose result I look out for first, although now that Bobby Robson is at Newcastle I will be watching out for his results.

After a trip to Antigua I returned to Taunton and was told that I was to be accommodated in the club flat next to the ground. Perhaps they thought that would help my timekeeping! I was to share with a couple of young players, Dennis Breakwell and, to my great delight, a young all-rounder I had become friendly with the season before, Ian Botham. He had come down from Lord's to join the ground staff and we had got on right away. We hooked up at one of the matches we both played in at Lansdown for the Under-25s. He was the up-and-coming all-rounder and I was the batting protege. We played against Glamorgan and I scored a duck and took five for 25 with my off-spin while Ian scored a ton.

He said, 'From now on I will do the batting and you do the bowling.'

He was given a contract at the same time but didn't break into the team immediately. His time was still to come.

Ian was to become a great and lasting friend, but the biggest influence on my cricket career in those first few months was the controversial Somerset club captain and professional Yorkshireman, Brian Close. He became something of a mentor to me. He seemed to see beyond the raw rookie and spot that there was something there. Brian took me under his wing and let me travel with him to the various county matches up and down the country. We travelled a lot in his car. He was a good driver and, because of his confidence, he felt that he could do anything. I was always afraid when we embarked on our long hauls up and down the country because he had a tendency to nod off. Amazingly, he would keep hold of the wheel and stay on track as though a computer linked his brain to the engine.

There were times when we had a few close calls and I would give him a nudge and say diplomatically, 'We had a close one there. Maybe we should take a little rest.'

He would simply tap me on the shoulder and say, 'Viv lad, don't fret.' And he would laugh it off with his very unusual giggle, and then we would be back on our way.

Invariably we would talk about cricket and where and how I needed to improve. In return I would pour him his coffee and wake him up when he nodded off at the wheel.

If we were in Yorkshire he would invite me to his home and we would stay the night with his family before driving up to Harrogate. He would constantly tell me, 'You have been blessed with so much talent but you must work hard to bring it out.' His attitude to the work ethic was unshakeable and, in addition, he was one of the bravest batsmen on the international arena. He was the perfect example to me at that stage of my development. He was a winner and would push me to the limits. I needed that because, although I was aware that I had an abundance of talent inside, it had never fully matured and had not been stretched to the limit. It was Close who helped me realize it.

As a fairly unsophisticated young black man living in an area where there was not a large immigrant community there could have been problems – but there were, in fact, very few. People were extremely friendly and I was able to make friends very easily, among them a young man named Peter McCoombe. To fill in the time I spent a lot of time going to the movies and so did Peter, who eventually introduced himself, saying that he guessed that I must be the young cricketer who had come to play for Somerset.

He admitted that he, as a Scot, knew next to nothing about the game. He explained that he had felt lonely when he arrived in Taunton from Airdrie, and he invited me home to meet his Finnish wife and his children, where he made me feel a member of his household just as if I belonged there. Incredibly, he became a cricket fan and, because of my influence, eventually found himself a job working on the lottery for the county.

International sportsmen, particularly professional footballers, seem to favour London these days. But living in Taunton proved to be the right move for me at that stage of my development. It was a good move for me and I am sure that, had I gone to London, I would have been wiped out. Taunton reminded me of the Caribbean: it was very relaxed and laid back and made me feel at home.

There was another aspect I also enjoyed and that was the company of the local ladies. A curiosity factor came into play where these ladies were concerned. There was only myself and fellow professional cricketer Hallam Moseley from Barbados resident in the vicinity, and the girls seemed quite interested to see the difference.

It was wonderful to be in an environment in which people adore you, and as I became more of a household name there came a new buzz about the place for me. Somerset had never had a football team and as the county cricket team began to improve and look for trophies so the interest and the following increased. We were the Manchester United of the West Country, capturing the head-lines and the crowds, as Gloucester weren't doing that well.

Just like in St John's, everyone knew everyone in the town. I would go into the Gardeners Arms or the Kings Arms for a glass of scrumpy or Guinness, and I seemed to know everyone. Cider, of course, was the local tipple as it was famously made in the city and we would regularly be invited by the brewery to lunches and launches. These people could relate to a kid from a small island. It was a blessing in disguise. I have seen cricketers from the islands go to the big towns and never quite live up to their reputations because of the distractions, boredom or loneliness, but I had no such trouble.

To be fair, there wasn't a great deal to do in Taunton and it enabled me to concentrate on my cricket. A big night out was finding a pub that went on serving a little after time or, even better, finding a party. It was a good environment for me.

Somerset cricket had been dismissed as something of a joke over the years, but suddenly there was a new life and impetus, which had started under Brian Close, with myself and Ian Botham seen as the two bright young stars to carry it forward. The new spirit had been built upon the foundations laid down by Brian Close and I always felt it was unfortunate that he wasn't around to savour the fruits of his labours. It was always unlikely that he would stay as he was not a young man when he came to the county – he was in his forties – but he could still live it up with the best even though he was on his last lap in cricketing terms. In my view he was responsible for transforming the attitude of the players, and that guided a ship that had previously been rudderless.

He was a tough, uncompromising man. I remember him getting badly hit in the box once. Unfortunately for him, he was wearing one of those old plastic affairs. When they broke they tended to splinter and snag in a very painful way. Even the brave Close was in agony as the doctors had to use a pair of pliers to prise the remains of the box away from the torn and bleeding flesh.

For some inexplicable reason, anyone hit in that particularly painful place tends to become the butt of black humour even though only a man can know just how it feels. But on this occasion the laughter was all the fault of the injured party. Close, in typical fashion, sat puffing a cigarette as the medical men completed their delicate surgery. Brian looked less concerned than any of those around him.

Funnier still was when Leicester needed 12 to win off the last two balls in a one-day game. Close had given the responsibility of the last over to Alan Jones and told him where he wanted the ball bowled. The instructions were not followed and both balls were dispatched over the ropes and we lost the game. The captain could not believe it and we had to rush in to stop him from grabbing the unfortunate, skinny Alan Jones, who had become the sole object of his wrath. Even so, as we reached the dressing-room, Close managed to reach over, grab his collar and shouted: 'You fucking pillock. My mother could have done better than that.'

It didn't look good for our reputation, with the captain having his fast bowler by the throat, and it needed our two enforcers, Budgie Burgess and Merv Kitchen, to step in and wrestle them apart as Brian tried to hang him up on a clothes-peg.

Close was infused with the sort of passion that I had. He was a guy who wanted the best out of his players for the sake of the team. If you are going to carry the burden and responsibility of captaincy then you want the very best out of your players. He wasn't that popular with the committee because he was so outspoken, but what he wanted to get done was to mould his team. He always put them first.

I learned a lot from him. I particularly liked the way he never flinched, no matter how fast the bowler or how often he was hit – as he often was when his reflexes slowed with the passing years. Some of us showed the world when we were hurt, wringing our fingers or rubbing the spot where we had been hit. There were times when I could hardly speak after being hit in the solar plexus or worse. Invariably someone would come up and ask if everything was OK, and the pain was so bad I could only nod because words would not come out. But Close never showed a flicker.

I loved him not only for his bravery but because he was a good bat and an expert close fielder. What I appreciated most about him was that he and the county allowed me to be a free spirit. I am sure they saw someone who couldn't be coached, someone who had a natural flair that coaching could only limit and damage.

I was pleased, however, to work with Tom Cartwright, the player-coach, who allowed me licence and helped me to work on my strengths. He was fun to be with and was a real good bowler who did just enough with the ball. He had been a fine county player with Warwickshire, but he suffered with injuries while he was with Somerset. Tom Cartwright was a very knowledgeable cricketer, an individual who talked a lot of sense in terms of what needed to be done with batting or bowling. He was pretty direct.

I could handle that and it was nice to hear experienced cricketers talk and pass on their experience. He had played with the likes of Rohan Kanhai and Lance Gibbs and with and against some of the best cricketers in the world, and he had plenty to pass on. He was definitely an influence on my development; he would tell me to be myself and work on my strengths. When things did not go well he was fine, but he was even better when things *were* going well because he could spot things that maybe you got away with and he made sure you did not do them again.

Brian Close was different altogether. A lot of players found him difficult to get on with because he was hard, brusque and went straight to the point. He didn't like quitters, of whom there were a few at Somerset at that time. They had enjoyed a cushy life and simply could not move on to the next level. Close realized this and would give those people stick. I thought that was fine because he was in charge and that was his job, but there were others who reacted and went behind his back.

He was a disciplinarian and his attitude to the sport rubbed off on me. I was a young man and having a good old sergeant-major type in the camp was good for me. I didn't look for an opportunity to be stupid with him around, and I tried my best. A young man like me, a bit casual and laid back and coming from the islands, needed a bit of a drilling in terms of being pushed to the limits, because you never know how good you are until you are stretched to the utmost. Brian Close recognized my potential and I benefited a hell of a lot from just having him around. He always wanted me to graft a bit more. He accepted that I had all the shots, but he felt that if I got myself well in and played around a bit, I would be the hardest man in the game to dismiss. This was true; because of the chances I took, I would be out to soft dismissals. I had a few of those and he realized that I had more to offer than that.

I remember when Muhammad Ali beat Richard Dunne. Close felt that the Englishman had been so lethargic that he had not done justice to a Yorkshireman's pride and at the end of the fight he stood up and offered to fight Ali himself. Mind you, a few slugs of whisky helped his bravado; he loved his Scotch. He was a real showman and after he had enjoyed a few drinks at the bar he would do tricks, for example balancing his glass on his head.

Perhaps he came to Somerset at the wrong time. There were a few who just weren't in touch with what he wanted to do. All he wanted was success.

This was a very determined individual who had no fear in facing Hall and Griffith. Most of my memories with him, however, were on the pitch. I remember him being hit by the ball when fielding against Gloucestershire. Mike Procter was facing Tom Cartwright, who dropped one a little bit short of a length, and Procter gave himself a bit of width, ready to dispatch it to the boundary. Close, standing at silly point, refused to take the normal evasive action and, instead, charged forward and took the ball right on that bald head of his. He slumped to the ground in such dramatic style that everyone thought he was dead. We all forgot about the ball as we rushed to him.

He gradually came round then said, 'Did anyone take the catch?'

'No,' he was told. 'We came to see how you were.'

'You pillocks,' Close raged. 'That was my ploy for the ball to hit me and give the catch. You bastards messed it up.'

Procter went on to get 100, and that annoyed Close even more. He was inconsolable in the bar, as he nursed his whisky and his inevitable fag, after putting himself on the line and no one having taken advantage of his cunning plan.

Somerset, lacking any success in their long history, had negative attitudes to him and what he wanted to get done. Those who had never been in that position before weren't able to help him when it was needed, and he was frequently at loggerheads with the committee over their bad decisions off the pitch.

I had almost three years with him before Brian Rose took over, and that is when we had our first success, in 1978, going to our first final and then returning to win in 1979.

One of my worst moments in cricket was the two-day period when we lost both the Gillette Cup and the Player's Sunday League title in the first weekend of September in 1978. We started as favourites on the Saturday to beat Sussex at Lord's, but we played poorly although we felt that our 207-7, thanks largely to Ian Botham who hit 80, would be enough. It wasn't.

All that work, all that preparation, all those dreams had come to nothing. I was in despair and hated having to parade on the balcony – and as for my medal, I threw it on the floor and never saw it again.

Beefy tried to lift everyone as we made our way back to Taunton where we were to meet Essex on the Sunday. A tie would have been enough and, even if Hampshire beat Middlesex, the title was still ours on run rate. But, again, it was not to be as Essex notched up 190-5. It was a large target but I had willed myself to make a big innings. After hitting five fours I was out to a terrible shot, caught changing my mind, a sin for any batsman.

The double blow was just too much. Both Ian Botham and myself were in tears. We were inconsolable and there was no losers' medal to take it out on this time, only my favourite Jumbo bat which I smashed on the stone floor of the showers, leaving it in splintered pieces. We locked the dressing-room door and refused to let anyone enter, while the cheering of our loyal fans outside made the bitter pill of defeat even harder to swallow.

The double defeat left me tired and jaded for a long time afterwards. But perhaps defeat like that prepares you to enjoy better any success that may follow. Certainly we at Somerset took nothing for granted, and triumph was all the sweeter when we finally ended more than a hundred years of cricket without a trophy.

Somerset's jinx was finally broken the following year when on 8 September 1979 we won the Gillette Cup by beating Northants by 45 runs. Those defeats of the previous year had taught a hard lesson. There was no flashing blade from Viv Richards this time. I had drummed it into my mind that this was one we had to win, not just for ourselves but for those fans who filled Lord's again.

Twice I was given the Man of the Match award, first when Somerset triumphed in the Gillette Cup and then against Surrey in the Benson & Hedges final two years later. The man I felt sorry for was my countryman, Joel Garner, as he could easily have won both himself. Joel bowled really well with six for 29 against Northamptonshire and then five for spit against Surrey – and he was still not voted Man of the Match because there was a guy there who scored a century and then went back and scored another. The conditions were good for Joel and at one stage in that second final he had five for 14. In any other team on any other day, he would have been totally successful, the hero of the day.

I grafted like I had never grafted before. I arrived at the wicket in the seventh over and left in the last, an innings of over three hours which yielded 117 and just 11 boundaries. It earned me the Man of the Match award from Cyril Washbrook, but I felt that it should have gone to the Big Bird, Joel Garner. The Doc not only took a match-winning six for 29 in just ten overs but he also helped me add 49 runs in what proved to be the difference between the two teams.

By great irony, we once again had a second title to chase on the next day when we clinched the John Player League. This time we could celebrate with the fans, and one of my most enduring memories in cricket was driving round Taunton in an open-topped bus. It was very emotional and will live with me for ever.

Suddenly we were a team to be feared, a county to be reckoned with, and there was another day for my scrapbook on 25 July 1981 when we beat Surrey to win the Benson & Hedges Cup. We were always in charge of this one, restricting their scoring and then passing their total with plenty of overs to spare. I was on 132 not out when we won, and once again I robbed Joel of the Gold award.

Once we won that first tournament in 1979 we became a more influential side, even though we did not fulfil our ambitions and win the County Championship. We did well enough at the three-day game, but it was in the one-day stuff where we really excelled and began to take an authoritative grip. We were a very exciting side and our loyal public appreciated the excitement we brought. We went to Lord's three years on the trot and this is what the fans pay their money for. Every final was like the FA Cup Final as those people dug deep in their pockets for the day out. We wanted to

win and we cared about those people who supported us. With
Gloucester not doing well and Bristol City and Rovers out of
touch, it was something the region needed at that particular time.

One incident I am not very proud of in retrospect was the infamous
ten-minute game against Worcester in the Benson and Hedges Cup
in May 1979. With two teams from Group A to qualify for the
quarter-finals we were top with nine points, followed by our
opponents and Glamorgan, who were both on six. It shouldn't
have been a problem, as we would fail to qualify only if we
lost and if Glamorgan hammered the Minor Counties and both
Glamorgan and Worcester significantly improved their wicket-
taking rates.

It was late May and the weather was, to me, like a bad winter.
Worcester's Sunday League game had been a complete wash-out
and the ground staff had toiled away to get a strip ready for our
game and they were not helped by further rain or by an accident
with the roller which damaged one of the strips they were preparing.

No play was possible on Wednesday, and Thursday dawned grey
and unsettled. Rose worked out a way by which we would be sure
to qualify in defeat by declaring after the first over. Although we
would be sure to lose, this way there was no chance of Worcester
overtaking our wicket-taking rate. It was clever and it was within
the rules, and everyone, including myself, backed him. Rose and
Peter Denning opened the batting for just the one over and declared
with the score at 1-0 – the single run coming from a no ball.
Worcester, through Glenn Turner, scored the two runs they needed
without loss off 10 balls. The entire match had lasted ten minutes
and a total of 17 balls.

> Somerset
> B. C. Rose not out 0
> P. W. Denning not out ..0
> Extras...........................1
> Total............................1-0 (declared)
> Bowling: Holder 1-1-0-0

Worcestershire
G. M. Turner not out 2
J. A. Ormrod not out 0
Total..............................2-0
Bowling: Dredge 1-0-1-0; Jennings 0.4-0-1-0

While it had seemed the right thing to do on the pitch, once we were back in the dressing-room the enormity of what we had done hit us. There was none of the usual banter and no laughter as we realized we had overstepped the mark. Any lingering doubts were erased as soon as we stepped out of the dressing-room to a chorus of abuse. It was a case of 'Oops, we have not heard the last of this incident.' And in our hearts we knew we had messed up badly.

The recriminations were instant as the handful of spectators – no more than 100 – protested, even after getting their money back. It was understandable, as some of them had been waiting around for two days to watch some cricket, while a couple of farmers from Somerset had made the long trip. There was also a group of schoolchildren brought to the game for a treat. Some treat that turned out to be.

The press and everyone else slaughtered us – and rightly. Even *Wisden* said that Brian Rose 'sacrificed all known cricketing principles'. It was a case of it being a good idea at the time, but it was not helped when Rose insisted he was within his rights and the committee backed him. A week later, the Test and County Cricket Board ruled that we should be expelled from that season's competition for not complying with the spirit of the game. We were totally in the wrong and I feel embarrassed at my part in the decision. It turned out not to have been even necessary, as Glamorgan's game was washed out. Next season the rules of the competition were changed to stop declarations in the competition. It was a blot on Somerset's pride, but the county recovered to win two of the next three Benson and Hedges competitions!

Somerset's success was helped because the guy in charge, Roy Kerslake, had the insight to ask the senior players what they thought was needed to get things moving. Apart from myself, Joel Garner came as the strike bowler, and with the new personnel came a new sense of urgency. The training sessions became like West Indies training sessions and people would come and clap at the end as we warmed down. It gave all of us the feeling that we were the team to watch. We started believing in one another and this self-belief gave players like Victor Marks the chance to go on and represent their country. I still believe, though, that it was Brian Close who built the platform for our success. There were some characters who didn't have the instinctive stomach for competition that he, Ian Botham and Joel Garner did, but he did his best to change that and turned us into a very formidable side.

There was a big clearing-out when Brian Close went. Cartwright was another who departed. He was player-coach and, because he was a bit injury-prone at the time, they weren't able to see the real Cartwright play and it affected the balance of our attack. The age factor had a lot to do with it as regards both Tom and Brian.

There were others who went and others who should have gone, mainly those 'professionals' who moved from county and county, picking up their wages and stopping young players developing and coming through.

Apart from Beefy, myself and Joel there were some good young-sters, like Peter Denning who formed the perfect partnership with Brian Rose to open the batting. Rose was a quiet, unassuming sort of individual. Close used to call him Dozey Rosey because he was always dropping off. He could sleep on a clothes line – still smoking a slim panatella!

Rose had a good group of players and he had an understanding with them and handled them well enough. It took him a little while to realize that it was not just himself he was looking after, and he became a little more open in expressing his views to people like Joel and myself and to Derek Taylor, who had a long career at Surrey before coming to Taunton. We were a group of strong personalities; we all loved our cricket and loved performing, so we weren't difficult to handle. We also liked competing and we were team mates and between us knew what needed to be done. We were determined that there would be no personalities who were going to get in the way of what we wanted.

I have a lot of time for the Big Bird, Joel Garner. He was very laid back and was the original gentle giant. He was another, like Close, who was always keen to drive. He was a fun-loving character who liked the outdoors and the open roads. There were times when Joel would fit himself into his car and drive all the way from Taunton to Oldham, where he had friends he had made while playing League cricket, just to have a few pints, and then he would drive back the next morning. We were amazed at this ability, but he thought nothing of it at all. I often travelled with him in his car. I would be sitting in the front seat, but he was so big it looked as though he was driving the car from the back seat with his legs almost up against the windscreen. As soon as I climbed into the car I would start laughing. It was the same story when we shared a room in a hotel. I would be lying down laughing as I looked over at Joel who would have limbs hanging over the edge of the bed. Fortunately he rarely took offence, as he was the kind of guy who would do anything for you.

He was an accomplished cook and would often make dinner for us. He took it very seriously, and we looked forward to him inviting us over for some typical West Indian cooking, something Hallam Moseley and I really enjoyed. It was a taste of home. One of his specialities was soup, and one day Beefy and I came out of the pub feeling peckish and ate most of a pot of soup Joel had made. That wasn't so bad, but then Beefy became naughty and put some stones in the bottom of the pot. When Joel came back home that night, hungry after downing a couple of pints, he discovered what had been done to his soup. He was furious and we had to keep low for a few days. He got over it and we were soon giving high fives again when he took his wickets – but we had to promise him we wouldn't put stones in his soup ever again.

Whenever we were all together, Ian and I would take the mickey out of him, trying on his huge size-15 shoes or putting on his blazer with the arms hanging down to the floor. He would say: 'Gor blimey you guys, always making sport of me.'

Whenever we were given our new kit, whether it was for Somerset or the West Indies, it didn't matter how much Joel had been measured, when the blazer and slacks came back you could see from his face that he was in trouble again.

Everyone was aware of the situation and would play up as they tried on their own kit, preening themselves in front of the mirror and declaring, 'Perfect fit, man.' Joel would sit there doing nothing because he knew that, once again, he was going to be the butt of the jokes.

I would wander over and say, 'Hey, Doc, haven't you tried on your stuff yet?'

He would reply, 'No man, I'm waiting until last because I know, man, whatever they do it will come back short, short, short.'

But everyone would linger because they knew they would see something funny, his new kit would be short in the arms and short in the leg. Eventually he would try the clothes on and I would shout across, 'The fit OK, Doc?'

He would suck on his teeth, the way people do on our island, and say, 'Smokey, do they think that I am some kind of idiot? Every time I come they always bring me clown suits. Everything is short.'

He might have been hard to fit out, but he was one of the best bowlers I have ever seen. A different style from anyone else, almost unique. He was a big, strong man at six foot eight. He had that classical action, very high, with a jump as well. It made him lethal, with the steep bounce of the ball as it came down from that great height.

He would completely tie down the best of batsmen and have them under his control. He would surround the bat with catchers and call down the wicket, 'I don't need no mid on and I don't need no mid off and all the batsman will need is a stepping ladder.'

The three of us got on well and, even when we played against each other at international level, we would carry on our friendship.

The Somerset team was not short of characters. There was Dennis Breakwell, whom Ian nicknamed the 'Severed Nerve' because he was real hyperactive, a man who could never sit still. Botham couldn't handle that: someone more fidgety than him! And as a result he took the mickey out of him unmercifully. Dennis was the regular target of Ian's jokes. Botham would pull at his ears and his nose so hard, I thought that one day one of them must come off. He was Beefy's stooge.

Vic Marks was a quiet man and you would never hear him say anything bad about anyone. When he talked he needed a megaphone so that you could hear him. He was a lovely individual who, when the cricket became tight or tense, would grab hold of his own ear and roll it between his fingers until eventually he wore away a piece of skin. But he was a very committed cricketer and he used to chip in with his bowling and take wickets. He consistently flighted the ball in one-day cricket and won us a lot of matches, and often when the batting would fail he would come along with runs.

The spirit was good with just the occasional bust-up, mainly when guys came into the team and wouldn't work; they wanted to eat off the rich man's plate, and Ian in particular hated that. But we never allowed them to divert or stop us.

The best and most lasting memories were of when we went around Taunton town in an open-top bus after we had achieved a double of winning the knock-out cup on Saturday and the League on Sunday in 1979. I felt that this was what I was being paid to do. Seeing all the people lining the streets, that was what it was all about. It was the icing on the cake. This wasn't about earning money, it was about helping to make the county a better team and winning something. I loved the feeling of winning and being successful as a team. We had a wonderful time, going to the Town Hall and the Mayor telling us how proud we had made Somerset.

Money certainly wasn't everything. I started off at £1 a day and moved on to £2,000 a year, and the most I ever earned with Somerset was £15,000. There were other players at bigger clubs who were not doing so well but were earning a great deal more. It didn't matter. That was all part of the job and I was totally embedded in that set-up. I felt I was part of the community and not just the cricket, and to be one of the underdogs who came good after more than a hundred years was something that made all of us feel good. Regardless of the money – or the lack of it – I felt fulfilled. All I wanted to do was to play cricket. I have never been a greedy man and I am of the opinion that when things come too easy you lose something. I believe in hard work, and if the returns are good enough – then I can cope with that as well.

What annoyed and hurt me, however, was that when I did ask for a pay rise, along with Beefy and Joel, I was turned down flat. We were scarcely asking for a lot, but I feel that from that time onwards for the next three years our relationship with the board members started to deteriorate.

The attitude within the team definitely started to change when Peter Roebuck was made captain. Roebuck is one individual I had a lot of respect for, in terms of his intelligence and his knack for being sharp, but not for other things.

When I first went to Somerset and we first got to know each other, Peter was not a very outgoing sort of person. For a young man with everything in front of him it was hard to understand why he was such an introvert. As a cricketer he is not the most attacking individual, but he has enormous powers of concentration. He is a hard worker and gritty and he works within his limitations and gets things done.

As captain, though, he was sometimes out of his depth and there is no doubt that the county went backwards when he took over. I don't think that someone with such a complex personality is suitable for the job. When we played and lost a quarter-final at Hove he refused to travel back with the person he had come with and walked all the way back. It was a very strange thing for anyone to do, but for a captain it was inexplicable. There were certainly occasions when his personality alone could create disharmony within the team.

I managed to go home fairly regularly while I was playing in England, although the first couple of years were quite hard for me because I was selected to tour India, Pakistan and Sri Lanka in the first year and then went to Australia the next, spending Christmas away from my family on both occasions. I also had a house in Taunton where the family spent five or six months each year. There were no worries about school as the children went to nursery and play school. My son was born in Taunton and my daughter in Canada, where my wife has relatives. I took time off from Somerset to fly over to Canada for my daughter's birth. It was great to have my family around me for those five or six months, but when the children were ready for secondary school I wanted them to go back to Antigua. It was important for me that they should learn about their background and their heritage. I wanted to give them the opportunity to know about their country, where their mother and father were born and what it meant to belong to Antigua and Barbuda.

There were still serious demands on my time though, and I didn't have the chance to see as much of home as I wanted. I would have liked the opportunity to go home and see family and friends and to play for my island. I played a couple of matches for Antigua and for the Leeward Islands, but they suffered as well because I was away and the domestic cricket was neglected by both myself and Andy.

There was nothing in my life that could have prepared me for life on the county cricket circuit. Dreams of lazy, hazy days in the English countryside, salmon and cucumber sandwiches for tea and sleeping in a four-poster bed in a historic country inn could not have been more removed from the truth.

For the average county cricketer it was more like cross-country car rides after a long day in the field, the boredom of another wet and fruitless day, a packet of crisps for dinner, a pork pie for breakfast and an intimate knowledge of the various chains of cheaper hotels. Without any question cricket is a very odd way of life, and I doubt that there is any other sport like it in Britain.

The hardest part of all was the travelling. I doubt if any other professional sportsmen travel as many miles as a county cricketer – and do it all by private car. The number of coach rides in my time with Somerset and Glamorgan I could count on one hand. Instead, the county would expect you to go from game to game under your own steam. We would find a partner, someone in the team with whom you would feel comfortable passing all those hours, and the two of you would share the driving. We always travelled by car, with the possible exception of a final when the county would hire a coach.

I am amazed that there have not been more accidents and fatalities over the years, with cricketers driving long distances after a tiring day in the field and a night in the bar. Maybe we were all aware of those dangers and the rough terrain and handled it as professionally as possible. But it was hard to adjust to sitting in a car after a match, maybe with your back in spasms or nursing a broken finger, getting ready physically and mentally for another game in another town and another county the next day. To me that was cruel, particularly for so little reward. In fact the wages were so small (and often for only part of the year) that the players, in fact, were happy to drive themselves so that they would pick up their car allowance, which helped boost their money.

A typical summer's day would see the team set off for an away match, driving overnight after play had finished and staying together at a medium-priced hotel, in those days somewhere like a Trust-house Forte, booked at a special reduced rate by the county. The choice of hotel varied season by season and according to the rates on offer, and the morning of the game would see us making sure we knew how to find the quickest way to the county ground. Often the receptionists wouldn't know or would send us in the direction of the football ground instead of the cricket ground. Despite the fact that many players played at the same ground year after year, we would still be driving round in circles looking for a sign saying 'County Ground'.

The first thing to be done on arrival at a hotel, after throwing the bag in the room, would be to find the best pub where we could have a drink and a cheapish meal. Favourite in those days were the Berni Inns, where we could get a pint of lager and a good steak for a reasonable sum in an environment that was relaxed and not stuffy.

The order of the day would be to build a base with a good meal first and then prop up the bar until it was time for bed, usually around midnight as far as I was concerned. In modern professional terms that, I suppose, was pretty poor preparation and you certainly couldn't imagine the likes of Manchester United or Arsenal doing things that way.

I enjoyed a drink and going out as much as the next man, but I knew that as a sportsman I had to take care of my body, and if there was a big match next day I would limit myself to a couple of pints after or with dinner and then watch some television or read a little in my room. Then there were other occasions when I knew it wasn't my turn to drive and I would drink a few more pints.

There was rarely anyone travelling around with us keeping an eye on our way of life or our diets, and I drew on my experiences with the West Indies to know what to eat and what not to eat. I used to see guys eating a steak and kidney pie or a pork pie in the morning because they didn't have time for a proper breakfast before a game. I preferred bananas, other fruit and lots of water. I would pick at things during the day and by the time the evening came I was ready for something solid, like one of those big juicy Berni Inn steaks. We did that run so often we didn't need to see the menu, we knew it by heart – and probably better than the restaurant manager!

Inevitably with an all-male cast, social life would centre round the bar of the hotel to start with, and then groups would move off to their various choices of venue. There were the odd teetotal players who wouldn't want to associate with someone like Ian Botham because you knew if you were around Beefy that you were going to indulge in a bit of drinking here and there. One could lead to two and two to three and so on, so those who wanted to avoid that sort of night would go off, maybe to a cinema or a quiet bar.

It was no problem to me. If I didn't fancy a drink that night, I wouldn't drink. Beefy would call me a 'little pup' and worse, but that never bothered me because I was doing what I wanted and not what Both wanted me to do. But others found his personality a little too strong and were sucked in when their brains were perhaps telling them to be sensible.

Then there were always the girls. They always seemed to know where the county teams were staying and they would be in evidence at the bar when we came down after checking in to our rooms. It really was a game for a single man with no ties, for the temptations were great for a fit, healthy guy and it is hard to resist a pretty face when you are away from home and wives or girlfriends for so much of the year.

There were girls we would see and remember every time we went to a certain town; particularly so once Botham started to become a cult figure, and his reputation went before him. This was when the different groups became even more marked, with those who wanted a quiet night, those who wanted a drink, those who pursued the cricket groupies and those who wanted to go on into the night by finding a club.

As far as I was concerned, clubbing was for when the sport was over. I found it hard enough as it was, getting up on dark English mornings, without feeling as if someone had dragged you through a hedge a couple of hours before you were due to play. What was the percentage in having a hangover and putting your very life at risk, facing fast bowlers who wanted to hurt you and enhance their reputation at your expense? I wanted to feel in the right frame of mind, especially if I faced a day in the field or maybe a big innings at the crease.

Fortunately, the ones who lack professionalism and try to burn the candle at both ends don't last – or at least most of them don't. But there are some individuals whose constitution is staggering. Joel Garner was one such phenomenon. His excuse is that he cannot sleep at night and he claims he needs to be up and about.

With the nomadic existence we led it was hardly practical to have a team curfew, but there have to be rules and if everyone did just what they wanted there would be total anarchy. As far as I was concerned, especially when I was captain, you couldn't have one law for one player and another law for another. Every member of the team should be a part of a professional unit with no exceptions.

That was easier said than done and control is not easy, with fines the best way to curb the errant player if he gets caught. I certainly wouldn't ruin my beauty sleep by waiting up to catch him out, but you can always tell in the dressing-room who is and who isn't behaving, especially those who use your time and the team's time to catch up on their sleep. Those individuals have to be told, and if they still do not respond they have to be got rid of. They can never be part of a unit and cricket is a team sport.

At times county cricket could be deathly boring. Rain, of course, was the biggest problem in an English summer, but also those dreadful, long-drawn-out and meaningless draws and, worse still, my pet hate: the contrived finish.

When it does rain, that is the time for me to go looking for the most comfortable place to have a sleep, but the competition in that respect could be fierce. There are some guys who spend much of their playing life on the physio's bench, whatever the weather; and it was always with some trepidation that I would look in the physio's room to see whether one of the permanently injured had claimed the bed before me. One of my biggest rivals and the man I jockeyed with most was Joel, who was always on the look-out for the best place to sleep, following his usual nocturnal wanderings.

Card schools were a common way to pass time during bad weather, but I was not in total favour of cards, especially when the gambling became too heavy. A big loss can affect a player's performance and prove to be a big distraction from cricket. Fortunately, with such poor pay there was rarely any trouble in that direction.

Music is another regular defence against boredom and, with the advent of personal stereos, everyone could listen to the music of their own taste. But even the Walkman could cause problems; the West Indies captain Clive Lloyd had such difficulty in trying to get his message across to people wired into their favourite music that he finished up banning them at team meetings.

The bad times were those dead days away from home. If it was going to rain, we prayed it would do a good job and wipe out play completely rather than see us dodge in and out of the pavilion, avoiding the showers, to bowl a couple of dozen overs. Just in case the weather did grant us a free day, we always had our golf clubs in the back of the car. Ian Botham was famous for winkling out the golf-loving umpire who thought the same way as him. We knew he had a result when he came back to the dressing-room laughing and rubbing his hands and saying: 'Off to the golf course, guys.' It was better to get wet playing golf than trying to play cricket in the rain.

I started playing golf because of Ian Botham. I started in the mid-70s, buying myself some clubs and playing in a pro-am tournament for Brian Close's benefit. I now love my golf and play regularly at home in Antigua.

The alternative to golf or a sleep was to read a good book. Peter Roebuck was a big reader and he claimed that it helped his concentration, something the experts agree with.

Players can also become very childish when they are bored and run out of things to do. It can be irritating when they throw water or talcum powder over you while you are trying to sleep, and it can often produce a bad reaction. It certainly did with me. Rainy days were the low points, but almost as bad was the ground with no atmosphere and no spectators on an overcast, cold day when you had to get on with the cricket. There are too many days like that in county cricket when players underperform because, psychologically, they are not motivated. There is nothing better than a game of cricket on a summer's day if and when county cricket is played properly. What is needed is more quality cricket, more competitive cricket. There should be serious incentives in the sport.

I never enjoyed those icy days at the start of the season when fingers and toes would be numb from the cold and the body swathed in sweaters; but as the sun came out and the summer progressed, so things looked differently and suddenly it was like playing anywhere else in the world.

Cricket was always very well organized in England from the point of view of the grounds, the locations and the organization; everything always seemed to fit into place. I never realized how pretty some of these venues could be in the sun after being so dull under grey skies. Suddenly they were like different grounds. Up north it always seemed to be grey and gloomy in Yorkshire, Lancashire, Derbyshire and, to some degree, Leicestershire; but in the sun you realized that these were real grounds and these were the conditions cricket should be played in. There are so many beautiful little grounds around the United Kingdom.

I felt comfortable as the summer wore on. There were still days when it was chilly and the ball stung the hands and could hurt you; a full-blooded drive would make it feel like your hand belonged to someone else. Sometimes it takes a few overs in the field to feel right, and during that time you are silently praying that the batsman will find some other fielder to hurt. But once the jumpers were off my back and the shirt was open, the grounds became sun-traps and I felt thoroughly at home.

It helped that, at the time, the cricket we played was of a very high standard. I hear complaints that there were too many overseas players involved in county cricket then, but I found that the players were very committed. If a youngster or any cricketer couldn't learn from playing with and against the likes of the outstanding batsman Barry Richards or, one of my all-time-favourite all-rounders, Mike Procter, there was something wrong with them.

At that time there were players from all walks of life in the county game, all with different styles. There were the likes of Imran Khan, Majid Khan, Mushtaq Mohammad, Sadiq Mohammad, Intikhab Alam, Rohan Kanhai, Glenn Turner, Richard Hadlee, all world-class players, and English cricket was pretty prosperous because of their presence. Of course there were always the odd one or two who weren't committed and who came just for the money. But they tended not to last.

Personally, I really felt part of Somerset and committed to winning things with them. I wanted to help them win something. I also thought I was playing the highest grade of cricket when I played in the English County Championship, but I don't believe that to be true now.

★

There were always sponsors during my years at Somerset and most of the senior players were provided with a Saab car to drive, which was very acceptable. These cars had just started to hit the English market in a big way and Ian Botham was full of it, telling me how good the safety record was and what good cars they were. After the experience of driving my Saab Turbo, I decided I would buy one for myself to take home to Antigua.

The advice I was given was not all it should have been and I was just delighted to be able to buy a car free of many of the crippling taxes they have to pay in England. It meant, of course, that I was not allowed to drive the new car on English roads. But the thought came into my head that I would try and run some mileage up so that when I returned home I might be able to show the Customs and Excise that it was not that new a car and thus save some import taxes as well. It was a bit naughty, and it opened the door for anyone having any reason for feeling a little vengeful to pay me back.

That is exactly what happened; someone must have spotted my different number-plates and reported me. Whether it was a jealous individual, a bowler I had made suffer or an excise official who had been in the right place at the right time, I don't know. But one morning I was amazed as I sat in my room, relaxing, to see this car pull into my driveway. I thought maybe it was a friend, but then I saw these two soberly dressed individuals, wearing typical English greyish colours and carrying matching briefcases. It spelled doom.

My initial reaction when I saw these two men climb out of their car and make their way purposefully up my drive was that they were a couple of hit men! My first instinct was to grab my baseball bat to defend myself! I was a little reluctant to answer the door, but I was quickly put at my ease by these good-mannered gentlemen. I looked at their well-worn briefcases, trying to guess what they were at my door for, but there was no clue until one of them announced that they were from Her Majesty's Customs and Excise division. They told me that it had come to their notice that I had been driving the car in my drive on English roads when it had been bought specifically for export.

I was numb and was feeling worse by the minute when they

informed me that the car was officially seized. They wrote up a few notes and gave me a telephone number I could call. They said that in fact they were being very lenient in only taking away the car, and that they could have taken me away as well.

I immediately called my lawyer and told him what had taken place. But there was nothing he or anyone else could do. I had gambled and had broken the law, and it was a fair cop!

I had to pay a fine of about £4,000 for being a naughty boy by having the car on the M5 instead of on the Geese Line, being shipped to the Leeward Islands. It was a very expensive lesson well learnt. It was a stupid thing to do and I paid a heavy price, not just the fine but losing the car I had paid for as well.

In many ways I am considered a perfectionist; everything has to be immaculate and in order. It was nice to be in a country where everything is in order and things are run properly and procedures have to be adhered to. England in that respect is second to none; it is a place where people queue up to get on the bus or in a shop, and there is not the mad rush where everyone pushes forward and the strongest wins.

When I moved into my house from my flat, I had one of those periods when I was away for a few matches and was unable to tend my gardens and hedges. My hedges had grown while I was away and had covered part of the bus stop outside my house. Someone reported it and the council wrote to me, insisting that I trim my hedge. I was not offended, I appreciated it. What is for one is for all, and that helps to breed a disciplined society.

But, clearly, I had succeeded in making one or two enemies along the way.

But this was nothing compared to the massive shock I got when I heard little whispers about my future prospects at Somerset, hearing things like the names of the players likely to replace me. It was mind-boggling after all I had put in. I felt that the very least I was owed was for someone to come and talk to myself and Joel, but no one did; the rumours were simply dismissed as speculation. But the speculation and rumour turned out to be true.

Somerset wanted the Kiwi, Martin Crowe. He was a decent man and it was not his fault that matters developed the way they did. It was the way the board went about it as though Viv Richards had ceased to exist and had never done anything for the county. I thought I deserved a better treatment.

When the axe fell, it was not done with any decorum. Joel called me from the ground and said, 'Smokey, I have just been sacked and they want you at the ground now, man.'

Incredibly, they had sacked him and had then had the cheek to tell him to ring me!

From the moment Tony Brown had come in as secretary, things began to deteriorate. Some people have the effect of being disruptive rather than helpful. Tony must have known at that time what was needed for the county – but after what happened they didn't go forward, they went backwards.

Board member Brian Langford was with Brown when I arrived at the ground, and the first thing they told me was that they wanted a letter written by them and signed by me saying that I wanted to leave of my own accord! I couldn't believe what I was hearing. They didn't just want to cut off my head, they wanted me to hold the axe!

I told them that there was no way I would sign something with which I didn't agree. I couldn't see any reason other than that their new captain, Roebuck, felt a little uneasy in the strong presence of Ian, Joel and myself. He lacked that sort of presence and personality, and it was his opportunity to start his own little club. This was when Somerset went downhill.

I wasn't that surprised. I'd had three years' warning and there were constant signs like seeing Martin Crowe arrive at the ground for a meeting while I was in the field playing. I knew then that my time wasn't long. Some of the committee were naïve and didn't know about the cricket and would listen to Roebuck, who behaved in an idiotic fashion.

No one bothered to talk to Joel or myself and say what he or she thought was wrong before that day when we were sacked.

I went back to Somerset during the 1999 World Cup in England, while I was working for the BBC. I was asked how I felt about the county, bearing in mind that I had previously refused to take up an offer of membership. The years had softened me, and when I remembered how much sweat and blood I had put in I realized that I was part of it and that now was the time to take my place. I was part of the history. This was the house that Viv helped build. It was self-defeating to go back feeling bitter and angry.

Beefy felt the same way and he too has taken membership and, while we have forgiven, we will never forget. Beefy knew how committed I was to Somerset when he made that huge sacrifice of quitting the county over the sacking of Joel and myself. That, I felt, was a gesture of true friendship. He was away a lot on his England duties, and often we had to carry his mantle in his absence. It was a measure of his personality and the respect in which he was held that when he came back he fitted straight in. It was a very big decision made by a very big man. What had Somerset missed? Well, he went to Worcester and played in a final at Lord's and won, while I eventually arrived at Glamorgan and helped them to win the Equity and Law trophy and finish second in the Championship.

Clearly there was something left in these players who had been forced out. Certainly there was enough left to spark up another team. I don't know if that proves anything or not, but I feel that it was Somerset's loss in the end.

But I had some great years there and I liked being part of the set-up, and in most of the big semi-finals and finals I was fortunate enough to be among the runs. That was my stage, it was the occasion when I could use my experience and knowledge of big games and my international experience. But the most important thing from the team's point of view was that others contributed by winning matches when it counted.

What I enjoyed most of all was being part of a team, a winning team. I have no regrets about my time at Somerset and cherish the friendships and the wonderful people I met. Success was helping Somerset overall to win trophies and to give them the opportunity to be a county to be reckoned with.

We were open in our dealings with our public and we played

our cricket in the same fashion. People felt that they knew us.

I would love to have finished my career at Somerset, but there were individuals and factors that helped to dismantle what we had built. It was a place where I felt comfortable.

3. The King and I

A continuous period of 30 days and 30 nights on the road with Ian Botham was enough to test even our friendship and it took us to the brink of a punch-up in Australia. Some 15 years after meeting at Somerset, the occasion was our tour of England and Australia in the winter of 1991 with a two-man show called *The King and I*. It paid well and for the main part it was great fun, except for the fact that it almost cost Ian and me our long standing relationship.

The problem was that everything had to be to Ian's agenda. Although there were two other big men, David English and myself, around as well, whatever Ian said, that was how it had to be. I didn't like that at all. As far as I was concerned, it was a partnership, a two-man show, and it should have worked that way.

One night in Australia I almost lost it completely and Ian along with it. I was watching a video in the wings shortly before we were due on when suddenly Ian said that I wasn't being professional. I was behind the curtain, the stage was dark and no one could see. I was seething. I told him what he could do with his comments and not to tell me what was professional and what was not. The manager had to step in between us and calm us down. At that moment I was tired and a long way from home, and I was ready to fight him.

We had thirty nights living in each other's pockets and working without a break, and that didn't suit my nature. I just don't operate like that. I like to have a rest, chill out now and again, and if someone had shown me the itinerary *before* it was all confirmed I would have made that point very forcibly and ensured that I had one or two nights off in between our shows.

Ian was making the decisions for me, and that I didn't like. He soon found out that while it might be all right for him to walk up and down Britain and do a pantomime season without a night off, I didn't work that way.

I raged at him, 'You are accustomed to all that with "Jack and the Beanstalk" and all that shit. I have to recharge my batteries. Don't do that to me.'

But that was cool. I had had my say and that was it. The beauty of the relationship was that we were able to have our shindigs and our little rows, but when we went on stage it was all forgotten. We are two explosive characters and things were always going to happen.

Another night, I had one or two too many Old Monk Indian rums on a promotion for Cathay Pacific. Ian had a guy called Jez working for him as some sort of partner, and I overheard him joking to Beefy, pointing at the Indians and saying something about 'When you were in charge of that lot'. It was clearly a racist remark and I hit back.

'What fucking lot you talking about, you see any of your land around here?'

He should have realized that he had touched a raw nerve, but he wouldn't let it drop as he added, 'When we had all these countries colonized, everything was in place and there was lots more discipline.'

I became increasingly heated and snapped back, 'I don't want to hear all that,' and dived at the man. Beefy had to jump in between us to stop us fighting. I stomped off to my room, but when I came down next morning everything was cool again and we were back on the road.

That was the closest we came to blows, but I cannot ever really imagine it happening. But I will never do that again, living out of a caravan for 30 nights, breathing in each other's fumes. That was not my style. I liked to do other things while I was working. Financially it was rewarding. We were paid around £30,000 and played to mostly full houses. The biggest audience we had was in excess of 1,000 in the big towns, with an average of around 400 in the smaller towns. We played some interesting venues on that tour, including the Wembley Conference Centre with 1,000 or more, and generally the crowds were damned good. The worst we had was around 50, one night in the West of England. Frankly I didn't want to go on with it, but Both drew on his pantomime experience again and said that if just one man and his dog turned up we had to go ahead and perform.

The shows in Australia tended to be much more rowdy than those in England. We operated mainly out of working men's clubs where the beers were swilled down with great enthusiasm before, during and after our shows. The drunks often tended to gather in the front row or the closest tables and one well-lubricated character became impatient when the introductions were being made and shouted, 'C'mon, cut the bullshit, Botham, tell us the full story, how many fuckin' women did you have?'

I almost fell off the stool laughing. It took the drunk a lot of energy to get the words out, and he promptly slumped back in his seat, completely out of it. Both turned to the audience and said, 'You see the problem you have when you have brothers sleeping with sisters.' It went over the drunken heckler's head because by then he had passed out.

Australia was so different from England and when we tried to give nice polite answers, you could guarantee that someone would stand up and give it the 'Cut the bullshit, Viv, tell us how it really was. You are in Australia now.' They wanted to hear effing this and effing that and when I went for a couple of answers without using a profanity another guy jumped up and shouted, 'C'mon, Viv, we're all mates here, y'can swear, y'know.'

The smaller towns were the funniest, liveliest and most enjoyable to play, particularly when the beer started to do its work.

After the show we would make sure the road manager had checked that he had a few beers in the back of the wagon for me, while Beefy would make sure he had a case of red wine at hand. He had read somewhere that a couple of glasses were good for the heart and the circulation. He must have worked on the principle that the more of it he drank, the healthier he would get. But seven bottles, Both? Do me a favour!

At the various cities in both England and Australia we would meet up with cricketers we had played with or against and friends we had made on our travels, usually going out for a late dinner after the show. We became real night owls, travelling and resting during the day and working in the evening. It could be very tiring and sometimes I just had to check out and head for my bed, like the night we were due to go out with a chef named Floyd who Both had met in Sydney. It turned out to be a good decision on my part as my showbiz partner arrived back at 6 a.m. the next day. He was full of what a great guy this Floyd was.

I thought 'Oh, yes, another new mate,' and I asked him, 'What was so great about this one?'

'We finished twelve bottles of red between us!' said Both.

I was glad I had missed out on that one.

It was like turning the clock back to the days when we shared flats near the ground in Taunton.

Before I moved into my own place, I first lived in a flat above the cricket shop at Taunton with Ian. Initially we shared the flat with Derek Breakwell who had moved down to join us from Northants. He was a man looking for fun after a divorce, but eventually he became serious about the lady he later married. The flat was hardly the place to bring her back to with two other fellows and their lady friends wandering about in various states of undress. We stayed there for a season.

After that I moved out to lodge with Hallam Moseley for a while so as to have some warm food, before Both and I found another flat to share.

When Ian and I shared our second flat, it was an investment. It had two bedrooms, a lounge, kitchen and bathroom, and at times it looked as though Hurricane Hugo had passed through. The focal point of the flat was the fridge, where I kept food and Both kept his liquid refreshment, mainly beers. The place was a bit like a tent, with people coming in at one door and out through the other as our friends would crash down after a particularly heavy night. There were four different rooms for occupation, apart from the wardrobes.

We led a hectic life and Both seemed to relish it, but he was sensible enough to slow down and mature. They were certainly memorable years, but no one could sustain that pace for long. That had worked well for a short time because we were so different. I was careful about my food and what I ate whereas Both was most interested in his liquid intake, whether it was wine, beer, gin, whisky or whatever. In our relationship I was the cook and he was the wine waiter. He would laugh at me and my quaint habit of wanting to eat regularly, but it always ended the same way: the food I cooked went down to his tummy to join the wine or the beer. If I didn't cook, it was down to the curry house, the Chinese restaurant or the fish-and-chip shop. Variety, they say, is the spice of life.

Most of the parties we had at the flats were impromptu. It was a bit like the fictional House of the Rising Sun from the '60s Animals' hit. The normal routine was that we would be drinking in a pub when the landlord would call time and ours was the natural place to go back to, with no wives or girl friends for us to worry about disturbing. The problem with that was the arrival of the cleaners the next day. People have no respect for other people's property, especially on top of a belly full of beer. After a particularly bad session I made a pledge that in future we would only go somewhere where they could cater for sessions like this, such as a nightclub. I reached this conclusion after finding cigarette burns on the carpets and the furniture and beer and food spilt everywhere after one get-together. It was not good to get up to in the morning and it was worse for the poor lady who had to clear up afterwards.

Eventually Ian and I went our separate ways. It would have been hard for me to carry on living in that style and at that pace. I was fortunate that I was of an age when my natural adrenalin and constitution could soak up that lifestyle. But while it was an enjoyable time, you cannot keep that pace up for ever and I can look back at it with pleasure and fond memories.

Taunton was usually a quiet town in those days, but it could also be a little wild. Now and then when we went out we would be chased home by a mob, often making it to our front door in the nick of time. Basically, there were some unsavoury yobs and the local village Rambos who fancied their chances against two people who were in the public eye. More often than not, the problems were over women. It was not unknown for a lady to ask Beefy or myself to dance at a nightclub and, being two gentlemen, it would not have been very polite of us to refuse. You dance, chat, then one dance becomes two, two become three. Suddenly you discover that, all along, she had a boyfriend with her and she has left him standing at the bar and, not unnaturally, he starts getting a bit cross and gives her a little tug. Anything can happen from then on – and usually did.

For me it was all part of the growing-up process. There was access to so many things simply because of what we did for a living. It was a different experience compared to that of the shy youngster growing up in the Ovals, skimming stones and hanging around Darcy's bar. What is more, there was no apprenticeship, as it were, nothing to ease us from total obscurity to a place on the big stage as both of us went to the top fairly quickly and were soon recognized around the streets and in the pubs and clubs.

Ian Botham's rise to the top was especially rapid. England had needed a character like him for a long time, there was just no one around with that charisma allied to so much raw talent. He grew into his public persona. It was a tiring life living alongside this human dynamo and I took every opportunity to catch up and get a good sleep. One day I managed to slip away during a game and slept like the dead on the physio's table next to the dressing-room. But when I woke I discovered that Ian had tied my feet together. There I was, thinking everything was cool, and the next moment I was down on the floor.

But it was difficult to be cross with him and his sometimes childish humour. Basically he was as good as gold. What I like about Beefy most is his openness. We hit it off right from the start, and what impressed me initially was what he did for me as a young individual. When he befriended me at the Lansdown club he didn't know me or have a clue that I was going to be a test player. When I came to England I was an unsophisticated young man, but he just embraced me and accepted me as I was. I met him for the first time at Lansdown in Bath when I was playing for the club side. When

I walked into the clubroom he was the one who came up to me and made me feel welcome. He has always had this wonderful attitude towards other human beings and none of his knockbacks have changed him or his attitude to life.

When we were living in the flat just outside the ground we did everything together. It was very spontaneous. He did a lot for the whole white race as far as I was concerned. Here was a naïve young black man with very little experience of being in what was virtually an all-white community, and this guy was just totally outgoing; his outlook was as laid back as that of any West Indian. But when it came to playing cricket it was 'All the other nonsense stops, now let's get on with it.'

People used to say he was my white brother. West Indians believed he should have been born in the Caribbean but, equally, Australians thought he would have made a good Aussie.

He is a very genuine individual. If he is with you, he is always in your corner, someone you can trust, someone you can call on when you have a problem. Look at what he did when Joel Garner and I were sacked at Somerset. He immediately quit in sympathy when he did not have to. He could have simply registered his complaint and got on with his job, but he felt strongly enough about his friends to walk out with us. You couldn't ask for much more than that from a friend.

As that action indicated, he is a very unselfish man. He made a few mistakes in his colourful past because of his joy in living and his attitude to people, and sometimes he brought people on board who were not always trustworthy or reliable.

Anyone who says they believe in Ian Botham earns his instant and undivided love; he takes them immediately to his bosom. Often he would come to me and say, 'Have you met my mate?' It would be someone he had just shaken hands with for the first time, they had enjoyed a drink together and already this new person was his close buddy. This was where we were often at loggerheads because it was all so alien to the Antiguan mentality. We are often considered surly or inhospitable in comparison with other islanders from places like Barbados or St Lucia because we have to really know someone

before we accept him or her as a friend and a confidant. By and
large you have to earn an Antiguan's friendship. But then it lasts
for ever.

Beefy was hurt several times by a few who came in the night
and slipped away with the dawn. He was simply too welcoming
and gullible at times and if we had a little argument it would
generally be over that issue. A friendship to me is a little bit deeper
than meeting a guy one night and sinking six pints together and
cracking a few jokes.

I remember when he first met up with the larger-than-life Tim
Hudson, who became his agent. He was going to change Ian's
world and make him a millionaire overnight. Tim was a member
of all the right clubs and he was going to take us everywhere,
including Hollywood. He told Both that the game lacked true
characters and that he could be the English equivalent of Errol
Flynn in Hollywood. (I suppose he meant a dashing swordsman
rather than any of the more unsavoury characteristics of the late
actor.)

Hudson's first problem was that Both never concerned himself
overmuch with how he looked. He was colour blind and never
looked in the mirror twice to see if his shirt was tucked in – or
whether he had one on at all – but Tim soon had him wearing
pretty striped blazers, a silk hanky in the top pocket and a fedora
perched on his head. I have to admit that he looked a bit odd to
me when he was properly shaved, with his fancy haircuts and
peroxide-blond locks. This wasn't the Ian Botham I had grown up
with.

He said to me at one stage, 'Viv, we are all going to Hollywood
and you can be my valet and bodyguard.'

I smiled and said fine, I took it all with a pinch of salt and got
on with my cricket. But he really believed it when Hudson told
him how he was lining up meetings with all these famous directors
and producers in America. I felt totally out of my depth with all
this talk and I did not for one minute believe all this rubbish about
acting. There are so many actors on the dole and it's the unions
that dictate who works and who doesn't.

At the time, Beefy was on a high with his dreams and aspirations and he laid out his plans in front of me and told me exactly what he was going to do. It didn't sound real, but he was in no mood to listen to me or anyone else. So I sat back and watched. When Ian jetted off to the States, the fares, the accommodation and everything else was supposed to be looked after by Hudson. But when he came back, Both found himself stuck with a bill for £70,000. This woke him up as quickly as a cold shower and he started to look at the entire project with a more jaundiced eye. It was not long afterwards that he realized he had been taken on a wild-goose chase.

I wasn't surprised. Both had been taken in before and it would, I was sure, undoubtedly happen again. If a Tim Hudson came around today, I doubt whether Both would give him too much time. He was very gullible and easily led in those days. I took a back seat and just waited to see what would happen. I didn't see any real harm in Hudson. He was a good chatter, either on television or person to person. I couldn't see much wrong with him, but I wasn't going to let him guide my career.

Bev Walker was another agent who promised Beefy the world and said that he could make him the cult hero of the '70s. It was all summed up for me when the two of them drove up to a function in separate cars, with Walker stepping out of his Rolls-Royce while Botham climbed out of his Granada.

I laughed at the irony of it all and asked, 'Who is working for who here?'

Basically, I suppose, it was because he takes everyone at face value, and it is only now as he matures and tastes the bitterness of being let down that he has learnt to be more circumspect. It is sad because his friends are his friends until death does them part.

He had another bad time when he was captain of England in 1981. He was the popular public choice but there were an awful lot of players in the team who did not want him as their captain, and a lot of back-stabbing went on. Some of the senior players in the England side did not back his decisions and he was pilloried when things went wrong and matches were lost. What people still don't realize is that his record against the West Indies is better than those of most of the other recent England captains.

Quite rightly, he wanted to do things his own way, the way he saw it. But to do that he needed the backing of others, particularly the senior players. They didn't help him and didn't do it for him. As far as I was concerned, he was not a bad captain. He led from the front and by example. Maybe he didn't have the astuteness of a Mike Brearley, who had a good grip on the psychological side but was not blessed with a great deal of natural ability. Ian had all the ability in the world, plus a naturally aggressive approach to the game and a will to win. For me he was always the sort who could inspire a victory either from other people or from himself.

To my mind he should have been given a longer opportunity as skipper. In the end he was hounded so much from inside and outside the dressing-room that he was left with no choice but to relinquish the captaincy. Such was the pressure heaped on him as captain of England that it affected his personal performances, and as his form dipped this added weight to those who wanted to get rid of him. I am sure that he was a strong enough character to handle his form and the captaincy, but there was also the negative side, where the committee was going to deal with him and deal with him severely whenever he took a step out of line. The same people who built him up forsook him and knocked him down. But then that was, and still is, a national pastime in Britain: to build a hero and then prove he has feet of clay. It is easy to blame the media, but the press is just a reflection of public opinion in the end.

It was a strange feeling when I was in a bar in Somerset and I would hear holiday-makers running Ian Botham or another player down. But I guarantee that if that same player walked in, they would be the first to go up and shake his hand, say he had always been their favourite player and could they have his autograph for their son. The player who was an idiot a minute before is suddenly treated like a best friend.

Apart from my family, Both is about the only person for whom

I would physically stand up and fight to defend. When he was on his way up and we used to go into a bar or a nightclub, there would invariably be some drunken oaf who wanted to show how big he was, betting his friends he could go up and stand on Ian Botham's feet and wind him up. I would hear them say things like that or shout nasty things at him, particularly when things weren't going well for county or country. Whereas I would shrug it off when it was aimed at me or ignore it if it was aimed at another colleague, if Beefy was the target I would rush back and say, 'Be careful. That is my mate you are bad-mouthing, man.' There were a number of occasions when it actually came to physical contact as I jumped in and grabbed the offender, telling them, 'If you know what's good for you, back off.' Fortunately they usually did. I watched his back in England and the West Indies when critics and fools lined him up.

When he was captain of Somerset he could be harsh with those who were not pulling their weight, but he was always fair and never bore a grudge. He left that to smaller-minded people. As a cricketer he was the brightest light England has seen for many years. Forget his batting records, his bowling averages and the many brilliant catches he took, I prefer to assess a player on how many matches he has won for his team and what he did for cricket in his country. Ian was a major influence and I cannot think of any other English player in my time who had such an influence and who could pick up a team from a losing position and put them in place to win with either bat or ball. Cricket was fresh again because here was a young man who, you felt, was capable of doing anything. I was grateful that I was around at the same time, because cricket was exciting – not just in high-profile test cricket but also on the domestic scene where it wasn't always nationally and internationally recorded.

When I am asked – and I frequently am – who I would compare Ian with, I struggle to answer because there is no one to compare Ian with. He is a one-off, like Sir Garfield Sobers, a complete natural with nothing manufactured about him. These players have a right to be in a category by themselves and not to be compared.

His ability to field, catch, bat and bowl was undisputed. He was always involved from the time of the toss-up to the last orders at the bar.

I was around when he first met his wife, Kath, and I was the one who vacated my room so he could spend a bit of time with the lady he was going to marry. I also went to Yorkshire for the wedding and drank a lot of champagne and was then driven back to Somerset to play in a county match. That's the trouble with these summer weddings – but with tours there was little alternative for a busy cricketer. When he had his son Liam, I was proud to be asked to be the godfather.

There were times when Kath must have felt a little left out because he always wanted to be with the lads and have a drink with them. It was difficult for Kath. She has always been a very honourable woman who stuck by her man, whatever the accusations – and there were many. It shows how much she thinks of him. She also knows that, at times, some of the things that were said and written were far-fetched to say the least. There were other times, however, when she knew that Ian had stepped out of line. It is a hard life for a cricketer's wife, knowing that her man is away so much with so much temptation thrown at him. But she always knew that, at the end of the day, Beefy would come home to her, and in that respect he's always been very good to Kath, the children, Liam, Sarah and Becky, his parents and his in-laws. He always had time or made time for his family.

When someone helps raise as much money for leukaemia research as he did with those long walks on Hannibal's trail and from John o'Groat's to Land's End, it shows what a good and unselfish person that man is. Those marches, quite rightly, received the full glare of publicity by the media, but there were also many things he did for the disadvantaged away from the press and the public gaze. He is genuine, not a publicity-seeker. Media coverage or not, he was willing to put his body through so much pain to help others less fortunate than himself on those seven walks. What he did was gruelling and it was other people, not him, who told me the horror stories of what he had to do to get himself back on the road the next day. I tell you, man, he is just a wonderful human being, hard to find and even harder to create.

'He who dares, wins' is his attitude. He didn't care if he was hit for four successive boundaries in an over if he thought he could get the batsman out with the fifth or sixth delivery. He would then be satisfied with a job well done. Too many bowlers these days want to be economically tight and look to their averages instead of taking wickets.

He was a smart bowler. He worked on the batsman's mind, often offering that bait. He wasn't as quick as Michael Holding or Dennis Lillee, but what he had in his locker was the ability to swing the ball both ways and a willingness to experiment. Today everyone wants to be hostile, quick, and even the best tend to move it only one way. He always kept the batsman guessing.

He claimed my wicket a few times in test cricket. The bitterest was at Lord's in 1984, when umpire Barry Meyer apologized afterwards for giving me out leg before. Botham also got me out hooking, and another time he clean bowled me at Old Trafford. When Meyer gave me out lbw, Both put his hand over his mouth to stifle his laughter. He knew there was no way I was out, and at the end of play Meyer came and apologized and said he didn't know what he had been thinking about.

This man took over 300 test wickets, so I wasn't the only good batsman he snared more than once. He didn't have it all his own way, though. In Trinidad, in the first test of the 1980–81 series, his became the most prized wicket of my career. It was a big game for him and he had predicted that if England lost this match, then heads would roll. He also used to say to me when we were at Somerset together, 'Don't ever bowl that little pup stuff to me or I will crucify it.'

When it finally happened, I bowled at the aggressive Beefy without either a long on or a long off. It was unheard of, but I kept floating it up and every so often I quietly signalled for Michael Holding to drop back a bit at a time. Sure enough, Both took the bait, he couldn't hold out any longer and took a big woof. It went straight up in the air and when Mikey took the catch I went totally berserk. It was the first time I had celebrated like that as a bowler even to the extent of doing a couple of cartwheels under Ian's nose because I knew that this was the last thing on earth he wanted in this extreme moment of grief and self-pity.

He had promised me that if I ever got him out with my pup bowling he would buy me drinks for the rest of my life. He was strangely silent when he walked off, shaking his head at my antics and saying, 'Fuck off, Smokey.' At the time he couldn't laugh because England were in desperate trouble, in fact so desperate that I finished with an analysis of ten overs, six maidens and that one wicket for just nine runs.

We loved playing against each other because we both had the same competitive, aggressive attitude. Botham versus Richards was always special. I wanted to tear him apart as much as any other bowler, perhaps more, and he wanted my wicket just as badly. We were able to define our friendship on and off the field. He is proud to be English and I, equally, am proud to be West Indian.

If I walked into the room during a series between our two nations, he would say to everyone, 'Here comes my rabbit!' It was good fun and good banter. Mind you, I wouldn't take it from anyone else.

It didn't always go his way and I remember one incident when I gloved the ball and he appealed, confident he had my wicket again. I vigorously rubbed my upper arm, ignoring his appeal and refusing to walk. He turned round to me, grinned and said, 'Got you.' And then, to hurry me on the way back to the pavilion, 'Fuck off then, Smokey.'

I started laughing, pointed down the wicket and replied, 'Look at the umpire, Beefy, he hasn't moved . . . and neither have I.'

His glee turned to abject disappointment as he snarled, 'Oh no, Smokey. You fucking cheating bastard.'

But, as with all our tiffs, it didn't last long and at the end of the over this funny man signalled to the dressing-room and asked for some pain-killing spray for Viv's finger.

I gave him some fearful stick when I scored the record-breaking 110 at St John's in 1986. He wanted one wicket to become the greatest English wicket-taker of all time, and I wanted quick runs. We both went at it hammer and tongs. That day he tried everything he had in his locker: his slower ball, his yorker and his famous wicket-taking long hop; but I kept whacking him to the boundary. I didn't mind being part of my mate's history as the record-breaking wicket, but I wasn't going to let him have it cheaply, so I just kept going for my shots. In the end the ball found the middle of the bat and not much else as I scored my runs in 56 balls.

He felt at home in the West Indies, he loved the Caribbean with its sun and sea and its relaxed atmosphere. He was always up for an invite to visit the islands, as he was when I took him to Jamaica as guest of the Shell Company to play in a special match in Montego Bay.

He had said to me, 'Look, Smokey, I want you to look after me this time and set me up. I want a real taste of the Caribbean.'

It is no secret that he liked a drink, and he was particularly keen to try the sweet-tasting rum punch. But, as in most things in his life, Beefy sometimes goes too far. He stood there, drinking his rum punches, then turned round and said, 'What sort of drink is this? I can't even taste the rum.' He complained that all people ever gave him in the Caribbean was fruit juice.

I spoke quietly to the barman and we mixed him a rum punch that he could taste – one with a real kick. An Appleton 150%-proof rum!

After the session he went to his hotel room, lay down and promptly passed out. I went out without him and when I came back I couldn't get any answer from his room. I found the chambermaid and had to spin a yarn about my mate having heart trouble and that I was worried about him before she would let me into the room with a pass-key. She opened the door, and he was still spark out, mouth wide open, snoring and in a terrible state.

I promptly went out, found a lady friend and borrowed her lipstick, eye-shadow, rouge and all the necessary equipment, and set about making him up. Throughout the entire time I was prettying him up he never moved a muscle. There are photographs recording the occasion: Botham in drag. What am I offered?

Eventually his eyes popped open and he said, 'Smokey, what the hell was that drink you gave me?'

I said simply, 'West Indian fruit juice.'

Normally he is renowned as the man to take over at the bar and drink everyone under the table, but now I had him pleading with me not to tell anyone he had been wiped out with what he thought was a ladies' drink. It was lovely to see him like a puppy that night, and for once I had a little of my own back.

He is always playing practical jokes and it could sometimes grate on the nerves. In the old pavilion we had at Somerset he would creep up with a water-pistol and shoot at the umpires through a knothole in the wood or squirt you in the eye when you least expected it. He even did it when I was receiving my Man of the Match award from the sponsors, sending a stream of water our way when we were trying to be dignified.

Not everything Both did filled me with delight. He would often go over the top and become annoying. At times his humour could become a little juvenile, to say the least. I was driving back from one county game with Beefy as my passenger when another driver upset him. When we pulled up alongside, he dropped his trousers and stuck his backside out through the window. It is a big backside and it must have been a pretty horrible sight to the people in the cars around him. That little jape didn't go down too well so far as I was concerned. But most of the time he was good for the spirit and very uplifting.

I was never very keen to test his driving skill to the limit, having been his passenger to and from various cricket grounds and other venues. His driving made me just a little reluctant to ride with him regularly, knowing of the pranks he gets up to while at the steering wheel. He would say to me, 'Come on, Smokey, get your seat belt on.' And I would know I was in for a hairy time.

He is one of those guys who like to take their hands off the steering wheel when they are doing 90 miles an hour. My heart used to be in my mouth, but to him it was fun and excitement. Coming back from Yeovil, he would delight in driving on the country roads and taking on the farmers' tractors rather than the speed cameras or the traffic cops on the main roads. On one occasion I was his reluctant passenger when he was going at some crazy speed through the little lanes. I was very aware that, if we met something coming the other way, there was no room to spare on either side. All I could see from his TR7 were the trees and hedgerows flashing past, when suddenly a tractor pulling a trailer loaded with bales of hay emerged from a hidden entrance to a field. There was no time to brake as Ian swerved. I closed my eyes.

When I opened them again, the tractor had disappeared, leaving behind a trail of hay. Ian had come so close that he had clipped the last bale of hay hanging over the back of the trailer. I came close to doing something that is not normally in my repertoire. I was shaking like a leaf as Beefy switched on the wipers to clear the strands of hay clinging to the windscreen.

Then there was the time when he had a sponsor's car from Saab. The directors from the car company invited him to test an expensive new car on the racetrack. At the time he thought he was the next Nigel Mansell and with typical enthusiasm was seriously considering driving racing cars for real. We went to the track together and he decided he was going to have the test run with the managing director of Saab as his passenger. Ian wrote off the first car in a crash and the MD was smashed up and left with a bad back. Undeterred, Ian went back for the reserve car and promptly wrote that one off as well.

Sometimes this man takes on the road the way he takes on opposing cricketers, and that is why I didn't travel with Ian as often as I might have done. I was wary of who I went with after suffering a bad experience myself when driving a Capri back to Taunton after watching a final at Lord's with my friend Peter McCoombe. It had been a long, tiring day and I should have stayed over when I realized that my entire system had slowed down. Jock had been drinking, so I had to drive and, before long, my eyes started to blink shut so I pulled in to a petrol station and went to the washroom to splash some water on my face. This held me in good stead for a few miles – but the next thing I knew, this almighty bang had woken me up as I swerved left, smashed into the crash barrier, swung back and landed in the ditch, just outside Swindon.

Peter somehow ended up in the boot of the Capri, breaking his nose and hurting his back. Stupidly, neither he nor I was wearing a seat belt. I was so lucky because I stayed exactly where I was in the driving seat, although with the car facing the opposite way to the way we had originally been travelling.

Relief at having survived turned to something closer to panic as I heard Peter groaning behind me and I caught the unmistakable smell of leaking petrol. Peter, sadly passed on now, was a little tubby man, but when he smelled the dripping fuel he prised himself out of his unusual seat at terrific speed, with me close behind. A car ahead of us had watched us disappear through his rear-view mirror and sensibly called the emergency services; they quickly arrived on the scene and whipped us off to a hospital in Swindon, where we spent the night under observation.

I claimed it was a tyre blowout. This was partly true – only the blowout came after I hit the barrier!

But Ian didn't need any help in landing himself in hot water; he had a penchant for finding trouble. He even managed to find problems at our local football club in Taunton at a benefit night for Trevor Jesty of Hampshire. After a while I told Beefy I was going home because the hands slapping my back were becoming increasingly heavy in direct relationship to how much the back-slappers had drunk. I had the usual insults thrown at me by Botham about being a wimp and not being able to hold my beer, but I ignored him and went home to bed for a fairly early night before playing against Hampshire the next day.

Next morning I was up and ready to make the short trip to the ground but there was neither sight nor sign of Beefy being ready. Then I heard a groan and, when I went into his room, there was Botham minus a big chunk of his hair. He had somehow managed to involve himself in a fight with some of the local yobs and one of them had grabbed him by the hair and pulled a lump out. His eyes were bruised black and blue. He looked up at me and said, 'Smokey, you must have read it. That place turned into the OK Corral. It was one of those fights I couldn't cope with. There were guys using chairs and another hitting me from behind just for the sake of it.'

The police came later and Beefy once again featured heavily in the *Sun* under the headline story of 'Botham in Brawl in Taunton'. It was nothing new. The news reporters, photographers and free-lances knew only too well where we lived and where we drank, and they would follow us back to our flat or they would hide in their cars, ducking down below the steering wheel. Sometimes, for sheer devilment we would pull up beside a parked car, knowing it contained a reporter or photographer, and would knock on the window and say something to the effect of: 'Hi! Were you waiting to see us? We've come to say hello.' Ian then used to give the car a little shake to let the journalist know that we knew what he was up to.

Ian Botham hit the headlines a lot more often than I did. Certain places where you go to you know you are vulnerable, and if I saw trouble I would avoid it. Maybe one of the reasons why Ian and I got on so well was because I had a nose for spotting the signs early and would warn him of impending danger. I would just say, 'I don't think it is too nice here,' and more often than not he would agree and we would go elsewhere.

Of course I was not with him all the time and he was certainly capable of getting himself into plenty of scrapes at various points around the globe without any help from anyone else. However, I never believed the stories about Beefy and serious drugs. If he took anything, it was no stronger than marijuana, and I don't think he had a problem with anything else. If anyone would know, I would, and I never saw him do anything other than smoke the occasional spliff.

Of course I do not know what he got up to when he was running with the superstars of the pop world like Elton John and Mick

Jagger in their sort of environment. In actual fact he said that Elton had been a great help to him with advice and stopped him wasting his money. Beefy gets too much of a high from life itself to need any outside stimulus but, on the other hand, he was always ready to give most things a try because life was, and still is, an adventure to him. But, as for injecting heroin, as some woman in New Zealand claimed, that produced a big laugh. Anyone who knows Ian Botham well will tell you that he is terrified of needles and injections. There is no way he would use one for fun.

I used to giggle when I read in the English newspapers back home in the West Indies about his latest so-called escapades. I am sure the newspapers used to set him up because he was such good copy and sold newspapers. They have tried it on with me, I know, because one or two ladies have owned up that they had been offered inducements to get to know me and learn my secrets.

Many of the people whom Both would trust I wouldn't, and that is the difference between us. I am always a little wary of people. As we say in Antigua, watch and wait, watch and wait. It has worked well for me because of my vision and because I was focused. Even Beefy says at the end of the day that I usually had it right. Perhaps it is no coincidence that I was rarely around when he was being turned over or set up.

Beefy always had the right remark for the right moment. I recall once, playing against Sussex, when he kept moving the ball past John Barclay's bat, five times every over. Eventually he wandered over and told him that he had brought out the wrong bat. Another time, when one of our fielders dropped a simple catch, he picked up a litterbin and took it across to him. Little things like that made him a law unto himself and different from other people.

He is a working-class man, and he often rubbed the cricket establishment up the wrong way with his straight talking. At the same time, he is a patriotic Englishman who did and would still do anything for his country. I hope they look at him again, because I think the man still has a lot to offer to English cricket. I would like to think that he might be put in charge one day. He is what the

English game needs: someone with guts, someone who will induce his batsmen to walk out to the wicket with an attitude. It would be the classic case of the poacher turned gamekeeper. Having been through just about everything and been in every scrape there could be, he is more than aware of the pitfalls facing young cricketers. He would certainly be able to tell the young bloods to beware of certain young ladies! He was a happy-go-lucky guy and maybe it is time for him to start spreading the gospel. He has become much more mature and has put his water-pistol away.

He has done well with his broadcasting, and that should have bridged the gap between playing and team management without losing touch with the game. Frankly, I cannot see Ian Botham ever losing touch with cricket!

When Ian is around, with his jovial, relaxed manner, you don't need people who are too stiff. When it comes down to the performing bit, he can be fierce and the others will hear him loud and clear if they are not representing England with pride and effort. They would be dead in the water and wouldn't be asked to represent their country again. In the role of coach, manager or administrator, he has much more than just the cricket to offer; he is someone who has been involved, who does and has done many things that others can only imagine. It is not even a question of whether the English and Welsh Cricket Board are brave enough to appoint him, because nothing else they have tried so far has worked.

We have discussed it and we both decided that we would like to be involved with our countries at a coaching or management level. I have always felt that Ian wants to put something back into the game that gave him so much. The one thing he is wary about is that the job in cricket, particularly looking after England's unpredictable lot, is so insecure, whereas his work in the media is much more certain and he can say exactly what he wants without fear of reprisals.

The man knows a lot about cricket and can lead from the front. I still see him on a regular basis and we are in touch by telephone. We have revamped our friendship over recent years, with time spent together working in Brunei. While we have gone our own separate ways and are often on opposite sides of the world, our relationship is more like that of brothers than friends, and it will undoubtedly last for ever.

4. The Test of Strength

I made my test debut aged twenty-two in 1974 against India, but while my father acknowledged that India had the best spin attack in the world he said that before he was prepared to baptize me as a fully fledged test player I had a further river to cross – Australia. And in particular the ferocious pace of Dennis Lillee and Jeff Thomson. My dad's opportunity to see me tested came quickly. My first tour to Australia in 1975–6 proved to be my baptism of fire. England had lost a series in Australia before us and had finished not only beaten but also battered and bruised by the most hostile fast bowling attack in the world.

After facing the Indian spinners in my first tour, this was a very different proposition, meeting not only Lillee and Thomson head on but also Gary Gilmour, Max Walker and others. Following the slow wickets in India it was an awakening and was very intimidating. The wickets were tailor-made for the fast bowlers and they were quicker than any others in the world at the time.

I had problems early on and scored 0, 12 and 12 in my first three test innings. In Australia I was looking to get forward on these harder wickets, but there were times when I needed to be on the back foot and watching the ball a little more.

My next three innings were an improvement with 41, 36 and 44. I was scoring my 30s or 40s but not going on to the big scores. It created some doubts in my mind as to my own ability at this rarefied level; in fact it was panic stations. I was hitting the ball in the middle of the bat and playing as well as anyone but was not scoring enough runs.

That was when I had a chat with Rudi Webster, the team psychologist; I talked to him about how I felt when I was in that zone and asked him how I could overcome that barrier on the concentration side. We did a whole lot of sessions and went through my thoughts during my innings to try and identify the problem. We were looking for the reasons for my success in the past which could be of use now. We discovered through discussion that I wasn't concentrating in the way that I should have been when I reached a certain stage of my innings. Then it was a question of discovering how I could do so and taking it on to another level, going forward step by step.

Gradually, as the tour went on, I improved both my concentration and my batting and in my youthful exuberance I even volunteered to open the innings! Gordon Greenidge was not having a great tour, scoring no runs in either of his two innings in the first test in Brisbane. He had quickly been labelled someone who couldn't cope with the ultra-fast bowling, and he had to carry the stigma around with him. Of course, it wasn't as straightforward as that. He had suffered some unfortunate decisions which, had they gone his way, could have changed the entire scene. When things start to go wrong, they usually get worse. The selectors were looking for someone to open because Gordon's confidence was shattered.

I asked to open in the zonal matches because I felt that I needed a lengthy preparation before the tests. I tried it and scored two centuries against Tasmania, giving me the confidence to carry on the experiment. But when it came to the crunch, opening at the Oval in the Adelaide test, I scored yet another 30 before getting out to Thomson. Lillee took my wicket in the second innings, but not before I had accumulated 101. He had me in the next two innings in Melbourne as well, but again I had gathered some runs first with 50 and 98. My confidence was growing, but I was taking nothing for granted against bowling of this pace and quality.

It was a good feeling, but I did not see opening the batting as a lasting career for me. I was a young man on a tour and this sort of gamble could make or break me, and I was determined to do everything in my power to help not just myself but my team as well.

What I appreciated more than anything else in Australia was that there were lots of quality beers to drink and the weather was conducive to a nice long cold one after play. Give an Aussie a luke-warm beer and it is just about the biggest insult you can offer him. They take tender loving care getting the Eskis filled with the ice, and the beers had to be well chilled. I would look forward to that beer at the end of the day with my team mates, or maybe even with the opposition.

I learned a lot from my little chats with the Chappell brothers. I was keen to learn and they were brilliant with me. I have always had a great admiration for Ian in particular. I liked his attitude, the way he went out to bat, the way he took you on. He had no fear and would hook at every opportunity, even when he suffered a bad run of being out to the stroke. Critics would tell him he should stop, but he carried on regardless. For some reason, Ian didn't get on too well with Ian Botham, but that was not my problem and it never affected my opinion of the Australian.

Lillee and Thomson were quick, very quick, but, over after over at any rate, no quicker than 'Whispering Death' Michael Holding. What really did us in those days was that the Australians had gone on to the next stage in their physical fitness, with their fast bowlers able to maintain longer and more hostile spells. We eventually came to realize what could be achieved when a fast bowler was superfit. That was the most important lesson we took back home from that tour. We felt that was what we needed to do in order to gain parity.

For that special delivery, no one could match Thommo for raw, lethal pace. Once, when I was batting with Lawrence Rowe, he was hit on the head and said he didn't see it.

I said, 'What do you mean, man, you didn't pick it up?'

'No,' he said, 'I just didn't see it.' Thommo had this action whereby he would hide the ball behind his backside before his delivery. 'Smokey,' Yagga declared, 'this man is delivering the ball out of his arse. I can't see it. He is bowling batty balls.'

But there were few better or quicker than my own Antiguan colleague, Andy Roberts, the first Antiguan to play for the West Indies. Andy was just the sort of inspiration that we needed at the time. When he was selected, I was in a little bar in the Ovals where we played bingo and pool. He came in that night to tell us that he had been selected to go to Barbados to play against England. Keith Boyce had been injured and he had been called up as a late replacement. I was awestruck and said, 'Wow, an Antiguan guy in the West Indies team.' There was no jealousy on my part, it was purely a spur-of-the-moment thing and, as we were team mates, it was almost as good for me as it was for him. I knew that this was what our cricket needed at the time to create confidence.

We all listened in with renewed interest to the third test and, on a very good batting strip, he took the wicket of Chris Old in the first innings when he bowled 33 overs, as many as spinner Lance Gibbs, in England's total of 395 and, had the West Indies team caught better, he would have had even more wickets. He scored 9 not out in our reply of 596 for eight declared – with my favourite player, Yagga Rowe, scoring a triple century – and then, to everyone's excitement, Andy and Vanburn Holder had England reeling at 29 for three in their second innings, with Andy picking up the top wickets of the Warwickshire pair, Dennis Amiss and John Jameson, in what was eventually to be a high-scoring drawn game.

The reports were that he was special – and the pundits weren't wrong. He turned out to be one of the best fast bowlers I have ever played with or against. He was a magnificent bowler. His action wasn't as smooth as Michael Holding's, but he had a wonderful arm. At the point of delivery his body was in the perfect side-on position to deliver the ball, and when he thumped it into the wicket you could see his body turn one side to the other to generate the maximum body swing and turn.

He was lethal in every way, and I have never seen any individual in world cricket who could hit the batsman at will the way he did. Andy had the knack of really hurting batsmen. No one likes to see a batsman hurt, but you could not help but admire the quality of those deliveries; there was more than one who suffered career-threatening injuries. The first time I saw it was when he hit David Hookes in a World Series cricket match and broke his jaw. The Australian Golden Boy was wired up for weeks and couldn't eat anything solid for a while. I also saw him hit Peter Toohey in Trinidad and break his nose, and then later he smashed his thumb

International Football – the Antiguan team in 1971. My brother Mervyn is fourth from the right in the back row while I'm second from the right

Domestic football – not as smart, but just as enthusiastic. Our local football team, the Ovals, with me second from the left in the front row

Happy families – my mother and father with my children Matara and Mali

Making my mark – taking on the Leicestershire attack in a John Player League match in 1974

Hitting the mango – all that practice in the Caribbean pay off with one of my three run-outs against Australia in the 1975 World Cup Final at Lord's. This time it was the dangerous Alan Turner

Up close – captain and mentor Brian Close, one of the toughest men in cricket

Who's grovelling now! – I celebrate the dismissal of England captain Tony Greig with Mikey Holding at the Oval in the fifth test in 1976

The dream realized – I raise my cap to the knowledgeable Lord's crowd as they give me a standing ovation after my innings in the 1979 Gillette Cup Final against Northants

The rebels – happier times at Somerset as Ian Botham and I congratulate Joel Garner after bowling Wayne Larkins for a duck in the Gillette Cup Final against Northants at Lord's in 1979

History in the making – World Series Cricket: Australia versus the West Indies at Sydney in 1979 and the first time in coloured gear

Only the girls wore white – I still don't think pink was my colour, but the drink was welcome. I'm second from the right

We won the cup – Clive Lloyd lifts the Prudential World Cup trophy in 1979 while I look on with the beaten English players

The King and I – this time with a crown, as Ian and I celebrate helping Somerset to beat Surrey in 1981 in the Benson & Hedges Final

Hair today, gone tomorrow – Vic Marks, me, Brian Rose, Ian Botham and Peter Denning see the funny side during the Benson & Hedges Final against Notts at Lord's in 1982. Looking at the facial hair, it was a good job it wasn't the Gillette Cup Final

Double the pleasure – hooking my old mate Both in the 1984 Oval test match

Fan power – our West Indian supporters, seen here at Headingly in 1984, were a great inspiration in England until they were driven away

In my zone – the arms swing free against England at Old Trafford in the Texaco Cup in 1984

Fetch that one – same match, different stroke, on my way to 189 not out

Hi, Dad – at home in England with my wife Miriam, son Mali and daughter Matara in 1983 on the eve of the NatWest Cup Final

Hi, Dad – my father, Malcolm, in Antigua in 1986

in the same game; he broke Sadiq Mohammad's jaw in a test match in Georgetown and Majid Khan's cheekbone in county cricket; and one of the more horrific injuries occurred when he hit Colin Cowdrey a sickening blow while Cowdrey was playing for Kent against Hampshire. There were too many similar incidents to mention. He was always accurate. When you missed, you were hit – and not just on the fingers and thumbs.

Yet although he was a very unassuming guy he knew his cricket and knew what he wanted to do when he was bowling. He never just ran up and bowled, he always used his head. He would often first offer the batsman one to hook, lulling his opponent into a false sense of security. That was the bait, and the batsman would eat well – and then he would make them suffer. I saw it so often. He would be hooked for four or six and I would say, 'Andy, you're not looking hot today, man.' He would say nothing but the next ball . . . bang, it would be game, set and match. They would be on their way back to the pavilion, either with their wicket in tatters or being helped off by the physio, wondering where those extra yards of pace had come from.

Andy and I virtually grew up together, playing against each other and practising together. I knew how fast and tough he was because he would even work me over in the nets; he could be a mean bastard and if you drove the ball past him too hard he would look at you with those slit eyes as if to say, 'Don't mess.' Then he would give you a little softening up just to make sure you were aware that this was practice and not a match.

Some said that watching the two of us playing against each other was like watching a bare-knuckle fight. At Somerset, when I was the new kid on the block, he was already the fast bowling find of the season at Hampshire. We first came face to face in a Benson & Hedges match when he hit Brian Close under the armpit. Close, who had been battered without flinching by the quickest fast bowlers the West Indies could throw at him, fell like a stone; he stopped breathing for a while and had to be resuscitated. Andy followed this up by hitting Ian Botham flush on the jaw and removing a tooth, free of charge.

The two old boys of the side, Graham Burgess and Merv Kitchen (the latter now a very good umpire), were doing a pretend radio commentary in the dressing-room, ball-by-ball and injury-by-injury. It didn't do the young players any good at all listening to them. Merv would have them quaking in their boots as he said to Graham, 'Did you see that! It's the quickest ball I have ever seen in my life.' Merv then took his false teeth out of his mouth and put them in his pocket, saying, 'I am not going to get these smashed up. I paid too much for them.' It did us kids no good at all; Andy seemed to be hitting our batsmen at will.

I only scored 20 or so runs, but one shot gave me plenty of satisfaction, when I got in position and hit him over the organ works. The fielders, all standing up close, looked on in amazement and were saying, 'How did that little bastard play a shot like that?' He didn't take my wicket that day, but I loved the challenge.

When we were kids from very early on after we left school we both played for the Rising Sun, so it was only in county cricket that we really came face to face. I would like to give him the credit by saying that we finished pretty even over the years. He will always be remembered as the first Antiguan to play for the West Indies, the father figure who laid the path for us to follow. He played his first match on 6 March 1974, and then in November of that year we both played together against India in Bangalore. He went on to play in 47 tests and he took over 200 wickets for his country.

Andy had his chance to coach with the West Indies team but he wasn't treated fairly. Sometimes people on the board don't want to listen to individuals who know the game, they were all too ready to challenge his experience and knowledge.

Andy is now with the Ministry of Sports in Antigua and I hope his presence can accelerate the erection of nets and facilities in all the areas around the country. He can also have a great input in coaching on the island.

Although I enjoyed playing against Andy, I was still glad that I didn't have to face him in test cricket. As it was, I have been hit a few times in these test battles, the strangest of all being by Greg

Chappell, hardly what you would call a front-line bowler at this level. He bowled a very good bouncer and to my surprise hit me on the forehead. Lillee hit me under the heart and Thommo hit me on the inside thigh, which hurt just as much. It is said that a black man doesn't show the bruises – I don't know about that but I turned purple afterwards.

I sniffed the leather on a few occasions, especially in Australia, and it smelled very sweaty. But there was no one who could persuade me to wear a helmet. To my way of thinking, I was going into battle for my country. It was a war, and if I was going to die for the cause then so be it. The fear of failure and losing was much stronger than the fear of being hurt. That never entered into it. God has given me this great power to tackle these guys and I always felt that all I needed was my bat and my reflexes. I was aware of certain deliveries that went by and I knew I had had a close shave. That didn't frighten me; it gave me the adrenalin to keep on my toes, ducking and weaving, keeping me alert and keeping me alive. One loose shot, one little mistake could mean getting seriously hurt. But the most important factor of all was that I enjoyed it. I actually looked forward to facing a really quick bowler and even one who bowled good bumpers. There was no more exciting shot to play than the hook off a rising fast ball. Facing bouncers was as much about technique as any part of batting, and if I was ducking well it was as good as hitting the ball in the middle of the bat. Ducking, swaying or hooking, I enjoyed it all.

Fast bowlers have this bully image and there are some batsmen who don't want to treat them with too much disrespect because they are frightened of what they might do with the next ball.

I remember Greg Chappell saying that I had the knack for competing and wasn't afraid and that was why I was roped in to play for Queensland. He liked the way I hit the bullies back over their heads off the back foot. Maybe because of the fact of having played under Brian Close, sometimes they hit me and it hurt like hell, but I tried never to show any pain. There were times when I would have killed for a glass of water, but that would have been a sign of weakness.

When Lillee hit me under the heart I couldn't even breathe and I remember Rod Marsh asking if I was all right; but there was no speech coming out, all I could do was nod my head. There was no sympathy from Lillee, of course, and I wouldn't have expected it. When I looked up, he was back at his mark; in fact there wasn't one Lillee ready to come snorting in at me again – I could see two! What is more, he was going back ever further while the crowd was chanting: 'Kill! Kill! Kill! Kill!' One Lillee is bad enough, but this was one too many and I felt it was about time to take the count. I stepped back and asked for a glass of water. I had no choice because I didn't know which Lillee I had to face, I was so dazed.

There were no complaints. Our side had had its share of really quick, hostile bowlers from the days of Wes Hall and Charlie Griffith onwards, so we could scarcely complain and, anyway, that wasn't our style.

The faster and more evil they were, the more aggressive I tried to be. We had to learn to take them on when we faced our own bowlers in the inter-island competitions.

One of the more explosive moments in Australia came in New South Wales at the end of 1984 when Alan Border was captain. There was an appeal against me for a catch behind and when I was given not out a few harsh words were said against me. Steve Rixon, the wicket-keeper, called me a lucky bastard, then AB (Alan Border) and Kepler Wessels came up and stuck their noses in. As they came menacingly towards me I said, 'What the fuck does it have to do with you?'

Everyone was pointing, gesticulating, talking and growing very animated. 'How the fuck did you get into it?'

'Am I talking to you?'

'You fucking stay out of this.'

Finally I pointed at AB and told him, 'I will deal with you after the end of play.'

Border agreed, eyes blazing, and retorted, 'Yes, if that's what you want, we will do it.'

I was usually too focused to get involved in a fight. If you get that involved, you let yourself and the game down, and I felt I had much more to offer than that.

I was still fuming at the end of the game and I was actually looking forward to the confrontation. I went back to the dressing-room, stripped off my wet things, put a towel round my waist and, to the utter surprise of everyone, stormed across the bar between the two dressing-rooms. I knocked on the door and there in front of me was a group of pressmen. Border had alerted them to the fact that I was coming and that I had threatened to do whatever to whomever.

There I was, caught red-handed. There was nothing I could do, and I had to back off.

The press had a field day – well, more like a few weeks than a day – bringing it up continually that I wanted to fight the entire Aussie team. Consequently I got stick everywhere we played, especially at Sydney where they would boo and jeer every time they caught sight of me. It was like a virus as it spread from town to town.

The series I played for the West Indies against Australia were always special to me, perhaps because I learnt so much in that first visit when we lost 5–1, in which Dennis Lillee took 25 wickets and Jeff Thomson 29. Between them they claimed my wicket eight times – Lillee five times – but I also had my say.

After that it was always tough, but in seven more series I never once finished on the losing side, although we drew a short series of three down under in 1981–2 when my contribution was fairly marginal to say the least.

We learnt an awful lot from that series in '75–6 when we took a physical and verbal battering, and by the time we faced the Aussies the next time we exacted our revenge with our own battery of fast bowlers, notably Andy Roberts, Joel Garner and Colin Croft, and the Aussies were twice rolled over for under 100! I played in only the first two tests and had only two innings, with my old mate Thommo getting me both times for 39 and 23.

But the return to Australia in 1979–80 was the most satisfying for, although it was only a short series of three tests, we won two and drew the other. Although Lillee claimed me twice, I guess I came out the winner this time with 140, 96, 76 and 74.

After the 1–1 drawn series in Australia in 1981–2, we restated our supremacy at home in '83–4 when, after drawing the first two tests, in both of which we were on top, we won the next three. The most memorable for me was back at home in St John's, when I joined fellow Antiguan Richie Richardson at 43–2 and we proceeded to put on over 300 as I scored 178 before falling to a catch from Rackemann's bowling, while Richie scored 154.

I had another good knock against them in Melbourne in the Christmas test, when I rattled up 208 after five disappointing innings of which my best was 42 in Adelaide. This series was Clive Lloyd's last as captain of the West Indies. And I was named as his replacement. There were some problems at first when some thought that I did not have the character to do the job, even though I had been vice-captain for so long. It was said that, once Clive Lloyd had gone, that would maybe be the end of our time as the best in the world. That was the challenge for me. I had done my apprenticeship and, as far as I was concerned, there was only going to be one captain and that was Viv Richards. I wanted to prove to other people, not to myself, that I could go and form my own dynasty and keep whatever we had had in the past. We had a good tradition under Clive and I wanted to show that we could still be a happy, winning machine.

When I quit the job, it was in the same condition as when they had given it me – and maybe with a little bit of interest. It was something I definitely wanted to do.

For any individual from the Caribbean who gets to captain the West Indies, it is like having the most important job in the region because of all the islands that are involved. When we win, we win collectively; when we lose, we all lose. It was the greatest honour, like a country being head of Caricom (the community of Caribbean nations) and what that means to the people of the Caribbean. It was a very responsible job and it was beholden to me that I should bear that responsibility with dignity and success. When I was finally appointed, I heard via the usual channels from the board and not through the media. They did the correct thing.

I learnt to be more patient with my players. What used to get me down initially was players not performing to their capacity and then I would show my anger. I treated everyone as though they were me, and not everyone could be. But when I became captain, I became more tolerant. Sometimes players who may not appear to be trying are, in fact, going as hard as they can. I learnt to realize that and to control the anger it generated. If there was individual slackness or if the team looked lethargic, then I would be harsh. The trick is to be professional and be hard when it matters but at the end of play it is time to relax and have a beer and not bear any grudges.

I know there were doubts about me being able to lead the side. I didn't mind them because they presented a challenge. I like living on the edge. I was always experienced enough, having walked the walk and talked the talk. There is nothing better than proving those small-minded people wrong.

My first series against the Aussies as captain was in 1988–9 and, again, we won 3–1 in their backyard, tying up the series in the first three tests. By this time I had relegated myself to batting at number five but I weighed in with some useful scores: 68 in Brisbane, where we won by 9 wickets; 146 in Perth in a 169-run win; and 63 in Melbourne, where we finished 285 runs to the good. I signed off with 68 not out in the drawn fifth test in Adelaide.

My last series against Australia was in 1990–91 at home, and my undefeated record as captain was maintained with a 2–1 series win, with the Aussies again winning the dead rubber in Antigua, where I sadly failed in both innings with 0 and 2! It would have been nice to finish with a big score on the Recreation Ground – but, as always, the most important factor was that the West Indies had won the series again.

The hardest and most satisfying test cricket I've ever played was against the Australians. What always brings the Australians back down to earth is a victory against them, because for them winning is everything. When you accomplish a win against Australia in any sport, you know you have beaten an individual or a team that would do anything to stop you achieving that objective. Generally, the Aussies are a good, sports-loving people, perhaps some of the best in the world, and appreciative of a good contest. If they are giving you a hiding, they will be unmerciful both on and off the field and will grind it in. I have seen that so often. If you get in there and give as much as you can they'll appreciate it. The fans like to see their team pushed to the limit – but not at the expense of defeat. At the moment, the position of best team in the world is held once more by Australia. My hope and belief is that the West Indies can win it back. The rivalry remains as intense as ever.

I suppose, if I have one regret, it is that I did not play more cricket in Australia. My one season in Queensland was all too brief, comprising just four matches, but in that time, on tour for the West Indies and playing World Series Cricket, I learnt to come to terms with Aussie aggression on the field and the strong social life off it. No wonder Ian Botham enjoyed playing down under so much, and no wonder they enjoyed having him over there.

The complaint down under is that there is too little cricket, but this is balanced by the fact that there is more time to recuperate, and there was a much more stable life as you could settle in one place for a good time rather than having to drive all round the country. After touring England with the West Indies in 1976, I went to taste the life of a domestic cricketer in Queensland. I was given this opportunity through local radio station 4IP, who sponsored a lot of sports people, including my mate Jeff Thomson, who had a ten-year contract with them. I was to be part of the radio unit and was to play four matches for Queensland, before returning home to the Caribbean for a test series against Pakistan. For that little venture I was paid around $US25,000, which compared more than favourably with the pay scale in county cricket at that time.

I found that Shield cricket was miles ahead in terms of commitment and competing, and this was just what I needed at the time. Although I had enjoyed the competitiveness of English cricket, it certainly lacked the intensity of Australian Shield cricket. There was so little top-grade cricket there that every player knew he had to shine and take his chance when it came. It certainly was damn good for me. The Australians have this die-hard attitude, and I fitted in quickly because I don't like to give a lot away when I am playing. It was great fun and proved a complete contrast to county cricket, which lacked characters, particularly as regards the aggressive nature of the game.

I see nothing wrong with playing to win, but sometimes they carried it too far in Australia, and some players needed to watch their tongues. Sledging, sadly, is a way of life over there: the youngsters start in domestic-grade cricket, hone it in Shield cricket and then lift it to an art form in the test arena. The protagonists do not care who verbally assaults whom.

A classic example was Lenny Pascoe, who played for New South Wales. Lenny and Greg Chappell had a particular thing going, even though Greg was his international skipper. It didn't matter a jot, for Lenny would try to rip his head off with the ball while abusing him verbally at every opportunity. Chappell would retaliate, and so it would go on.

Personally, I always found Greg to be too quick a talker and I couldn't always understand what was being said, and as Lenny had a Yugoslav background I needed an interpreter to really appreciate the vitriolic exchanges between the two of them. But I got the idea pretty quickly! Lenny would taunt Greg by calling him a little boy, and Greg would respond by telling Lenny he had no brains – only not in such polite terms.

Yet off the field Lenny was a gentleman, and it always amazed me how different he could be on the pitch, cursing, swearing and telling you that the next one you missed would put you in hospital. Whereas in England the batsman would usually turn away at such abuse, in Australia the batsman turns round and gives as good as he gets. That, for me, is how it should be. Fast bowlers are basically bullies who try to intimidate batsmen. My attitude over there was: don't treat me like that, I have a bat and you only have a ball.

Lenny, however, was not the brightest bloke on the field. He was a big man and he would follow a bouncer with a comment and then a glare. But I could match him in that. Staring at bowlers and mouthy fielders was one of my hobbies. I loved to stare, and I could glare for the world.

There have been all sorts of stories and rumours about how the famous Viv Richards 'stare' or 'glare' began; it was even suggested that it was Jeff Thomson who taught me. I am sorry to disappoint all the rumour-mongers, but the glare just developed naturally through my competitive nature when facing extremely aggressive fast bowlers like Andy Roberts from a very early age. They could waste their breath on words – I was happy just to stare them down, and if they still stood in my way I would do a little gardening with my bat by their feet and just beyond.

The glare also worked well when I was fielding at forward short leg. If it intimidated batsmen, then I had succeeded in what I was trying to do. When you stand and glare back, you cannot lose as a batsman because you are in your ground. The bowler is always the one who has to break eye-contact, turn his back and walk back to the start of his run-up. When Lenny or any of the other quickies overdid it, I would stare and say, 'Fuck off back to your mark, OK?' I wanted to show them who was master.

Graham Whyte, an off-spinner, was a real character in the Queensland side. He would stand there and say, 'Come on, Thommo, rip the fucker up him . . . Fucking give him plenty . . . Hurt the fucker.' But his batting was as limited as his vocabulary. When it was his turn and there was some pace about, the same guy who gave all that crap suddenly went deathly quiet. I turned to Thommo and said, 'Hey, Jeff, it doesn't look as though our man is too tough.'

Thomson responded, 'He's as weak as piss, mate. He talks a good game but when it's up his ass he runs like a thief.'

And this was with team mates! Out there he had all that chat, but when it came to it he displayed cowardice, and there are a lot like that in Shield cricket, good talkers when they are in the field but when they come in to bat it's a different story.

I enjoyed my cricket and scored a ton the day after I got off the plane in a centenary match for Queensland against the Rest of

Australia, which included Dennis Lillee. I then notched up 141 against a Pakistan team that included Imran Khan. No wonder I enjoyed it out there with all those runs under my belt.

Geoff Boycott was invited to play for the Rest of Australia against Queensland at the Gabba when I was making my debut for the State. He was as polite to me as ever and when we met he said, 'Good morning, Viv, congratulations. I heard that you had a contract with Queensland. Well done, you will enjoy batting on this wicket.'

The conversation continued as we strolled out to the middle together and he continued to tell me all about the ground, that it took a little spin and that there were lots of runs to be had. What Geoffrey did not know was that there was a new curator at the Gabba and his speciality was making slow pitches into fast ones. I knew this, but I wasn't going to tell Geoff.

Then, as now, he always had a cricket ball in his hand, like the old pro he is, ready to test the playing surface by bouncing it on the wicket. To me it looked a little swift at first view, but still he went on about how we should both be able to score runs on it. Then he bounced the ball on a length – and it flew straight back up over his head! He grabbed the ball, stuffed it in his pocket and whistled off to the dressing-room without another word.

It was only when I returned to the dressing-room that I discovered that Geoffrey was reputed to have deliberately avoided Lillee and Thomson in certain games. As I walked through the door, still chuckling at what had happened in the middle, I found a raging Thommo spitting nails and saying, 'I am going to kill that Pommie bastard.'

'Who's going to be killed?' I asked in all innocence, not being aware of the background.

Thommo was like a snorting bull and he retorted, 'I am going to stick it right up that bald-headed bastard.' I began to have an idea of just whom he had targeted.

Thommo didn't slow down as we walked out to the middle, followed by Boycott and his partner. Thommo had read all the pre-match hype and as we went out he was still raging, 'I've waited all these years for you, you Pommie bastard! Trying to avoid fucking pace! There is no place for you to run now.'

Thommo then proceeded to tear into him from the first ball. I have never seen the ball fly so much in an exhibition match, as Thommo followed up his express deliveries, saying, 'Hit that one then, you Yorkshire bastard . . . You're not playing those little fucking pie-throwers now . . . C'mon, have some of this. This is what you've been fucking missing . . . Welcome fucking back to the big time' . . . And more.

Geoffrey was out for a duck, caught at slip, and he couldn't go quickly enough, with Thommo's words ringing in his ears, 'Now fuck off! This is what the real game is like.'

But Geoffrey had the last laugh. Thommo put so much into his bowling that he overdid it and damaged himself, forcing him to miss the next few matches.

I loved every side-splitting minute of it, but it remained a job unfulfilled. I would love to have played more of that cricket and I loved the pace of life in Australia. That's my kind of cricket: raw-to-the-bone stuff, the fire to compete and so different from the quieter English game.

It was fun all of the time, off the field as well as on. Thommo's girlfriend Cheryl was working for a modelling agency at the time and they persuaded me to take part in a big mannequin show on the Gold Coast; I was to wear a white caftan to promote and advertise the new 300 ZX Datsun. I was supposed to make my appearance on the catwalk with two Labradors. What is it they say about never working with children and animals? Whatever it was, I didn't listen, even though it was my first time and I was nervous in case anything should go wrong in front of all the media.

The dog-handlers arrived with the dogs and assured me how well behaved and thoroughly trained they were and that they were totally used to this sort of work. It was explained to me that I would be escorting top model Tina Derby, helping her and the dogs out of the Datsun and then walking them up a ramp. As simple as that.

I drove the car up to the ramp, climbed out and opened the

door for Tina. I helped her out, then opened the door for the two dogs. I was supposed to have the girl on one arm and the dogs on their two leashes in the other hand. No chance. That was when it all fell apart. No sooner had I opened the rear door than all hell broke loose. The dogs jumped out and started running about all over the place. I didn't know what to do, as one went left and the other went right.

The dog-handlers were furious and I was embarrassed. I didn't know what to do next, so Tina and I just jumped in the car and drove on to allow the next models on to the ramp. It wasn't as if it was just for a film – this was live, there was only one shot at it and I had been bowled a googly first ball!

Thommo, who was also in the show, told me it brought the house down and was voted the best part of the entire event. It also went down well with the rest of the Queensland team when Thommo regaled them with the details on our return. They were a good bunch with Martin Kent, who went on to play for Australia, Phil Carson, Malcolm Frank, a leg-spinner from Sri Lanka, Johnny McLean, the wicket-keeper who played for Aussie, plus, of course, Jeff Thomson and Greg Chappell.

The Aussies are a much more fun-loving people than the English both on and off the pitch. Every Aussie believes he has to give as good as he gets. I was very at home in Queensland with the beautiful seawater, the lovely seafood and some serious beer drinking. The XXXX went down well. On a long journey to somewhere like Perth they always made sure there were enough beers to go around.

Sometimes matters could get out of hand, as they did when we played against Dennis Lillee's team, Western Australia. We bowled them out for 71 and they responded by bowling us out for 69.

That night the committee came back to the hotel and a number of players were pulled up for poor discipline, with the committee claiming, quite rightly, that they had drunk too much. I never did find out what their excuse was!

It was incredible, like nothing I had ever experienced before. I went into a nightclub with one of the guys, and the first thing he did was stand up and shout, 'Anyone for a root!' This was their way of having fun, but it surprised and shocked me to start with. Unlike England, everything was done together as a group. Because of the distances, there was a lot of flying; but even when we played just across the water we would all jump in a minibus and stop at the first off-licence to stock up with grog, usually two cases of XXXX. The only one not to drink was the driver.

They also eat well and, while the English guy would save on his meal allowance by having a bag of chips from the fish-and-chip shop or a packet of crisps so that he could afford to buy his round, in Australia eating is almost as important as the drinking. The Aussies make sure they take in their proteins, usually a big piece of chicken, serious-sized steaks or the fabulous fish. Food was cheaper and there was a lot more variety in the players' price range. Thommo and Lillee were, not surprisingly, amongst the biggest trenchermen.

In those days sportsmen took precious little notice of what to eat and what to avoid affecting their performances, but happily this attitude has made something of a U-turn in recent years. I have always wondered what difference it could have made to me, but I was by no means the worst and made an effort to eat and drink the right thing. I always carried around the supplements, shakes and vitamins. It was so necessary and I was grateful to football, of all sports, for teaching me that.

The Australian is basically a confident individual. Because of the country's history as a penal colony, they now have a fierce national pride in everything they do and even how they present themselves. It is not just in cricket but in everything, and especially in sport in which, despite their small population, they dominate many of the team games. They're determined not to lose. Sometimes they go over the top with their 'C'mon, Aussie this' and 'C'mon, Aussie that', while others put on a macho front which isn't really in them. They do it because it is what is expected of them and they feel that they have to live up to their reputation of being aggressive.

It wound me up to such a point at first that I just wanted to say to them, 'You have all that chat, let's see if you can mix it a bit.

Let's see whether all those foul things that come out of your mouth make you as tough with your fists as you are with your words.'

Racism was another matter altogether, and the Aussies were never slow to say what was on their minds. In England most people seemed to know better, as well as being naturally more reserved, so nothing much was said in Yorkshire except by the odd idiot.

In parts of Australia though, some people simply weren't sophisticated enough. You only have to look at their treatment of the Aborigines, whom I saw getting some harsh treatment in Queensland and other places. You might have expected Aussies to have some respect for the indigenous people of their land. I put their bad behaviour down to sheer ignorance. I experienced the problem at first hand, usually when I went outside Sydney and the other major cities. I found myself being looked at real funny, with that strange old 'sun' look that comes from being in the bush too long, as if to say 'I haven't seen your likes around here before'. I also experienced this lack of education where races other than Aborigines were concerned. They use insulting words like Abos, Spics and Wops, showing their ignorance and immaturity.

I found it pretty hard on the cricket field to start with: playing this gentlemen's game, standing waiting to bat when I would suddenly be called 'a black bastard' just as the bowler was in his delivery stride and 'a fucking lucky black bastard' whenever I missed a ball. It was the repetition, black this and black that, but usually black bastard. I used to ask them if they had slept with my mother in order to discover that information. They are people who have not taken the time to work out other people's culture. They are naive and need to learn so much more.

For a while I was an angry young man, but I have mellowed a lot and I can see that there is racism on both sides. I would like to see us deal with it collectively rather than itemizing things. No one would tolerate, for example, an association for white sportsmen, so why should there be a black sportsmen's association? All this does is to achieve the opposite of what's intended and it encourages division. Both are equally racist. We need to address the things that we feel angry about now – and not because of any perceived divine right, because of the suffering of our forefathers. The only way these problems are going to be solved is for us to look at the problems together, especially where sport is concerned. Racists of all colours make themselves look silly – and none dafter than the so-called fans jeering a black person in the opposition when they have black players in their own team.

Racism wasn't confined to Australia either. When Somerset played against Worcestershire at Weston-super-Mare, a group of visiting supporters were continually chanting, 'Vivian Richards, you are a black bastard,' and growing progressively worse, the more they drank.

Suddenly I snapped. I couldn't cope with it any more and I jumped into the crowd and confronted them over their foul language in front of the children who were there with their parents. I said, 'This is a family outing and you guys are behaving like yobs. Call me black, but how intimate are you with my family to call me a bastard? Whoever is shouting it, stand up and be counted.' Like all cowards, they hid, and the rest of the crowd applauded me for my reaction. It brought the game to a halt, leaving a mystified Ian Botham searching the boundary for his sweeper! Fortunately the police moved in and took the offenders away. But maybe that was what they should have done in the first place, before I was provoked beyond reason.

Even in the short time I was in Australia I managed to have a brush with the law, once again over driving too fast. It happened after a party on the western side of Queensland. On the way home I looked at this long expanse of empty road with not another car – or even a kangaroo – to be seen. I put my foot down and as the speedometer crept up a police car appeared from nowhere. I was stopped by a traffic cop who, fortunately, recognized me and contented himself by telling me to cool it down.

Thinking about the fact that lightning does not strike twice in the same place and how fortunate I had been, I put my foot down again – only to be halted further up the road by a second patrol. The original cop must have been on his car radio, telling his mate how he had pulled Viv Richards over. The second policeman, aware that I had been stopped for the same offence just a few miles down the road, told me that this time they had no option but to book me, whoever I was, and asked where they should send the speeding ticket to.

Feeling smug, I told him I was leaving Australia the next day. He said that, in that case, the next best thing would be to lock me up! That brought me down to earth and really shook me up. I said that wasn't such a good idea and, with fingers crossed, suggested it would be much better if he could see his way clear to ripping up the ticket if I promised not to do it again – not a difficult promise to keep, considering the circumstances. To my relief, he agreed to my proposal.

Sometimes being a celebrity can be a pain in the backside, but sometimes it can help. I can honestly say of my experiences with cops in Australia and England that they have been very good, and my brushes with the law have left me unscarred because I have dealt with decent people. There were times when I have been out of order. One policeman in England told me that if his father hadn't been such a big Somerset supporter and a fan of Viv Richards and Joel Garner, he would have booked me. Another time I was in Cardiff and Glamorgan had just lost in a quarter-final to Middlesex at Lord's. I was tired and depressed and all I wanted to do was get home and go to bed. I suppose I was travelling at around 60 in a 30 m.p.h. zone. Sure enough, I found myself being pulled over and I went through the usual routine until the policeman said, 'Are you the guy who plays for Glamorgan?' I said I was, and he told me, 'Count your lucky stars tonight. This is not my normal job and we are far more interested in the theft of cars. But don't do it again.' Remembering what had happened in Australia, this time I crawled home, and I was fortunate to escape again.

When I first played cricket in Australia in 1975–6 and was on the receiving end of a 5–1 series defeat, Australia were the best team in the world. The hostility of their attack, their aggressive, win-at-all-costs attitude and their superior approach to fitness all contributed to their dominance. It took the rest of the world some time to catch up, but it was the West Indies who first challenged their position and took their place at the top. The Australian cricketers are proud people and I felt the same. There were always going to be personality clashes. I respected their cricket and their ability to perform and compete at the highest level, but I didn't feel they were my masters in any degree. I always felt that I was on a par with them and wanted to compete at that level. If for any reason they tried to prove they were better than me, that just pumped me up. I've since enjoyed going back to Australia with Ian Botham for our exhausting 'King and I' tour and I feel lucky I have been able to experience and appreciate getting to know the workings of a great sporting nation.

5. Something Special

Despite the intense and increasing rivalry between the West Indies and Australia, any series against the oldest enemy, England, remains the biggest prize of all. This is the one all West Indian cricketers want to play in. There is a long tradition between the two countries, which has always been made more special because so many of our players have performed in England, either with the counties or in League cricket. This means that there has always been a considerable rapport between the players from the two sides, while we are fortunate to know the local conditions, having been given the opportunity to exhibit our skills in the four serious competitions.

The conditions and traditions remain a great attraction. Even as a child I would always tune in my radio to listen to the great John Arlott who, to me, epitomized the English game and had such a way of describing not only cricket but everything surrounding it. He was the voice of cricket, and not just of English cricket. Because of the time difference, we used to listen to him early in the morning, usually at around five a.m. before school time. It was worth rising with the sun just to hear the way he described the scenery, the weather, and the colourful sight of the West Indians and their contrast with the English players. His commentary painted a picture in my mind that stayed with me and made me yearn for the day I could play in England. It was something I looked forward to and, when I eventually played in a test match against England, it was made more special for me because I knew that John Arlott would be commentating to a completely new generation of West Indian schoolchildren.

The matches were also very competitive. What was intriguing to me was that the critics would have their doubts as to whether the West Indians could perform as well on the green English wickets as they did on the hard, rolled, sun-baked West Indian tracks. It was nice for successive generations of us to disprove that theory, not least in my case because I had become used to frozen fingers and toes during my time at Somerset. There were also the usual question marks on the circuit about those of us who hit across the line at the ball that moved in the air or off the seam. It also used to be said that when the West Indies were down they couldn't come back, but in a five-match series that is always a dangerous thing to say. There is always time to come back when you have quality players.

It was not often that these doubts were raised openly in public, but they were in 1976 before my first tour of England. We were all sitting around prior to a team meeting, relaxing in a hotel room and having a fruit punch or an orange juice, when our attention was drawn to the television screen and an interview with England captain, Tony Greig. We were about ready to switch off the television for the start of the meeting when Greig uttered his immortal words about making the West Indies grovel.

Everyone was stunned. Some of us were not exactly accustomed to the word 'grovel' and I asked what it meant in this context. It transpired that it was very much a derogatory expression used specifically in South Africa in the apartheid era. With Tony being a South African by birth that, as can be imagined, went down like a lead balloon. In other words, he was going to have us down on our knees, begging for mercy! Both that team meeting and every subsequent one on that tour was instantly made redundant; this was the greatest motivating speech the England captain could have given to any West Indian team. Greig was foolish in what he said because he was about to confront a rampant West Indian team. What helped us was having had the tough series in Australia and then the different series on the Indian subcontinent. I grew up on those tours and by the time I was in England I felt I was a test player and that I belonged. Even before Tony opened his big mouth I was in good nick and I felt I was going to score runs. It was good to be back in England and Tony's stupid remark only added a sharp edge to it. Confidence is an important asset at this level in cricket – or in any other sport, come to that – and I felt good about my game and myself. Australia had been forgotten and we had enjoyed a good tour of India and Pakistan. You only have to look at the names: Roy Fredericks, Gordon Greenidge, Alvin Kallicharran, Lawrence Rowe, Collis King, Clive Lloyd, Deryck Murray, Andy Roberts, Michael Holding and the rest. It was a good team, a damned good team. You can imagine, even all these years later, how Andy Roberts, Michael Holding and the other pace bowlers reacted. Everyone felt that he had to make a contribution to put this man and his team down.

Despite my brief absence through illness, this was my best series ever and I don't think I am going to make a comeback now! In fact it was a great time, with 1,710 runs in the calendar year, a record I believe. It was my first tour of England and I followed up my three consecutive centuries in India with over 800 runs. I started off with a big double-century (232) at Trent Bridge, then my highest score in first-class cricket, followed by 63 in the second innings; a century in the third test at Old Trafford; 66 and 38 at Headingley and 291 at the Oval as we won the series 3–0 after drawing the first two tests.

I might have scored more, but I was struck down with, of all things, glandular fever before the Lord's test. This was the one I had dreamed of playing in ever since I had heard Arlott talk about the batsmen going through the little white gate at headquarters and the capacity crowd rising to applaud a century by a player, no matter where he came from. I had dreamed of stepping through that gate and raising my beloved maroon West Indian cap after my maiden Lord's century. At first I felt a little on the 'fluey side, very weak and lethargic. They sent me for tests, and it transpired I had glandular fever. I was devastated. I couldn't even go to watch as I was confined to my room at the Waldorf Hotel in London in case I passed on the germ to the other players. I was really miserable after making such a good start and I even wondered how big a part I was going to be able to play in the remainder of the series. I felt so down. I also lost a great deal of weight and, for someone as conscious of his dress as I was, it was a shattering experience as my trousers were loose around my middle and my blazer hung on me as if I was a scarecrow. It was a really sad old feeling.

I felt so weak that when I was finally cleared and allowed to travel by train to rejoin the team, I couldn't even grip the bat properly. Gradually I clawed my way back to normal weight and something like fitness and I started to feel that much stronger. Most importantly, I started eating solid meals again; they had had no taste for me while I was ill. But it was a difficult time because here was a great opportunity for me to fulfil my personal ambitions and help my team crush this bigoted South African-born English captain and his team. I need not have worried for, in the end, it spoiled nothing, as I picked up exactly where I had left off and I was able to continue to stack up the runs.

Despite our experiences with sledging on the previous tour of Australia we did not give it back to Tony Greig. The bowlers didn't need to. The quickies couldn't wait to get the ball in their hand when he came in; he was quickly softened up with a couple to sniff at as they went past his nose and then he was given a really quick yorker.

Not only were England on the end of a drubbing, but Tony was heading for his worst series as Andy Roberts bowled him for a duck in his first innings; Roberts and Holder took him out in the second test for a handful of runs, and Wayne Daniel and Holding for even fewer in the third. Despite this, I grew to respect Tony's fighting spirit. In the fourth test it was largely due to him that England held us to a 55-run defeat as he steadied the boat with Alan Knott in the first innings when they both scored 116, and then he top-scored with 76 not out in the second innings. In the circumstances and with our bowlers howling for blood, it was a quite remarkable performance. But Michael Holding had the last word in the fifth and final test, bowling him twice for 12 and 1.

As for myself, the Viv Richards glare was enough when he bowled at me. The staring match was one battle I always knew I would win because he would have to turn back for his run-up. If he stood in my way when I was taking a run I would tell him what to do in very graphic terms. It was not at all like the aggravation we faced with the Australians, however.

Tony Greig proved over the years that he could handle the

sledging and give it back with bonus, as he proved every time he came face to face with Ian Chappell. They hated each other. Time has healed the rift between the two of them, but when they were playing they would curse and shout at each other. When they faced each other in a Packer match between Australia (captained by Ian) and the Rest of the World (led by Tony), Ian would shout out, 'What's that man doing in this team? How can he be captain? You are not good enough to be in the team, Greig. You are out of your depth.'

Tony would give it back and I would be standing there at short leg to Tony's off-break bowling, trying not to laugh at the exchanges when Chappell, batting with a broken finger and sweeping every ball Tony bowled, suddenly said to me in a very loud voice, 'Viv, you better fucking get out of here because that idiot of a captain you've got is going to get you killed.' Then, turning to Greig, he shouted, 'You can't bowl, Greig.' That was it. I just burst out laughing.

But it was serious, because this was winner-take-all cricket with nothing for the losers. What was said was meant.

Personally, I got on all right with Tony Greig. Sometimes we say silly things and regret it afterwards. I know now that Tony was only trying to hype up the series, and what he said and the way it came across was perhaps not the way he meant it. He was a fierce competitor and I didn't mind that. Sometimes it is nice to have an individual like him who goes to extremes because it spices up the series. As a player he was always ready to try little tricks, varying his bowling and playing unorthodox shots. When he bowled at me he used to chatter, and if I tried to hit one to the offside and it went to the onside he would tell me how I should have done it. My job was to deal with whatever he bowled at me, and his little antics gave me strength. I would say to him, 'I'll be a good student if that is the way it should be done.'

He was a useful bowler but he did not hold too many terrors for me. There were other English bowlers who were better and who posed more problems. One of them was Mike Hendrick. I also liked him. This was one fast bowler who was no abusive bully. I thought he was a nice, honest human, a guy who I felt should have played a lot more for England. He was a rhythm bowler and as good as any English bowler I faced. He had a high action, hit the seam, and on his day he was hard to play and he deserved to be chosen more consistently by the selectors.

It was also a good social tour – although not quite as good as some of the newspapers made out. The night I was 200 not out at the Oval, it was suggested that we had a riotous Caribbean jump-up in my hotel room. The truth is that there were a number of Antiguans who used to travel around the world watching cricket, including Prime Minister Lester Bird's brother, Ivor, who owned a radio station in Antigua called ZDK and who came to my hotel to congratulate me. Ivor was there with some friends, along with another Antiguan friend of mine, the late Milton Samuels, with whom I had been in partnership and who had done pretty well for himself. It was wonderful to see all these people when they came around, and we had a few drinks with Andy Roberts and his fiancee, an air-hostess named Janet, and her friends from Jamaica.

Everyone came in and offered their congratulations and we all talked cricket. They were all up on their statistics and were talking about whether I would break Sir Garfield Sobers' records. Everyone had a good time in our room and more than a few drinks were consumed, while I drank orange juice. I was very proud because they were there to salute this little Antiguan boy who had done quite well out in the middle that day.

I eventually walked through that famous gate and doffed my cap when I scored my century at Lord's on the next tour in 1980. There is an old groundsman by the name of Jim Fairbrother who worked at Lord's and with whom I had a wonderful rapport. He used to prepare a pitch that got the best out of both bowler and batsman. He would tell me, 'The first hour and a half you may have to worry about feeling the movement, but as long as you can bat, master, you can see that off and after that the show is yours.'

I had great respect for Lord's and its great traditions. You could almost taste it in the dressing-room, the Long Room and out there in the middle where there had been so many great games. It focused my mind that Lord's was such a highly traditional place when it comes to cricket and, whenever you did well there, it would be well and truly recorded, historic in every sense. Having been to the north London ground with Somerset, I had pictured everything in my mind, right down to raising my cap and lifting my bat in front of a packed house. It came true in the cup finals, but now here I was with my country at last. In many ways this was, I thought, my destiny.

After we had lost Gordon Greenidge fairly cheaply I went out and remembered what groundsman Jim had told me as I carefully watched those first few deliveries. I was so switched on about wanting to do well that my focus on the ball became big. It was so damned big that I could not miss it. I had pictured this moment so many times that I was almost on automatic pilot. It was as though the good Lord had told me that everything was in place and I just had to do it. I had so much time to make up my mind whether to hit on the on side or the off side. I played shots all round the wicket, hitting the ball so sweetly. I felt in total control. I raced to 100 quickly and it was flawless. I was seeing the ball so big and I was starting to think about coming back the next day and lighting up the place. I had handled the best that England could offer: Bob Willis, Ian Botham, Derek Underwood and Mike Hendrick; and then Peter Willey came on, just before the close of play. I tried to be too clever, too cute; rather than sweep full-bloodedly, I paddled the ball and caught the top edge. I saw everything in slow motion and my heart stopped as the ball looped up and Graham Dilley, the twelfth man, took the catch.

I had scored 145, but it felt for the whole world as if I had scored a duck. I was really thinking about a big day at Lord's on Saturday, seeing off the first couple of overs and then going to town. This was to be my big, big innings. I was sick. Des Haynes, with whom I had shared a stand of 223, did what I had hoped to do and went on to score 185. We had such a good bowling attack that, more often than not, I had to do it in the first innings because there would rarely be a second knock, even for a number three in the order. That was true at Lord's that day in the second test, and in the remaining three tests as well because we had posted a big total or because rain took away so many days in that series.

It was the same story in the next series in the Caribbean, a year later. We played only four tests because the second, scheduled to be played in Guyana, was called off when the government withdrew Robin Jackman's visitor's permit and served him with a deportation order. There was a lot of controversy and so many things were happening because some players had played in South Africa. There was no overall mandate and every island had its own interpretation. It was crazy. We flew to Guyana and then flew back again. It was very frustrating; we didn't care about the politics – we just wanted to play cricket. All we wanted was consistency and not stop-gap solutions over apartheid. There were people with placards trying to disrupt the tour. These were worrying times for us, and it was handled very badly. It all overshadowed what we came for: the cricket.

In the end the tour continued, thank goodness, because if it had been called off we would not have had that first ever test match at the Recreation Ground in St John's on my home island of Antigua. Antiguans had come from all over the world to watch the game and it would have been a shame if that had been spoilt.

Once again there was generally only the one chance for Viv Richards to shine. In the first test in Trinidad I contributed just 29 out of a total of 426, and then in Barbados Ian Botham, of all people, caught me for a duck off Graham Dilley. Fortunately that was the one game where I had a second chance, and I took full advantage of the fact by hitting 182 not out in quick time.

But the one that really mattered to me was St John's. It was a good wicket and I played well, and it was nice to do it in front of my home crowd with everyone cheering and people running on the ground stuffing my pockets with money. It was a great feeling for my country and for me, and to do it on the ground where I played as a child meant something special. That was one of the truly great days of my cricketing career. I would have to rank my century in St John's first ever test right at the top of the pile of my most rewarding and satisfying innings. I was the little boy who grew up playing on that particular park, the Recreation Ground, so it was a serious factor in my life. I was in awe as I walked out to bat – to develop from those crawling stages to playing in front of the Antiguan public. This time they did not have to read about me in the papers or see me on television in other countries. This was something they had wanted to see for themselves.

In dialect, the locals would say, 'Look man, I wanna see, dowanna hear nothin', wanna see, man.' That created a lot of pressure on me, but I loved the challenge. We need challenges in life because they can give us inspiration to go on to better things. It makes you alive, aware. Scoring a century against England here in Antigua made it extra special.

A great deal has been said and written about that historic day – and not much about the remarkable build-up when the local black magic practitioners tried to use the occasion for their own benefit. Before that first ever test match in Antigua a lady appeared at our doorstep and warned us that there were certain evil forces at work on the island that didn't want me to do well. We told her to go away. But it didn't stop there; others came up and told me and my parents that my image was buried out at the graveyard. Their game was that they saw an opportunity to manipulate my funds, to try and suck me into their group in order to bleed me of my money and to increase their credibility. They tried to convince me that they were keeping me alive, protecting me and stopping other evil forces from getting to me. They warned my parents that if I didn't go with them, I would score a duck. Someone else, who heard these lurid tales, told me at my parents' house that when I was batting I should put a lime in my pocket.

My father would listen until his patience ran out and then he would say in his abrupt manner, 'Are you finished?' Then in his big deep voice he would shout, 'Get this damned rubbish out of my house.'

Unfortunately there were plenty of others who swallowed it and took stupid advice and lost all their money. Sadly, Antigua seems to be a centre in the Caribbean for witchcraft. Recently there a story came out of an area called Otters, in which objects were seen flying about the house of their own accord. I didn't take the time to look into these strange goings-on myself, but I spoke to many people who said they did see them, including reporters and police officers. It made the front page of our local paper for several days. It was even claimed that the devil had taken over an eight-year-old child. There are a lot of people who believe in the Jumbies and witchcraft in our region, but fortunately there are many more with a strong faith in Jesus.

There were none of these distractions in 1984 when we returned to England, but I did suffer a loss of form. Not that it mattered. We won every test by a very large margin. I started well enough with 117 at Edgbaston and 72 at Lord's, but it went downhill for me after that. But it was still memorable as we recorded our first ever 5–0 victory, against David Gower's side, that summer. Everything fitted into place. We were on a winning streak and our supporters loved it.

When I first toured in England in 1976 the support was tremendous as the West Indian supporters came out in droves. A few years after that they tried to take away our support when they banned our people from bringing their drums and musical instruments to the grounds. It had a big effect and helped to take away the true support we used to get when we came to England. Cricket can be a dull game unless you get the right people in the grounds and then it can help, but this decision took away their rights. When we look at modern-day sport, music is involved in football and in other sports. When you are used to the music, the noise and the atmosphere, it takes something away when they are missing. The music helped our rhythm. For a while we did not have the same support because the West Indian felt that his rights had been curtailed just because someone had complained about it. It is now even worse, with hardly any West Indian supporters going. It is one of the saddest developments in modern cricket. I know this is why the West Indians based in England stopped going to test matches because they used to write in to the newspapers to say so. This was the reason and it had nothing to do with when the tickets were on sale, as was claimed. I read recently that the authorities are thinking about an experiment where they will allow the music to be played in a certain area of the ground. Perhaps it would be sensible just to have the instruments confined to a designated section.

The situation is now completely reversed because there are currently a lot of package tours to the Caribbean and everyone looks forward to the English supporters coming because it is more than just about filling the cricket grounds, as they spend money on hotels, taxis, meals and drinks, and everyone benefits. What I find enjoyable is that they love our music and they join in the fun at the end of the day, whatever the state of the game.

The atmosphere in our grounds is special and since the music has been introduced into cricket the feeling has changed. At first people complained that it wasn't cricket but gradually, when the timing was right, it became accepted and now music is such a big part of our life. If you have it you should flaunt it – in the same way as the Brazilians play the drums when they play football; people accept it and come to expect it.

But in 1984, while our supporters revelled in it, England were panicking and, as usual, making far too many changes for their own good and making life difficult for the new players coming in. The selection played into our hands. Our confidence was sky high, we were playing so well, and we beat England convincingly.

We did it again in 1986 in the Caribbean when I skippered the side to another 5–0 win. My most notable contribution with the bat came on my old St John's wicket again. I had failed in the first innings and I moved up the order in the second when Gordon Greenidge couldn't bat. Richie Richardson opened with Desmond Haynes, but things weren't going as quickly as I wanted, since I had in mind a declaration that afternoon so as to put England in for a while and then have a full day after that to bowl them out. The openers put on 100, but not as rapidly as my calculations demanded. So I went in when Richie was out for 31 and I immediately launched a massive attack. As captain, I had given myself permission to go out with all guns blazing, even if it meant sacrificing my wicket.

With Chickie's hi-fi blasting in the background, I set about the England bowling. Chickie has become well known as a local character. His music creates an audience that can extend beyond the true cricket lover. It is highly successful and as long as it lasts I am going to be totally supportive. To go to a ground and not hear the music there makes me feel as if something is missing; I like to think that Chickie was one of the first to start it. I remember him coming to my first test match at home against England, and he is still going strong.

On this occasion it was just one of those days when everything I hit went straight to the boundary, even my miss-hits. I was in good shape, and what made it more interesting was that my mate Ian Botham wanted one more wicket to break a bowling record. He expected me to be in my shell to deny him. Man, was he surprised.

In a sense I did everything to get out; when you are playing so many shots anything can happen, but, luckily enough for me, everything started to flow off the middle of the bat. The crowd was jumping and the car horns were blowing all round the island. It was a magnificent feeling as I scored 110 in 56 balls. It wasn't my fastest. I hit one for Somerset in thirty-something balls, but this one was so special.

Beefy took it well, but the England team were on their knees. Considering the circumstances, he took it pretty well; he was good about the whole thing, even when I hit him high into the back row of the stand. Both's reaction was to tell Graham Gooch to go and field in the stand! The game was played in a tremendous spirit. Both finished with 0-78 off 15 overs and John Emburey 1-83 off 14. Neil Foster and Richard Ellison were the other bowlers to suffer that afternoon.

It was on that tour that I had my falling out with my opposite number, David Gower. England were looking to waste time and I felt that they were overdoing the gardening, prodding down the pitch after every ball. Admittedly, it's the normal thing to do when your back is up against the wall, but with the adrenalin flowing and a win in my own backyard in the offing I wasn't going to let the occasion pass without comment. At the time of the confrontation I definitely felt that he was wasting time. After the event, some people exaggerate what was said. I know that I was trying to get him to hurry up as he tried to use up time to help England to draw the match. I told him, 'Get on with the fucking game. Stop the mucking around' – the normal kind of thing you say at that stage of a game when you are pressing for a win and are battling against the clock, and the other team are naturally trying everything they can to slow it down. But since then the story has developed, depending on who is making the after-dinner speech!

David wasn't the sort to stare you out. He just said, quite rightly, that he was doing what he was allowed to do. His remarks were like his batting. Quite casual. I rated David as a very good player. A lot of people thought he was an under-achiever and was too casual in his way of life and his batting and that he wasn't serious enough about the game. But I like to think that anyone who wears the three lions is committed and he went about it in his own way, according to his character. He was always relaxed and very comfortable in the way he played.

Make no mistake, he was a brilliant player. Some look more urgent than others at the crease and in everyday life too, but perhaps he got it right because he still looks in great shape and he still takes everything in his stride. I must admit that we always fancied his wicket the way we did that of any attacking player. On certain days he could take you apart and on others he could look less than ordinary, perhaps like myself in some ways. When you are blessed with natural ability you do not do things like a normal individual, and that goes for someone like David who is such a flamboyant character. He was such a good batsman you could forget or at least forgive his bad days. He was out soon after our exchange of views and we won the game without a great deal of time to spare. Happily, we were friendly enough when we met for a beer afterwards.

David Gower also supplied one of the funniest moments in the test series that year when he was captain during a 5–0 defeat in the Caribbean. There was a calypso song called 'Captain, the ship is sinking', and this became the theme tune on all the grounds where we played the tests. When we cleaned up the last wicket, David was interviewed in front of the crowd and television cameras. He started off his speech by saying, 'Now that the ship has finally sunk.' It brought the house down and he showed good wit and humour which, along with his flashing blade, endeared him to the West Indian folk.

The 1986 series was to provide another of my most satisfying innings. At my home ground, St John's in Antigua, we were looking for quick runs in the second innings to make England bat again if we were to accomplish the 5–0 whitewash we were looking for. The opening batsmen, on that day Desmond Haynes and Richie Richardson, did well as they put on exactly 100 and I was able to go out with free arms again and hit 110 off 56 balls out of 146, which they reckoned was something of a record. It was not just doing it in front of my home crowd, but also – what was specially pleasing – one of the local companies, Courts, offered what I thought was an enormous amount of money to go to charity for every six that was hit. They say you don't think about things like money when you are playing cricket, but on that day I was aware of the rewards with every ball that went over the boundary ropes. It felt great to know that, added to all that fun and entertainment, there was a spin-off which helped the local needy. I just went out and attacked the ball. The right hand was coming off the bat as I was hitting balls one-handed for six. There was no problem about following the captain's instructions this time as I was the captain and gave myself the licence. It was always good to do something for people at home and it was special to let your country see what you were all about.

As usual I stuck to the pattern I thought was normal. I am a simple individual about what I needed to do on a cricket field. Too many people put undue pressures on themselves. Sometimes I would hear them worrying out loud about the elbow not coming up and other technicalities. You cannot be textbook correct every ball you face from an express bowler or a top spinner. There is no time to be pretty. It is an instinct thing. If you are able to prepare yourself quickly enough and make quick decisions, these are the solutions for reacting to a quick delivery. Even great batsmen like Brian Lara or Sachin Tendulkar are sometimes out through not thinking quickly enough and that has nothing to do with technique. It is often enough to be sharp and to read bowlers' minds, not just watching the arm and the grip on the ball; sometimes there is a need to watch the pattern of the feet, which often give an insight into the sort of delivery about to come.

Personally I was heavily into these little things. I would watch feet, hand, body action and body language. I always knew when a bowler was on song – but you cannot let him know that. Just the way the ball hits the bat lets you know that this man is bowling real quickly. But you have to stay focused and make what you do count.

These are the challenges. Like the bowler who doesn't normally move the ball back into you and then suddenly does. It can play games with your mind. There are a whole lot of little things that go towards making or breaking an innings.

Occasionally mind games are even performed – albeit unwittingly – by your own players, shaking their heads and muttering what the ball is doing as you cross on your way to the wicket. I can accept comment from batsmen like Haynes and Greenidge who were good judges of what needed to be done and what was happening in the middle. But there were other times when some batsmen got out and looked for someone to console them, saying, 'Viv, be careful. He is swinging it in the air and turning it square off the pitch.' Maybe the batsman didn't have his feet in the right position or he lost concentration, or whatever; no one should put demons into other batsmen's minds. Alvin Kallicharran was one of the worst in this respect. He would come out and tell you that the ball was doing all sorts of things. I had great respect for him and he could read the spinners better than most, but I couldn't allow his judgement to affect my game. I knew that if a guy overspins one and you read it as a leg-break then, of course, you are going to have problems against that delivery and I always felt that, while it was nice to be that technical, it was even better to judge for yourself and to be able to assess what you think is happening.

One of the great things about going to sleep before I batted was that I had a picture in my mind of what the opposition could do, and only the outgoing batsman could further influence me. What could be very unnerving would be watching a turning ball or a fast bowler going past the bat; from the pavilion it could look ten times as quick or be turning far too much. That's when it starts playing tricks with your mind. That was another reason why I preferred to sleep. It was never as hard out in the middle as it looked from the pavilion. That is something youngsters could learn from: stick to the basics and don't clutter the mind. Sort out who to listen to and who not to listen to. Someone tells you the ball swings in and then turns the other way, and you are dead before you face a ball. Better that you sort it out for yourself. Back your own judgement.

But sometimes circumstances change, and you have to change with them. When I became captain, my game had to change a whole lot. I was no longer able to sleep. I had to sit and watch. Whether it was psychological I do not know, but my batting suffered a great deal. It was not solely the change in preparation but as captain. I have a natural aggressive instinct to attack and if there was a bowler who was kicking up and causing the team problems, I always felt that I should be the sacrificial lamb to go out and kill or be killed. That entire scenario changed when I took over from Clive Lloyd because of the responsibilities of captaincy. I suppose I still played a lot of those loose shots and got myself out when I shouldn't have done. But this style was tempered according to the team's needs, as was my position in the batting order. I had to sit and watch every ball when I was captain to see what individuals of both sides were doing. You cannot pass on information to your own players if you do not know what is happening. Sometimes I watched so much cricket that I needed matchsticks to keep my eyes open. It certainly killed off much of that natural instinct. A lot of emphasis was put on other players and I felt that it was my job to be the father figure. Even when there was net practice, I let others go in front of me, often batting last, which meant facing the bowlers when they were tired and past their best. When I organized fielding practice, I gave the catches instead of taking some myself. Of course, this was before we had all those positions of coaches and technical director. I was coach, captain, player, disciplinarian and father confessor. You can imagine the responsibilities placed on a single player's shoulders. When I compare the situation today, the captain does not have nearly so much to do. This is no bad thing! Because of my responsibilities I was not as sharp as I should have been. It was a heavy burden to carry personally. It almost certainly hastened my retirement from the international arena.

I didn't score a century in the tour of England in 1988, but we still won it 4–0 with one drawn. That series the late Malcolm Marshall was devastating with the ball and he even scored a nice little 72 with the bat. This was some great player for a captain to have at his disposal. Everyone thought he was primarily an away-swinger, but on that tour he developed an inswinger, a beautiful delivery. He took out quality batsmen like Graham Gooch and Allan Lamb, leaving the ball outside the off stump. He made a huge contribution, scoring 72 runs in the first test and taking seven wickets; ten wickets in the second test; nine wickets and a 43 not out in the third; five wickets in the fourth and four in the last. Whenever we needed wickets or runs, Malcolm seemed to be there. But once more the English selectors helped us no end, and they must shoulder some of the blame. You have to make a choice, picking someone you think can do it. Sure you will pick a wrong one now and again. When you pick someone to play for England it is a big step. Any player needs a run of games to be given a chance. You have to crawl before you can walk. It's a step-by-step process. Some develop more quickly than others do, some come very late. These are the things the selectors must be aware of. Selectors have to shoulder the responsibility; constant change shows that the selectors are not sure themselves. It creates a fear factor, when batsmen are afraid to play their shots because it might cost them their entire test future.

In that series their top order was constantly changing, starting with Graham Gooch, Chris Broad, Mike Gatting, David Gower,

Allan Lamb and Derek Pringle; Martin Moxon came in for the second test, David Capel for the third, Tim Curtis, Bill Athey, Robin Smith and Chris Cowdrey for the fourth, and Rob Bailey and Matthew Maynard for the fifth test. Those were just the specialist batsmen! Below them the bowling changes were chaotic. The whole selection process was in a shambles.

Mark Ramprakash is a prime example of someone who's suffered from this panic-driven decision-making in more recent times. He was in and out of the side so often that he must have felt that he was playing for his place every time he was selected; yet in county cricket he was consistently good and always looked to me to be an outstanding international prospect.

Players need to be given a chance to settle and improve. This is why some international players go on for 12 years. After baptism they take their holy communion, and so on. Now is the time for the England selectors to get their act together and get it right for the new millennium. This has got to be the focus. The young individuals are an investment for the future and they must be given their chance. If they do that, England can come good again. There is too much talent for them not to. To use as an excuse that you have too many players to pick from, as I have sometimes heard for both English cricket and football, is ridiculous. The more the merrier as far as I am concerned.

A player needs a whole series to find out whether he has the makings of a true test player. The selectors have to look at how well a new player fits in. Even if the player does not score his 50 or take five wickets, look at the circumstances. Look for the pedigree and, if it's good, keep it going. Sometimes a youngster might score a good, solid 20 and then receive an unplayable ball. Rejecting him at that point is stifling something he can build on. It can be shattering for his confidence to be axed for something that is not his fault.

The influence of the media in England is also sometimes too strong. If ever there is a series when England start well, everyone says that this is the dawn of a new era. The same thing happened when the selectors decided on two teams, one for the one-day and one for the test matches. The one-day team won a couple of tournaments and everyone got excited and said that this was the way to go. It was another false dawn. Judgements are made too soon and heroes are made too early without a lot of substance. Some individuals believe their own publicity and get carried away; then they want to know why the same press guy who built them up is now knocking them down. Nothing will change that and sportsmen and women will constantly be under pressure in England. All they can do is choose carefully which newspaper they read.

My last series against England in the West Indies was in 1989–90 and I again missed a test match through illness, this time with an acute fistula. I missed the Port of Spain test and had to watch the cricket from my hospital bed. I had hardly had any cricket at all in the build-up, but I climbed out of my hospital bed and flew that night to Barbados because I wanted to be with my team.

I had one day of practice and played the next day. I knew that my strength would not carry me through a long innings, so I blasted everything, scored 70 and ran out of gas. My arms felt tired, my legs felt tired – I felt tired from head to toe. Even so, I was very annoyed at getting out and I sat on the steps for half an hour after being caught behind by Jack Russell off David Capel.

Having lost the first test in Jamaica by nine wickets – I was out twice to Devon Malcolm – and drawn the test that I missed, the team and I were desperate to get back on level terms and, thanks to a knock of 164 by Carlisle Best and eight wickets for Curtly Ambrose in England's second innings, we won by 164 runs. With the second test in Guyana having been rained off, everything was down to the fifth and final test in Antigua. Although Devon got me again, this time for just 1, our fast bowlers gave England a battering, with Ian Bishop, Curtly and Courtney Walsh sharing the bulk of the wickets in an innings victory.

My final series against England was in 1991, defending my record of remaining unbeaten as captain. It was one of the best series I had played in, especially as it followed another nasty round of games against Australia. We needed to clean up our act a bit because of what we had been involved in with the Aussies in the home series, when we had given as good as we got. Not surprisingly, the media were focusing on how we were going to react against England. There had been lots of individual confrontations, notably between Desmond Haynes and Ian Healy, whom Des called a cheat for claiming a catch; there was also a famous war of words between Craig McDermott and myself.

I had made a pledge that we were going to clean up our act. It was down to the captains, and so Graham Gooch and I spoke about it. I was mates with a number of the team, with Allan Lamb and with Robin Smith, a nice man, as is his brother Chris. I even knew their parents. I spent some time with them all. This was not a series for all-out war. It was a very good test series, with just one match drawn and four results, a great advertisement for the game of cricket and all played in great spirit.

I was sad that I couldn't win my last test in England at the Oval, but we still drew the series 2–2 and what made that last test special for me was that England brought back my old mate, Ian Botham, for the game. Typical of Ian, he went out in style – but not quite in the way he would have wanted. He was hit on the toe by Curtly Ambrose, tottered backwards, and not being a ballerina, hit his stumps as he tried to lift his leg over them, causing famous hilarity from Brian Johnston in the BBC commentary box and no less mirth among the West Indies fielders. But despite this he made his usual contribution with a few runs, a few wickets and a couple of catches.

The series was set up when England won a low-scoring first match by 115 runs, with my first innings 73 being the second top score to Graham Gooch's outstanding match-winning 154 not out as he batted throughout England's second innings. We drew the second test but levelled things up with a nine-wicket win in the third at Trent Bridge; we won the fourth but then lost the fifth to level the series, a fair result – although, of course, I would like to have won my last test and my last series. Although I didn't score a century, my form wasn't bad with 73, 63, 80, 73 not out and 60 in my eight innings – not too disastrous for someone they were saying was finished!

I always liked Allan Lamb; he was one of my favourites, always jovial and always up to something. He would invariably have something to say when he passed you, like, 'Fuckin' 'ell, Smokey, it's fuckin' seamin' a lot today,' in that thick South African accent and through the inevitable chewing-gum. He was so honest with it. Fielding in close when one whistled past his head, I would follow it up by saying, 'You had a good one there, Allan.' Unfazed, he would respond, 'Yeah, Smokey, a real snorter.' I liked Lamby, and he and Both together were a hilarious combination.

Robin Smith was another cool individual who wanted to learn more and find out more about our marvellous game. A real student and a fine bat.

I also had a lot of time for big Syd Lawrence. He used to make me laugh a lot and I even found the way he moved funny. He looked to be a very aggressive man, a typical fast bowler, and so he was on the cricket field. But when you meet him off the pitch and hear the way he speaks and realize that he is quite intelligent, the impression is totally different. I have known him for a while, ever since he was a youngster at Gloucester and then when he made his debut for England. Out there, he is aggressive and doesn't care who you are, and he has a big heart, a good attitude and he always believes he is going to roll you over. A confrontation with him was the sort I enjoyed; he was real mean on the cricket field.

Mike Atherton and Graham Gooch were from a different school and were fairly quiet, but John Emburey always wanted to talk a good game about cricket and was pretty sure of what he wanted to get done and how he was going to get it done. Phil Tufnell was another who made me laugh, while Mark Ramprakash was a cool guy. I had heard about him being a rebel and clashing with authority, but I found him cool. Sometimes he would react when confronted, but it has to be remembered that he has a bit of West Indian blood in him!

I also respect the current England captain, Nasser Hussain. He is an outgoing guy and I hope he does well for England. When he first came on to the scene, I stood back and looked at him, and I liked what I saw. He came to the West Indies to play for the

University of West Indies as an invited guest against New Zealand. Although I was long retired, I was also guesting in that game and it gave me a chance to chat to him and watch him at close quarters. I was impressed by what I saw and heard. He is a regular guy and I think he will make a good captain; he is keen about his game, desperate to do well and he bears responsibility without obvious stress. He can also perform well and he can take the glare and make this a better era for English cricket.

I also admire Graham Thorpe. He looks a bit distant, but I think that is because he has a shy streak; you only have to look into his eyes and you can tell. Sometimes people see that the wrong way and think he is either stuck-up or arrogant. I perceived it as basic shyness. He is someone who likes to watch what is happening and he will stay in a corner and look. He doesn't step over his boundaries. I have been a little disappointed and he has let himself down a little in the recent stages of his career. He is one of the better English batsmen in terms of his commitment. You can see it every time he plays forward to a quickie. I don't know how much the back problem has hurt him and affected his performance, but over the last couple of years he has not fulfilled himself.

There was no one in the English side who was really nasty in the manner of the Australian test teams. County cricket doesn't seem to breed that type of cricket, at least not until chirpy Dermot Reeve got Warwickshire at it, and later Adam Hollioake had the same effect at Surrey. That said, I admired the way Dermot made things happen. He was very inventive and didn't mind taking a chance here and there. And Warwickshire won silverware with him – which speaks for itself.

England tours have become increasingly important to the Caribbean, not just in a cricketing sense but for the tourism they bring as well. Every tour seems to bring more and more English supporters to enjoy the cricket, the sun and the hospitality. Their influx is great for the game. The English love the atmosphere and there is never any trouble. They like the difference in the atmosphere compared to their county grounds at home and to be part of the after-match jam. Everyone, black and white, jams for hours afterwards. It all ties in nicely with the tourism and the economy of our island.

When I took over from Clive, the West Indies already had the Indian sign over England, winning 5–0 over there. I was then in the position to follow it up, and the motivation was to do it on our own soil in front of our own supporters. The series against England is always the epitome. It was one of the better places to play and we wanted to drum home the fact that we could play winning cricket in our own style and not the way we were told to play. My belief is that cricket should be about placement of the ball, beating the field and finding the gaps; but to hear critics in England go on about the way we hit across the line and then watch them try to play the game themselves sometimes made me wonder where they earned the right to give us lip about how we should play. Getting your eye in can mean different things to different people. Hitting the first ball for four off the meat is as good a way as any of looking at the ball, but incredibly that sort of aggression is frowned on in some quarters. If the ball is there, hit it! In my view the game is, and always will be, simple. It's about adapting to the conditions. Historically, the English never paid a lot of respect to West Indian cricket, and that gave us the strength of character to overcome whatever odds there were supposed to be against us. There was always something to prove.

6. Out of India and into Africa

I love India. It is a beautiful country with so many cultures. They worship their sportsmen, and particularly their cricketers. While it is never easy there, I love the passionate people. If I step out of the Hilton at Hyde Park in London, I am able to go for a walk; I may be asked for the occasional autograph, but there is minimum fuss, an acceptable degree of hassle. I could never do that in India. The moment I walk out of the hotel door I would be recognized and stopped, with the word spreading like wildfire. Before I can move I become a pied piper and the street has become a carnival. That attention can be rowdy and crowdy. When I was younger I found it difficult and embarrassing, but I now appreciate it when people show that amount of enthusiasm. I have no problem with it and I am delighted that I was able to give them pleasure. It is a strange feeling, but it makes me proud to think that I've achieved this level of recognition coming from an island as small as ours. There are times when I observe the following I attract in the streets and I can't help wondering whether I should open my own commune!

My test career began in India, in 1974, so the country will always hold cherished memories for me. When I was picked for the West Indies my father, who was living in the United States at the time, was so thrilled because he had been brought up in the era of the three Ws. He was full of advice to me. Everyone was really proud; the brothers in the USA were able to share the feeling enjoyed by the West Indies population. My mother could hardly believe it and my friends marvelled at the honour. Mervyn knew the value of having a brother playing for the West Indies. It was a big thing for Antigua to have two of us, me and Andy Roberts, in the same West Indies side after years languishing in the shadows of the larger islands. As a basically shy youth, the attention was hard for me to take during those early days. There were huge crowds to meet

Andy and myself when we came back from our first tour of India and Pakistan. It was something I had never seen before, nor had either of us expected it when we stepped off the plane. In fact I was embarrassed. I preferred to be in the background and, strangely, I have never liked to be in the middle of too many people, those big uncontrolled crowds. I have never minded autograph-hunters when they have lined up. But when there are people left, right, centre and behind your back – that still bothers me.

As a young cricketer I was also disturbed at having to make speeches in front of those big crowds. For a personality like mine, going up on to a platform was a very hard thing to do. I thought it was wrong, because I was a sportsman and not a politician. But it is all part of the learning process. It was hard to see the point at the time, but later in my career when I was a public figure and was made captain and now that my playing career is over, it has stood me in good stead.

Indians' enthusiasm for all things comes as a surprise initially and it's not just confined to cricket. When we first went to India we were invited to a lot of functions, but the trouble was that they had all the chat and the speeches first, with the food not served until 11 p.m. or even midnight. It was usually a buffet-style meal and, when it was announced that the food was served, everyone would dive in and we would be left wondering if they remembered that they had some guests attending who might also be hungry. They didn't mean to be rude, it was just the way things were done in that part of the world. This whole-hearted approach to life was never illustrated better than by my experiences with the Indian team physiotherapist. It was 1983, the year when we lost the World Cup to India, and we were due back for a full tour in October. The physio was cool, a nice guy, and when he asked me if he could bring his family to meet me on our return to the country, I told him, genuinely, that it would be my pleasure and that I was more than happy to say hello to his wife and children. I thought no more about it until we returned to Bombay. The team was staying at the Taj Mahal Hotel and on the afternoon before the first day of the test match I was relaxing before going to the team meeting, just having a few private thoughts, when the doorbell rang. I wasn't expecting anyone but when I looked through the spyhole I saw it was my friend the physio. I told him I remembered him and I asked him if it was now he wanted me to say hello to his family. He beamed his delight. I opened the door, turned to go to the lounge to put a shirt on and, when I turned back, I saw him ushering people into my room like a swarm of mosquitoes. Then someone else unplugged my television in order to plug in his video. I stood there in amazement, looking at all these people who were still pouring into my room. There were aunts, uncles, cousins and friends, and I stopped counting when I reached 50. I was as polite as I could be, but I was cursing under my breath at the sheer cheek of it all. They wanted autographs and pictures taken individually. I let it go on for a little while, but then I told them they had to leave because I had a team meeting. It wasn't funny at the time, but looking back on it makes me smile and there was a sharp lesson for me in the danger of saying to a casual acquaintance, 'Look me up some time.'

Caribbean crowds are perhaps the only ones to rival those in the subcontinent for passion and enthusiasm, although on occasion this can spill over. This happened most memorably during a match against India in front of an excitable Jamaican crowd. I felt that I was close to fulfilling a dream in the fourth test against India in 1988–9. I was going sweetly, I had scored a ton and felt this was it. I was ready to explode, I desperately wanted to cut loose and show the Jamaican public what they had come to see of Viv, to be everything the crowd hoped and expected me to be. Suddenly it all turned sour when Kapil Dev bowled me a delivery that was just too good to get away. It cut back viciously and clipped the top of my pad. Kapil Dev was always a good appealer. He went up, the wicket-keeper Kiran More went up and, unfortunately, so did the umpire's finger. I didn't even know what I had been given out for, leg before wicket or caught. The scorebook later revealed that I was supposed to have edged the ball.

My disappointment was huge. I stood there in total disbelief, looked at Dev and the umpire and stamped my feet. Admittedly it was all a bit childish for a thirty-seven-year-old captain of the West Indies. I was wrong for showing dissent, but these things happen in the heat of battle, especially when you are as competitive as I was. I couldn't believe it – to be given out at a time like that, having paved my way for a really big score with what for me had been a careful innings. How wrong it was I was quickly to find out. My reaction started a bloody riot!

In Jamaica the police are always ready for trouble, as they are used to the violence. They were so well prepared that they were armed not only with their usual batons but also with tear gas. As I watched it unfold there was a touch of *deja vu* as I said to myself, 'Oh no, Viv, you have done it again.' There was an instant flashback to St John's in Antigua and the time when I brought my first big representative game to a halt when I was a kid. The passionate Jamaican cricket public wore their hearts on their sleeves that day. They must have sensed how I was feeling and they, like me, let their anger show. Play was immediately suspended.

I was feeling remorseful and guilty as I sat in the pavilion and watched them climbing over the fences and setting fire to newspapers and anything else that would burn. When someone came up with the suggestion that I should go and speak to the troublemakers in the eastern stand, I never hesitated; I was involved and it was me who had sparked off the bad behaviour. I had never expected it to escalate to such a pitch.

As I went out in my role as peacemaker, flanked by the police, I couldn't help feeling an enormous sense of power. Where it came from I do not know, but I could almost taste it as I strode towards the fans who were rioting because of my ill-judged actions. I had started that riot and now I was stopping it. I have to admit that, terrible as it sounds, it felt great: having the power to tell a mob to cool down and seeing them respond. I realized that whatever I asked them to do they would do. Oh man, I thought I understood in that instant how Caesar must have felt when he stood on the balcony in front of the Romans. This was serious power and a bit frightening. I could sense at that moment how easily it could turn heads and create monsters. All other authorities had tried to calm them down, but I had stopped it with just a little wave. I was pleased that we were able to cool things down, not only for me, but for West Indies cricket, for the game and the series; but it drove home to me the reality of my position and the consequences of my actions.

We lived to fight another day, and I lived to put my hand in my pocket to pay a big fine, something around $US 500 – a great deal of money then.

It's hard to think about India without talking about the dreadful poverty of the country. From the moment you are born you can be told that you are doomed for life, and that strikes me as being unfair. Certain classes of people have no chance of knowing anything that is going on anywhere else in the world or ever making anything of their lives. We hear about all these great people – inventors, philosophers and philanthropists – but not one of them has been clever enough to solve the problem of hunger and poverty around the world. It is never wise to back away from things that you may not like, and it is from this sort of experience that you learn. When I hear people at home complaining that things are tough, I suggest that they might exchange places with someone from the streets of Bombay and see how long they last. I look at these things and compare them to life in general and maybe take inspiration from some people having so very little but still making it work for them. It amazes and humbles me to see them not only getting by but still maintaining their dignity. My great respect for the poorest people of India only underlines my high opinion of the whole country. Sadly, the rich tend to be very rich, exaggerating the gulf even further. If something cannot be done, then at least it is up to everyone to make the problems known. I have observed in recent years that more and more people and businesses are prepared to put themselves out to try and do something about the problems and give the support that every government needs. That is a promising development and I hope it continues.

When I first travelled to India with the West Indies team, I couldn't have anticipated the pressures that touring would put on my family life. It is very difficult being a father and a husband when you are away from home for so long. It destroys relationships in a big, big way and makes life extremely difficult. Every father wants to see his children grow up and do those special things with them. You try to make as much time for them as possible, but it is near impossible when so much of your work is thousands of miles from home. But that is the job. It is what I do best and the reward it has brought has helped build them a good life.

Certainly being away from home all the time eventually affected my relationship with my wife, Miriam. It's created a gulf and gradually, because of the continued and extended absences, in a sense you become strangers, with each forming his or her own way of life. Inevitably it creates a serious strain. To be honest, all you can do is hope for the best, that time will prove to be the crucial factor and that our decisions made will send us in the right direction. I contemplate all these diverse factors and hope to come up with the right answers. It would be unfair and improper to go too deeply into our personal relationship, as there are certain things that Miriam has to protect because of her religion. It is a very delicate subject, but the important factor is that we have worked hard together to bring up our son Mali and our daughter Matara.

But with my being away from home so much we have had our problems. When travelling you need the company of other people more than ever and there's always the chance that you will meet someone else, someone you enjoy being with. Everything can escalate from there. I met the second lady in my life, Neena, at a dinner at a maharaja's palace in Jaipur. I was the only cricketer among the celebrities and film stars. The film industry in India is huge and every bit as popular as cricket – which is saying something. Neena is a very talented lady, an actress, a film producer and a director in Bollywood. A relationship developed and I am proud that we have a healthy daughter, Masaba, who's now eleven. I see them both as often as possible, helped by the fact that my profile in India has endured, meaning that I'm fortunate to receive regular invitations to go there.

My ties with India are especially strong, considering I played only three series there. I've always felt, though, that I've enjoyed some of my best and most memorable performances against them, and it was in India that I played my first ever test match. That first test was at Karnataka State C. A. Stadium in Bangalore in November 1974. We batted first and I just couldn't watch. I had to convince myself that once I was on the field it would be fine. Cricket, I thought, is cricket wherever it is played, but then came the first test and that was the most frightening experience of my life. Every time a batsman took a ball on the pad the entire crowd would jump up and down, shouting, appealing and putting incredible pressure on the umpires. Judging by the noise and tumult, it seemed that something was happening every ball and I was due out there in a short time. Despite the apparently unplayable wicket, however, I had to wait as Roy Fredericks scored 23; Gordon Greenidge scored 93 and Alvin Kallicharran 124.

As time passed I began to relax and went and lay down and tried to close my eyes. The roar from the crowd told me when the two wickets fell and when it was my turn to bat. But immediately things began to go pear-shaped. My legs, numb from nerves, were not working properly and as I stepped on to the big bamboo step leading from the pavilion to the outfield I stumbled and fell right to the bottom. I picked myself up and dusted myself down, but my nerves were hardly settled as firecrackers flew past me, while someone in the crowd shone a mirror straight into my eyes from behind the wicket.

My mind was in turmoil. I was totally overawed by the occasion and was out for 4 in that first innings and 3 in the second, both times to Chandrasekhar. Fortunately we won the match handsomely and I took catches at short leg to dismiss both openers, Sunil Gavaskar and Farook Engineer. I found myself in that suicidal position because I was the youngest and if I hadn't volunteered someone would have volunteered me anyway. Those two catches were crucial, for they meant that I was there for the remainder of the series.

I went to the second test in Delhi with my debut behind me. My confidence was in tatters but I was determined I would not fail again. I didn't. I went in at number five and hit 192 not out. This was no shy, retiring innings. As my confidence grew on a true pitch I went on to the attack and started to hit boundaries. We won again and I felt that I had retrieved my position somewhat after the embarrassment of the first test. It was a good knock because we had been in a little trouble at 73 for three, and I shared good partnerships with Clive Lloyd, Bernard Julien and Keith Boyce to help us post a total of almost 500.

The Indian spinners soon brought me back down to earth in subsequent tests, but I enjoyed my first tour. It was to prove to be an exciting series for, after winning those first two tests, we promptly lost the next two. We won the series in the last test in Bombay, although my contribution in the first innings was only 1 before Chandra had me caught behind the wicket; but I was at the crease with an unbeaten 39 when we won the match with Alvin Kallicharran at the other end.

That tour was a great experience and held me in good stead for the future. I have never felt or seen such support as in that part of the world. The constant noise, the stifling heat and the intimidation of the umpire by the crowd all hem you in. It could be extremely intimidating, but it helped me; it broadened my perspective and widened my whole area of performance, and I was all the better for that.

Australia had big partisan crowds as well – but what are 40,000 drinking Australians compared to 80,000 frenzied Indians? There is no comparison. One event that made a big impression on me during that tour was provoked when, in that deciding test in Bombay, Clive Lloyd scored a crucial big double-ton. Someone ran on to the pitch to offer congratulations. He was caught by the police just as he was about to jump back over the fence and was given a terrible beating. The crowd was incensed, they thought this action was unfair, and we found ourselves back in our hotel a lot sooner than we had expected. A riot quickly spread and, before I knew what was happening, they had set one of the stands on fire.

That was my first experience of how intense these people can be. I did not dream that this sort of thing happened. But I must confess that I loved the intensity of the atmosphere. Cricket is not the liveliest of sports and I appreciated having spectators displaying an avid interest. During the World Cup in England they showed that they are the sort of people who can help the game go forward.

The 1974-5 tour was also my first experience of the wickets that were specially prepared for the spinners like Chandrasekhar, Bedi and Prasanna, who had me both times in the fourth test at Madras, which we lost by 100 runs. But if the Indians were happy about producing wickets to satisfy their own specialists, they were less than pleased with some of the quick tracks we produced for our pace men in the Caribbean a few months later. I scored 142 in the first test in Barbados, which we won by an innings; 130 in the drawn second test in Trinidad; and 177 at the same venue where we surprisingly lost the third test by six wickets, thanks largely to the batting of Gavaskar and Viswanath, who both scored tons when chasing a target of 400!

But it was in Jamaica that the Indians collapsed against our pace with *five* absent hurt in a second-innings total of 97. That gave us a 2-1 series win. It happened when the West Indies played India in Kingston in April 1976 in the fourth and deciding test of the series and ended in absolute farce. Over there we played on wickets made for spinners, so when we had them in the Caribbean we produced wickets for our pace bowlers. There were no complaints from us when we were in their backyard but their actions showed that they only liked it when they were on top. We had to put up with a great deal in India, not just wickets, but bad umpires as well. Admittedly the wicket was a little unpredictable and two-paced, and it created fear in the Indian batsmen, who were ducking into balls instead of under them or away from them. Bishen Bedi, the Indian captain, had some harsh words to say about our bowlers and called the test a war. But it couldn't have been that bad, as they scored over 300 in their first innings and we scored almost 400!

Michael Holding, playing his first test on his home island, bowled tremendously. His first casualty was Viswanath, who fractured a finger when Julien caught him at short leg. Gaekwad, who had batted for more than seven hours, was then hit on the ear by Holding, sending him to hospital for two days. Michael then saw a ball to Patel deflected off the batsman's glove and into his mouth, and that injury required three stitches. That was the last we saw of him that match.

Bedi was moaning about intimidating bowling and he declared the first innings closed with six wickets down and two players retired hurt. It seemed that Bedi was protecting himself and his fellow spinner Chandrasekhar with the declaration. It didn't do the Indian captain a lot of good, as he damaged his left little finger trying to take a caught-and-bowled chance from me. Then Chandra injured his hand in the field, while Surinder Amarnath, one of six substitutes used by the Indians, was rushed to hospital for an emergency appendix operation. None of those three mishaps could be blamed on our fast bowlers or the wicket! But it meant that when India batted for the second time they were all out for 97 despite losing only five wickets!

I can remember England doing it to the same India side when they produced the greenest wicket I have ever seen in England and Bob Willis rolled them over twice for around 100 each time. The wicket certainly didn't suit Bedi and Chandra – but then they hardly gave Willis a track that suited him when he visited the subcontinent.

I missed the '78–9 series that we lost 1–0 in India, but I was back for the home series in 1982–3, which we won 2–0. It was in the first test of that series that I enjoyed my all-time favourite innings of 61 that helped us to an unexpected win in Jamaica. I was out for 1 to Kapil Dev in the second test and I scored a hundred in a rain-ruined third test after we had totalled over 400. In Barbados I scored 80 in a ten-wicket win that was won with a no ball bowled by wicket-keeper Kirmani with the first and only ball of our second innings. It gave us the one run we needed to take the series, with the fifth test in Antigua drawn. My contribution with the bat on my home ground was 2 after waiting for an eternity as Gordon Greenidge and Desmond Hayes put on 296 for the first wicket.

Not even the spinners' wickets in India in 1983–4 could blunt our battery of fast bowlers as we won the series 3–0 with three games drawn. The lines of battle were drawn in the first test in Kanpur when we won by an innings, with Malcolm Marshall taking a total of eight wickets and Michael Holding six. After a drawn second test in Delhi, where I scored 67, we won again in Ahmedabad by 138 runs, with Holding not only taking six wickets but also top-scoring in our second innings with 58.

I lost my wicket to Shastri twice in the drawn test in Bombay, but not before I had scored 120 and 4; but in the fifth test in Calcutta the honours were shared by skipper Clive Lloyd with 161 not out and our fast bowlers again. But while Marshall took a total of nine wickets and Holding six, they also did serious damage with the bat, with Andy Roberts scoring 68 and Marshall 54 in another innings win. The drawn final test in Madras fell a victim to bad weather.

I went back as captain in '87–8 and we drew 1–1 with two drawn. We looked to be heading for another series win when we took the first test by five wickets, as I steered us home in the second innings with 109 not out with considerable help from Gus Logie and Jeffrey Dujon. We drew the next two in Bombay and Calcutta, but we were denied a series win when Hirwani skittled us out for 160 in the second innings in Madras, leaving us 255 short of our target.

Honour was restored in '88–9 back home with a resounding 3–0 success, with only the first of the four tests drawn and that because of the rain in Guyana. We won by eight wickets in Barbados and by 217 runs in Trinidad when Malcolm Marshall took eleven wickets. The captain's contribution with the bat had been 5, 1, 19 and 0, but I made amends somewhat in the final test in Jamaica with 110, which contributed to a comfortable seven-wicket victory.

Nowhere else other than on the Indian subcontinent does the game seem to be supported with the same burning intensity. It matters so much to people. I wish I'd played more of my cricket in India, a country I love. These days, with so much more test cricket, I might have had the chance. Nevertheless, even though

I'm long retired, the crowds soon gather whenever I visit, even if, now and again, they sometimes mistake me for Richie Richardson!

If I didn't get to play as much cricket in India as I'd have liked, at least it was only for reasons of scheduling. I was never to play a test match in South Africa – and the reason, by contrast, was one of principle: taking a stand against apartheid. I was very humbled when I went to the new South Africa to meet Bishop Tutu and the Minister of Sport, Steve Tshwete. They wanted to tell me to my face how much I had helped them in their cause. Bishop Tutu told me that they prayed for me on a regular basis because of the decision I made not to come to South Africa and how I had helped fight apartheid in my own little way. When I visited I had my lawyer, Harold Lovell, with me. He was always strong in his opinions on apartheid and I thought it perfect that he should be with me and see what the new South Africa was all about, now that apartheid was dismantled.

The decision not to play there hadn't been too hard for me. We were playing in Australia when there was talk of certain rebel tours. South Africa was hungry for cricket after their long absence. There were all sorts of tours going over there and having everything paid for. I was asked to make a trip by Ali Bacher, who was putting together a major tour featuring a lot of big names. He was travelling all over the world putting his team together, and when we met he made me a huge offer, well over $US500,000. I was told that everything would be cool and that when I signed, others would follow. I made the decision there and then that it wasn't for me. The money was not a consideration. I was simply not interested in such a thing. I knew of the sufferings going on in South Africa and was insulted when it was suggested to me that if I went I would be called an honorary white. That is as low as you can get in selling your soul. I wasn't going to be a human being who was restricted to being in certain places at certain times. I am a free bird and where I come from we ran that entire thing away when the slave trade was abolished.

I have no tolerance for that sort of rubbish at all and I just felt that coming from this environment I would be likely to express my opinions out loud and, by so doing, even put my life in danger. I would rather die than lay down my dignity. It would have made me so angry that I would have wanted to kill someone myself. How can anyone deny that you are an individual and a human being? I wasn't going to take any rubbish from anyone. I won't throw the first stone, but if I am called a pig and told I have no right to be a human then watch out.

I talked to some of the West Indians who went on that tour to South Africa, and some not only felt humiliated but were also utterly ashamed of themselves. I can accept that people do make mistakes; and there were also others who claimed that they were able to work wonders for the people of the townships. That is looking on the positive side, and I have no reason to doubt their honesty. There may have been positives that came out of their tour. I don't want to act as judge and jury but, like everyone else, I am entitled to my opinion and I have no regrets about my decision at the time. I am not going to say that all those who went were wrong, but I know that I wasn't going to go, however many noughts they put on a cheque.

Those who went have to live with themselves and decide whether they were right or wrong. They will know it every time they look in the mirror, whether they were black or white players who went on that tour. All of them had their own reasons and maybe some of those reasons could be explained in dollars and cents; while others, perhaps, weren't good enough to play for their country on a regular basis. Everyone who went had their own agenda and we have to respect it, even if we don't like it. I am sure, though, that the sporting blockade played a major role in the breaking down of apartheid.

Looking at the attendances and enthusiasm, it is easy to see that South Africa is a sporting-mad nation. The ills of the past won't be cured overnight. They are still solving the problems and, because it went on for so long, it will take years to resolve. Obviously it will take time to develop and integrate black players into the cricket and rugby sides, but they have a good example with the white players who have been integrated into the football team which had long been considered in South Africa a preserve of the black people.

The more that happens, the more it will spread to the other sports. Football has set a fine precedent, where you have a football team representing the colours of the nation. Ali Bacher and the cricket union have helped develop cricket in the townships, forming leagues which never existed before. The benefits will be reaped from those initiatives in the years to come and, more importantly, they will be achieved naturally. I don't believe you can force the issue. To represent your country you have to earn it and not be put in the side because of the colour of your skin.

I would like to think that Nelson Mandela represented a dream after the trials and tribulations he went through. His background made people sympathetic to him personally, but I believe he will have prepared for the future and I hope his successor, Thabo Mbeki, will carry it on and fulfil his vision. South Africa is on the right road now and they cannot afford to turn back. South Africa has so much to offer and share. Just because the black people now have the majority, they cannot run wild and have everything they want 'yesterday'. If progress is carried out irresponsibly, it would just play into the hands of the people who maintained apartheid. It is extremely important that knowledge be gained from past mistakes and that divisions are broken down. They must integrate, bringing people from all backgrounds together to make certain that what hurt the country so deeply never happens again. There's a long way to go, and the anger and deprivation caused by the bad old days has meant that many of the cities are dangerous places. Even the President of the West Indies Cricket Board, Pat Rousseau, and his wife were mugged on the eve of the historic series between South Africa and the West Indies. There are still huge problems there, which only time and a collective will can heal.

It was a great shame that the West Indies were never able to play a test against South Africa while I was in the team, but I don't regret it for a second. The real shame, of course, was the racist system which gave rise to this situation. At a purely sporting level, though, I would love to have played cricket with some of the biggest names in South African cricket at the time. There were none bigger than Graeme Pollock; sadly, the only time I ever played against him was in a 'Legends' match in India, where two old beaten-up warriors limped along. From what I hear, he was a great batsman. I wish I'd seen our fast bowlers against players like Pollock, Barry Richards and Mike Procter when we were all in our prime. It would have been some series between the two countries. They would have made a big impact on cricket. The world missed some great players, but it was all for the greater good of fighting the evil of apartheid. That cricket suffered was a small price to pay. As a player, some consolation to me was an opportunity to play with a handful of some of South Africa's best players who emerged from an unexpected quarter: Australia.

7. The Packer Years

The controversial Kerry Packer was a visionary who brought a great many changes to the game of cricket, most of them for the good; and many of them live on today, embraced by the very establishment which ridiculed the Australian and tried to destroy him. I feel privileged to have been personally involved in something which shook the cobwebs out of our game, breathed new life into it and elevated the professional cricketer to a financial status he had never before enjoyed.

It all began for me during a test series against Pakistan in March 1977 in the Caribbean when the England captain, Tony Greig, acting as an agent for World Series Cricket, made contact in secret with our skipper, Clive Lloyd, in Trinidad during the second test. After their initial discussions Clive spoke to Andy Roberts, Michael Holding and myself about the prospect of joining him in forming part of a Rest of the World team to play a proposed series against a very strong Australian team. When Clive told us that this Australian television magnate, Kerry Packer, was prepared to put up a great deal of money, it immediately captured our interest and the bottom line was that I would come out of it with around £75,000, a staggering sum of money for a cricketer at that time.

The prospect of mega-bucks took our breath away and there was little or no hesitation because we trusted Clive's instincts and we decided to put our signatures to the private and confidential documents. I sat there thinking to myself, 'Wow! Let's get into this as quickly as possible.' We signed not only a contract but also a document that swore us to the strictest secrecy. No problem there. My only doubt was that Packer and his men should have looked for a whole West Indies team rather than a handful of individuals. I also had some worries about what Somerset would say about it, but these proved to be unfounded as the majority wished me well

– but with a warning to be careful since I was stepping outside the security of the establishment.

That was not, however, the case around the world and, when the news finally broke a couple of months later, the repercussions were felt around the globe, with its epicentre in Australia where the battle lines were being drawn between Channel 9 and the Australian Cricket Board. I discovered later that this war had broken out because the Australian Cricket Board had twice rejected big bids by Packer's channel for the exclusive rights to Australian cricket, preferring to accept lower bids from the traditional Australian Broadcasting Commission.

It transpired that the secret talks had seduced 35 of us from five different countries to sign contracts for the next three years, with the Aussies to be captained by Greg Chappell and the Rest of the World by Tony Greig. We were scheduled to play 54 days of cricket in that first season, including one-day internationals, five-day tests and three-day matches. The tremors were felt when everyone realized that official tour schedules would be thrown into chaos, with England due to tour Pakistan and New Zealand, while Australia were to entertain India and then visit us in the Caribbean. The Australians had lost 13 of the 17 players who were currently on tour in England. But what really upset them was that Greg Chappell, Doug Walters, Rod Marsh and R. D. Robinson were on their sub-committee, set up a year earlier to give the players a stronger say in the running of the game, including much higher salaries and rewards.

In England Greig was immediately kicked off the English team, but it was decided that the others, Alan Knott, John Snow and Derek Underwood, would not be barred from selection. Tony Greig, who had acted as Packer's undercover agent, was the one most vilified in the media for his part.

It looked as though the stormy affair might be calmed when the two parties met in London that summer, but the talks collapsed and full-scale war was declared between the two factions. The International Cricket Conference responded by trying to bar all of us who had signed to play for Packer in what was now very definitely pirate cricket, since they issued a statement saying, 'No player who after October 1977 has played or made himself available to play in a match previously disapproved by the ICC shall thereafter be eligible to play in any Test match.' Worse for us was that they also tried to persuade every country to ban us at domestic level.

This was escalating way out of our league and over our heads, but Packer was quick to reassure us that the ICC had overstepped the mark and made a bad legal error and that there was no chance of them carrying through their threats in the courts of law, especially with the team of lawyers Packer had ready to fight them. He took them to the High Court in England where, after seven nerve-racking weeks, Mr Justice Slade came out on our side and declared that it would be a restraint of trade and that we and our contracts were entitled to the protection of the law.

Meanwhile we were underway and Richie Benaud had further shocked the world's cricketing establishment by announcing the innovations: restrictions on defensive fields at the start of an innings; night games with black sight-screens and white balls and coloured outfits instead of the traditional whites. But the biggest change as far as we were concerned was that Packer and his men had listened to our pleas and had added a West Indian team to the set-up – and not just a team but enough for a few of the 'extras' to play for the World XI.

The West Indies Cricket Board were not nearly as harsh as the other associations around the world, but when they left out Deryck Murray, Desmond Haynes and Richard Austin, three players who had signed for Packer, Clive Lloyd promptly resigned his captaincy in protest and within days the rest of us involved with Packer had withdrawn in solidarity. Joel Garner, who thinks himself a good negotiator, took it upon himself to lead the talks with the board on behalf of the aggrieved players. Andy Roberts and I stayed in Antigua; I wanted to go to Guyana, as I thought it was the best place to negotiate from, but Joel and the guys who were representing us told us to stay put. I was concerned that I might end up as the fall guy.

I have always tried to do what is best for the team. If we were all doing the right thing, then I was with it. I stayed in Antigua and chilled out. In the end I was glad that I was in my own backyard because some of the other guys had the humiliation of being thrown out of the team hotel in Guyana when they arrived. Most of the cricket lovers in Antigua seemed to be behind us and thought that the West Indies Board had handled it all very badly. A lot of bad feeling was created. A lot of the board members seemed to take the entire matter personally; they felt that we had let them down, and they kept that monkey on their back for a long time. Many of them did not forgive or forget for many years afterwards.

It could have been resolved a lot more easily with discussion. As far as we were concerned, we were all perfectly willing to continue playing for our country, in fact I desperately wanted to because there is nothing better in cricket than representing your country. It was all so silly, because we had one team in the West Indies and another in World Series Cricket where the best and toughest cricket was played. As far as we were concerned, we were still the West Indies and we bonded in the same way. I remember watching television one evening when English journalist Robin Marlar made a complete ass of himself, running down the WSC as men wearing pyjamas. I was glad that, in the end, the pompous fool was made to look silly and had to eat his words.

Kerry Packer himself became involved, flew into the luxurious Sandy Lane Hotel in Barbados and invited all his West Indian players to join him for dinner, sending out his private jet to collect us. Packer also spoke out on Caribbean television and gained massive sympathy for us from the public when he explained the impoverished state of their favourite players and how he was redressing the balance.

The other problem with the West Indies Board was over the use by Packer of South African players not involved in organized authorized cricket around the world. It was fine, for example, for Barry Richards, Mike Procter and Eddie Barlow to play because they were regulars in county cricket, but the West Indies Board, fighting a fierce battle with the despicable apartheid state in South

Africa, would not agree to us playing against South African-based players like Graeme Pollock who, despite his personal stand against apartheid, was deemed unacceptable. The West Indies Board won that battle, and the Packer organization was forced to pay off the left-hander's contract without him ever appearing in the games.

While all these legal battles were being fought in courts and boardrooms around the world, we were getting on with our cricket. Our first concern on arrival was the new coloured gear; it wasn't that we were against playing in coloured clothing, but we had been designated to play in pink! Hardly the colour for the macho men from the Caribbean. England was playing in a triangular tournament that year and the establishment decided that they would not get involved; when we played, they wore white and we wore pink. It didn't look right at all.

When the series started, it was very competitive. There was huge prize money, with winner take all. That was genuine; there were no arrangements, no secret agreements. We were paid our flat fees, but the prize money went to the winning team. Packer had gathered the cream of international cricket from around the entire globe. It was, without doubt, some of the toughest cricket I had ever played in, before or since. There were the South Africans who had been banned as a team and were desperate to compete. They had players of the genuine quality of Barry Richards, Eddie Barlow, Garth le Roux, Kepler Wessels and Mike Procter, a group of diversely talented cricketers who could hold their own in any company. Every country was represented from the world of cricket, and I just felt that we were at the pinnacle with the best of the crop. We had to perform at our best in very evenly contested, tight matches, perhaps some of the best ever played on a cricket field.

The critics knocked the event, particularly about playing night cricket. Kerry Packer and his public relations team were instrumental in developing the idea that we would start at 2 p.m., take a break, and then resume so that people who finished work at 5 p.m. could come and watch until stumps at 10 p.m. We were not allowed to play any later as that was the cut-off time for the lights.

I felt that cricket had a new commercial image. Cricket needed a face-lift and Kerry Packer gave it to us. As part of our deal, the players did a number of promotional adverts for television and for radio, with slogans that were picked up by the crowd, things like 'C'mon, Aussies, c'mon' and 'There's going to be thunder Down Under'.

It was like a Hollywood affair. It looked wrong and out of place at first, but eventually it worked, with the white ball, the coloured gear and the floodlights being accepted as a step forward in popularizing the game. It proves that you never know what you are creating and, although we may have looked like prats at the time, we were eventually seen as pioneers. I would remind all the knockers – and there were many of them – that most of Packer's innovations are now a recognized and accepted part of the establishment's one-day games and the World Cup.

Kerry Packer was responsible for putting his money where his mouth was and he was not only responsible for changing and modernizing the face of the game, but also the fees became better for the players. It put us on proper salaries and, when the dust settled and everyone fitted back into their own folds, they enjoyed improved remuneration along with those who hadn't joined the venture. Even the county cricketer in England felt the benefit.

The establishment had a serious scare. Here was a guy who was brave enough to come up with an idea, invest his money and back it to the hilt. The establishment fought and squirmed but, in the end, had nowhere to turn but to go the Packer way. It was tough at first as the headlines denounced us as Rebels on a Rebel Tour. But I firmly believe that if Kerry Packer had not come along and improved the lot of cricketers around the world, then the players themselves would have had to do something about it along the lines of the baseball and basketball shutouts in America and the end of the maximum wage in football in England. I am talking about strike action. This would have seriously damaged the game and it would have taken a lot longer to get over. Although they may not agree, the establishment have a lot to thank Kerry Packer for, along with every professional cricketer.

It was hard when the West Indies forced us briefly out of the fold. It robbed me of a few runs towards my final total and it would have been nice to be able to include the five centuries I scored in the World Series. One day I may ask the authorities to add those runs to the records as I scored them against some of the best bowlers in the world, while lesser batsmen were scoring runs against inferior bowlers in the 'real' tests! It would have given me a final total of 29 centuries, which would have been damned good. It was a tough three years' cricket but very satisfying to have gone there and made that impression. I missed a six-test tour to India, one against Sri Lanka and three tests against Australia, but I never once felt that I had made a mistake.

Kerry Packer was totally honourable in everything he promised. When he took us to dinner at a time when we were having problems being reinstated in the West Indies team, he flew not only us to Barbados but our families as well. He was a great believer in family values.

WSC created a new lifeline to cricket supporters, especially in Sydney, where people who were not able to watch normally because of their business commitments were able to enjoy a session later in the day when they could relax and put their feet up. How many new supporters did we bring to the game in those three years?

The Aussies, in particular, loved the competitiveness and aggression of a winner-takes-all situation. The decision to adopt this cut-throat form of cricket was made because it was thought that if we were all paid the same bonuses, there wouldn't be the same level of competition. It was hard to argue with that theory. We fought out each match for around $US100,000.

The West Indies had some good kitties and good bonuses with our hard-won victories. That first season was not totally successful as far as Packer was concerned and he lost a great deal of money, some said as much as $2 million Australian. But, at the same time, the Australian Board lost money for the first time ever in an Ashes series against England in which the second-string English team hammered the third-string Aussies 5–1. While our gates were not all that might have been hoped for, there was an instant interest in the day–night games and there was a crowd of over 50,000 at the SCG.

But for me personally it was tremendous; I relished the quality and the aggression and enjoyed one of my best ever seasons. I made the top scores of 79 and 56 in the first of the 'Super Tests' as we won against Australia at VFL Park in Melbourne. I top-scored again with 88 as we won the second at the Showground, but was disappointed when my 123 was not enough to stop us being defeated in the third game. In the fourth game I played for the World XI against Australia and again picked up a century and a nice win bonus, but the best game of all was the next in Perth, where the World team slaughtered Australia by an innings. It was sensational cricket, with Barry Richards and Gordon Greenidge sharing a first-wicket stand of 369. I have never slept for so long! Gloucester Park has never seen better batting before or since as Richards (the other one) scored a double century, Gordon weighed in with 140 and I scored 177, having been given total freedom to go for my shots because of the enormity of that first-wicket stand. We totalled over 600, but the batting feast did not end there as Greg Chappell scored a magnificent 174, as good as anything that had gone before. But it was not enough, as we forced them to follow on and then bowled them out for 159.

Unfortunately we lost the final game, but again I managed 170 before being given out lbw. Perhaps the umpires were sick of the sight of me by then, as I had amassed over 700 runs at an average of 90.

There were a lot of good players about, among them a youngster named David Hookes who was a young coming cricketer, the Aussie golden boy who scored heavily in the series, but who after that never fulfilled his potential. Dennis Lillee, as usual, was very impressive, as was Garth le Roux, who went to Sussex; Eddie Barlow, a very competitive sort of individual; Barry Richards, a brilliant player who scored a lot of runs; and one of my personal favourites, Mike Procter.

The wickets were good and hard with bounce so if you could bat you scored runs, while the pitch helped the quickies. Admittedly, when we went on our travels around the country to places like Townsville, there were some dubious little grounds where the pitches weren't of the same standard as the big city wickets. They could be quite dangerous and not many of us chose not to wear helmets on this part of the circuit. I remember Colin Croft hit Rod Marsh when the Australian tried to hook and duck at the same time. The ball ran off his bat and under his visor on to the side of his cheek. He was dazed and was running about like a wild boar. Ian Chappell, a good friend of his, was at the other end on his hands and knees and then on his back, rolling about with laughter. Whenever we were in Sydney we all stayed at the Commodore Chateau, where they boasted a big suit of armour that you had to pass going in and out of the hotel. Eventually Ian got his breath back and shouted out 'Hey Baccus, I'm going to send for that fucking suit of armour from the hotel for you.' Marsh, for some reason, failed to see the funny side of the incident. With friends like Ian you didn't need enemies like Colin Croft.

It wasn't just the Aussies who could fire off a mouthful. There was the night we went out for dinner with the Jamaican, Richard Austin, and a group of friends and players. Austin was a very straightforward guy and sometimes a little on the crude side. As we sat in the famous restaurant, O'Doyles on the Bay, my Jamaican mate thought that the waiters were not paying us due attention. Richard stood up and surveyed the scene, then pulled out a big wad of money and shouted, 'Waiter . . . do you see any blood on this?' I just wanted a big hole to open up and swallow him – or me! He had the attention not only of every waiter and waitress but of every customer in the place. They didn't need to say a word; their stares said it all.

It was a real travelling circus as we criss-crossed the states of Australia, living out of our suitcases and going from hotel to hotel. We took cricket to some parts that weren't involved with the Australian Cricket Board. They appreciated it and so did we, what with the parties and social life. One of the better parties was at Kerry Packer's mansion. I have never seen so much to eat and so many interesting people. He was a good man, Packer; he would arrange Christmas parties to keep the spirits of the guests alive and to ensure that the foreign players were not left feeling lonely and unloved. It is always difficult being away at that time of the year. He made sure that players who served him were happy and well looked after above and beyond the financial commitments he had made to us. He was successful in what he aimed for: earning the right to televise Australian tests in the future. That is what this was all about, and he employed the best cricketers to achieve that end. There was only the odd one like Jeff Thomson who, like Alvin Kallicharran, changed his mind after signing a contract. There was never any need for Jeff to throw in his lot with us as he had such a good contract with his radio work and his cricket.

Everyone eventually realized that the project had been a success and the West Indies Board was eventually forced by public demand to change its opinion as the Caribbean public began to demand the return of their stars to the national side. The board finally capitulated because they had no other choice. Gates were seriously affected and the supporters were losing interest in their second-string team, while we were doing so well for the good name of our country in Australia. The spectators welcomed us back with open arms, but there were some members of the board whose welcome was grudging and their memories long-lasting, as rebels Clive Lloyd and then myself went on to captain the side.

I don't feel bitter. The three years were beautiful years. I would like to have done it officially, but it was not imperative and I know that had I not gone I would have regretted it and so would my bank manager. We not only felt we were the West Indies when we played, we believed that we were the original and real West Indies.

In the last year of WSC we actually returned to the West Indies and played Super Tests at the regular venues in Barbados, Jamaica and Antigua with the board by then having caved in, probably with the help of financial inducements from Kerry Packer. So, when it came to the crunch, they were really no different from the players. They liked good money, too! He offered rental fees to the financially embarrassed West Indies Board and we began our West Indies tour in Kingston, Jamaica, where Dennis Lillee hit Lawrence Rowe, who had enjoyed a fabulous second year in the WSC, on the helmet. Rowe was unsighted by the building work still going on at Sabina Park. The impact was so great that, despite the protection, Rowe suffered a depressed fracture of the skull. He went to hospital but was soon back playing in the series with no ill effects.

We moved on to Barbados, Trinidad and Guyana, and finally to my beloved Antigua, where we drew to keep the series level at 1–1, with the brave Rowe back in action scoring a remarkable 135 against Lillee and Thomson, who had been allowed to link up with the Aussies this time. Rowe had a great second year, but I was tired and flat and reached 50 only once. By this time the opposition to Packer had run out of steam and all the players in England, Pakistan and India had been restored to their 'official' teams in time for the World Cup in England in that summer of 1979.

There had been several meetings between the ICC and Packer's men, but the ACB remained the stumbling block until, to the joy of us all, peace broke out in April of that year, with Packer winning everything he had demanded at the start, including an exclusive ten-year contract for TV and the marketing rights. Cricket in Oz was never to be the same again and it went from success to success after being deep in the doldrums. Typical of the man, Packer ensured in the contract that the players who had supported him would not be punished in any way.

The legacy of Packer to cricket was immense: the increase in salaries, the further projection of the one-day game and day–night game, coloured kit, white ball, black sight-screens and many new sponsors injecting money into what was becoming a bankrupt game. It has given cricket a new lease of life. Everyone was asking what could be done to market the game, and he did it in such a professional manner. You have only to look at the World Cup to see the impact he had, right down to the punters holding up the cards with '4' and '6' on them, a simple expedient for getting the crowd involved. Packer had a vision of promoting and improving the game and he did it to such a degree that cricket is now as attractive a game as there is on television.

One-day cricket is now a crucial part of the game in general. It funds the four-day cricket in England and fills grounds all over the world. It is all about marketing and selling the game to as many people as possible. Attendances at test match cricket matches have dropped, but one-day cricket is here to stay – just like the fast-food business. People are more impatient these days and want to see a result.

Of course there are still the purists around who dismiss the limited-overs game as irrelevant and are only happy when watching the complexities and strategies of the longer game. There is a place for both. If the game is not only going to survive but also to prosper, we must look forward and sell the game, using music and anything else to attract the new generation.

I am very proud of the part I have played in the twists and turns that cricket has taken, particularly my years with Packer. I know for a fact that the West Indies team came out of that WSC series a stronger, better and more professionally equipped side under Clive Lloyd, as results subsequently proved.

In 1979 we were to defend the title we had won in 1975. My great memory of that campaign was, of course, the World Cup final itself at Lord's against England, when I scored my runs when the team were in trouble. I enjoyed every moment because I seemed to be involved from start to finish. We batted first and lost our classy openers, Gordon Greenidge and Desmond Haynes. I came in after Gordon had been run out and then watched Desmond go to Chris Old, Alvin Kallicharran to Mike Hendrick and our skipper, Clive Lloyd, caught and bowled by Chris Old to leave us on 99 for four. Collis King joined me and I met him halfway to the wicket and said, 'Hey, man, take it easy. We have plenty of time.'

England's captain Mike Brearley had not handled his bowling well and, at the time, was using Mickey Mouse bowlers like Geoff Boycott. 'Kingdom' said to me, 'Smokey, I ain't gonna let Geoffrey get this man. Smokey man, in the League there would be no mercy, so why should this be any different?'

Boycott was using the full psychological bit. He was clearly thinking that we wouldn't want to be out to him because no one in his right mind wants to be stuck with that label; you would be remembered for the rest of your life for getting out to Boycott in a World Cup final. There was a silly little smirk on his face as he ran up to bowl. It soon vanished as the ball kept disappearing around the ground. Collis ignored my advice completely and played magnificently well. Every time I told him to take it easy, he hit the ball further and further. He was in that special frame of mind and in the end I just relaxed and let him tear the bowling to shreds and, rather than the two of us going berserk, I took time out and worked around him while his fire raged. I didn't feel that I should try to match him. There was the more important issue of the West Indies reaching 200, and I was happy to support and play second fiddle. Collis is a very jovial guy, very high-spirited, and one of my favourite people – and not just as a cricketer. He is naturally strong and believes in his ability. I scored 138 not out, but it was Collis who came in and took charge.

I was a little nervous as we had lost wickets, but he lifted the burden off my shoulders and every time he put bat to ball it seemed to go for six or four. He scored his 86 in about 50 minutes off 67 balls. We put on 139 in 77 minutes and I was totally relieved. Once we had gone past the 200 mark I was more relaxed and I knew then that we could go on and top 270. In fact, we scored 286 and that was always going to be too many for England. I'd finished the innings with a big six from outside the off stump from Mike Hendrick. It was a shot that stood out for me. I had nothing to lose with over 100 on the scoreboard against my name and I had sussed that Mike would, with his long on and long off back, bowl a ball of fuller length to allow me to stroke for one or, if we pushed hard, two at the most. It was the correct ball, a much fuller length but slightly off the line and I just stepped to the other side and flicked it. It went off the meat to perfection and sailed over the fence. I left the field thinking, 'That shot is my invention.' I was very proud of the option I had taken. It wasn't arrogance. It was pure one-day cricket.

England were all out for 194 despite the fine start given them by Mike Brearley and Geoff Boycott, who put on 129 for the first wicket. Boycott scored 57 and he did it so slowly that we weren't too worried, not even when our captain, Clive Lloyd, contrived to drop him off a sitter, prompting claims that we were deliberately trying to keep him in. It was a good solid start, but we were happy to have the two there and my gentle off-spin cost just 35 runs off my full quota of 10 overs. It left the rest of the order too many to get too quickly against top bowling and they lost their last eight wickets for 12 runs as Joel Garner with five, Michael Holding with two and Colin Croft with three got amongst them.

In that final I was also able to make my mark in the field with a deeply satisfying catch. Ian Botham was beginning to look as though he was in the mood and I was posted, for a change, at long on just a couple of yards in from the boundary. Ian rifled one from Colin Croft about head high to my right; it was going for six, but I saw it early and I had that rhythm that I looked for. My last step took me to within reach of the ball. But I still had to make a dive and I was so worried about dropping the ball when I hit the ground that I flicked it up in the air as I fell. Everyone, players and spectators alike, were looking in the stands for the ball and when my team mates realized I had caught it they converged on me because in getting Ian out they knew that we were on our way to victory. The catch meant almost as much to me as my century.

We won the game and the trophy, and my 138 still remains the highest individual score in a World Cup final and won me the 'Man of the Match' award despite Joel Garner's spectacular five for 38.

I have never been able to understand why so many critics remain firmly entrenched against one-day cricket. Personally I love it. I relish the atmosphere, the crowds it attracts, the certainty that a result will occur and the aggression in the strokes it evokes. England was my introduction to the serious one-day game with the 40-over John Player League on a Sunday; the 55-over Benson & Hedges Cup and the 60-over Gillette Cup. I enjoyed it, and the more I played it the more I liked it. At first I felt I had to go out and blast the cover off the ball from the first over but then, when you consider the number of overs at your disposal, the realization comes that it is not only possible but preferable to bat properly, occupy the crease and work round it. Going in and blasting a quick 20 in one over isn't enough, there has to be continuity. For that reason the longer games suited my style, but the 40-over matches added that touch of variety.

There is no reason why top-order batsmen cannot build an innings and work at their game. It also encourages players to develop as allrounders, although sometimes I feel that too many can upset the balance of a side rather than help it. I believe that one or two allrounders are needed at the most, but specialists remain crucial. There was also a time when the one-day game, particularly in England, wiped out the spinners altogether, as everyone appeared to be a medium-pace trundler. The rest of the world woke up before England, and now spinners are seen as a critical part of any attack, with bowlers like Shane Warne, Muttiah Muralitharan, Anil Kumble and Saqlain Mushtaq respected as match-winners who can have a dramatic effect on the game. In England the spinners were left behind. Now England are paying for that and are having to search for world-class spinners to match the other nations, not just for five-day test matches but for all forms of cricket.

There are a lot of players who have personal success in a one-day but, as in the longer game, what is the use of personal success if it doesn't help the team to win consistently? To many, just reaching the final of a knock-out competition is enough, to win that semi-final and to take part in the grand occasion is sufficient. But that has never been the case for me. Winning is what it has always been about. Who would have remembered what was achieved at Somerset or Glamorgan if we had not gone on to pick up the silverware? No one remembers the runners-up.

With Somerset I went to Lord's on a few occasions and when we got there some would freeze. I used to say to the skipper, Brian Rose, and the other players, 'You guys take me there and I will fix it up on the day.' I relished being in those finals, and if you are in touch with the game you remember who took you there. That is where the collectiveness came in. The final was where I came in with my experience and my passion for that great cricket ground which never failed to inspire me. That was my stage and that was where I was going to excel. I felt I had every right to succeed and I believed I could not fail, even though there were times when I did. I liked playing to the big house and letting the world know what I could do. That was one of the great things about the one-day game: there were always big houses, finals or not.

I loved the atmosphere created by the Somerset supporters as they travelled up from the West Country dressed in their smocks and floppy straw hats, sometimes even carrying a bale of hay in case there was any doubt who they supported – and, of course, always the scrumpy cider. They looked as though they had come to scare the pigeons off the square. On one occasion when we were playing Northants in the final, one of our regular supporters got married in London in the morning, left his blushing bride at the hotel and rushed to Lord's to watch the final. He enjoyed the day and the victory and joined in all the celebrations, until finally he went over the edge with one cider too many and collapsed, rat-faced, on the boundary edge. As if that wasn't bad enough, he was dragged off to the Tavern by a few supporters who recognized him; they propped him up in a chair, then let him lie, undisturbed, on the ground until it was time for the buses to depart for Taunton. They found his address in his pocket and promptly took him back home, leaving his bride fretting in the London hotel. He was left with an awful lot of explaining to do after he turned up, comatose, on his mother's doorstep.

There were quite a few memorable moments for me in the one-day game, such as the record 181 against Sri Lanka in the 1987 World Cup in Karachi and the 150-something in Melbourne against Australia's Thomson and Lillee at full throttle. But the bottom line was that I enjoyed scoring runs and, more importantly, helping West Indies to win, as much in the one-day game as I did in a five-day test.

In the first World Cup in 1975 I had hardly set the world alight in the one-day game at international level and had no reputation for anyone to take me that seriously. I was scratching about, scoring my 10s and 20s, when we had a very significant first-round game in which we were struggling against Pakistan at Edgbaston. We were all sitting in the dressing-room biting our nails, and at the time we felt that it could be all over with the last pair at the wicket. Andy Roberts and Deryck Murray enjoyed a famous partnership which, against all the odds, put us through to the final. They took us to the winning total.

It was hard to take that in as a youngster, but it set the scene for the excitement and the importance of the one-day game and the World Cup in particular. My contribution in those days was my fielding, and I took a great deal of pride in it; in fact, my major contribution to the West Indies' World Cup win in 1975 was in the field. In the final I ran out three top Australian batsmen, the Chappell brothers and Alan Turner. The bat didn't work that day but, by fielding well and running out three top-order batsmen, I felt that I had made my point. I had scored only 5 before being bowled by Gary Gilmour and when Australia replied to our 60-over total of 291, they were soon going well, with Alan Turner looking solid and Ian Chappell quickly into his rhythm. Then a misunder-standing left Turner in trouble and I hit the stumps with an underarm throw. The Chappell brothers were also looking good when Ian played a ball towards me out square on the offside, and I hit the single stump I could see to run Greg out. I got lucky, but I guess the harder you work the luckier you get. Ian continued to go well and looked set for a ton until he hit one to my left and I fumbled the ball. He forgot the old adage about not running on a misfield and I whipped the ball in to the bowler's end for Clive Lloyd to take the bails off and leave him high and dry. We had actually discussed it before the game and had decided that they were not good runners between the wickets and that maybe we could pick up some of them that way. To run out any of the top batsmen would have been a major contribution, but to run out three – that is special. In fact, that day we ran out five of the Aussies to win by a meagre 17 runs. That is what being part of the team is all about.

That day I was there for my fielding and it goes to show that, whatever part of the game you are playing, you can still enjoy it and influence the result.

One of the most important aspects of the one-day game is the fielding. Its significance has led to an exciting new athleticism. Being a good fielder is no accident, either; it is the result of a great deal of hard work. It was a Caribbean thing – but now our fielding has taken a backward step while others have progressed. We are still an athletic nation but we have ignored that side of things. I always practised before and after a match, asking team mates to hit long catches to me in the deep at the end of play when most were showering or in the bar. I would also ask the wicket-keeper to take a few throws from me. I would have the ball thrown to the left and then to the right so that I could chase and flick the ball in. I would throw overarm, flat from the side and sometimes with a flick of the wrist from the boundary, a throw which surprised the batsmen and produced several unexpected run-outs. No one told me to do it, it just became natural. In fact, I enjoyed it and I couldn't get enough fielding and catching practice. West Indies was traditionally the best in the field and we were rightly proud of it, but other countries have specialized since, and both Australia and South Africa have passed us by. You only have to watch the top teams to see how hard they have worked at their fielding, although I do feel that the sliding stop on the boundary, such an integral part of fielding these days, is often exaggerated and not always necessary. I always thought it best to be on my feet as long as possible in order to chase and save. If the situation became desperate, then the slide came out. But I felt that my rhythm took me to the ball as quickly as the person who made a spectacular dive. To me, my anticipation and rhythm were more important. When I chased, I would always work out the steps needed to reach the ball smoothly. Too often you see a fielder get his feet too near to the ball and so lose the chance to explode and throw in the ball in one motion. It's this kind of action that the one-day game delivers so much of.

Another one-day match that particularly stands out for me was against England at Old Trafford in 1984 when I scored 189 not out in the first of three Texaco Cup matches. And this time it was Michael Holding who helped me out as we recovered from a horrendous start on a good pitch and some fine bowling from Bob Willis and Geoff Miller.

Mikey came in as the last man and said, 'Smokey, what are we going to do, man?'

I said, 'Just keep it going, Mikey, and we will see what happens.'

'I'll just try my best, man,' he said casually.

I felt the tempo needed stepping up. We had no more wickets to play with and I played with great freedom. I started hitting some big sixes and, once again, we scored over 200. Everything worked out well, I felt totally in control and able to take a single and give Mikey a few balls. It was just fantastic to be able to accomplish these things in the face of adversity.

These are the sort of innings I liked to be associated with. These were the challenges when people were writing the team off. To succeed and go on and win from that position is very special. You can see the heads of the opposition drop. There are certain totals which you reach and you see the heads start to roll. When we were up to 220 we all knew that we had the bowlers to fire at that. You see the field-placing disintegrating as the captain tries to chase the ball, but you know they are gone from the look in the eyes, in which you can see the hurt and frustration. Michael kept an end going as we put on 106, of which I scored 94. In all I faced 170 balls and managed to hit 5 sixes and 21 fours. It allowed us to reach 272 in our 60 overs. It was again too many for England, and we won by 104 runs.

When limited-overs cricket was introduced, there were many, and there still are, who derided the one-day game and refused to take it seriously. To me it was always part and parcel of my profession and, whatever game I was asked to play in, it was my duty to go out and play, and play it properly. Now if it weren't for the growth of the one-day game worldwide we might well have seen the death of test cricket. The one-day game has sustained it and kept it robust and I say this as a traditionalist who loved playing in the test arena better than in any other. We have to recognize that many people find our longer game dull and boring, and that is often reflected in the attendances at domestic cricket around the world. If you find a solution that helps to keep the game alive and pays the wages, then it is stupid not to embrace it. Some find it hard to admit but, in terms of spectator support and finance, the one-day game drives the game of cricket and provides the finance and, thank goodness, it continues to grow and become stronger and better because it is entertaining. People who are busy don't have time to attend a three-day game; it is expensive both in costs and in time spent. There is not even the guarantee of a result, even if you come back on the last day. It is up to the professional to sort out his strategy and play both games. I felt that the one-day game was great for cricket and if the game is to stay alive we have to make it exciting – and the one-day game is as exciting as any other sport. It has been important to my country and to me. Being world champions meant a huge amount to people in the Caribbean. To me it was our Olympics.

And it's because of this that it's particularly disappointing to me that we did not and still don't have an anthem. There was nothing that could be played for the ceremonies before the final. All the islands have their own tunes, but the West Indies as an entity has nothing – and this despite our love of music and the part it has played in our history. I felt badly that, after they had played 'God Save the Queen' or 'Australia Fair', there was nothing for us. Someone should have been wise enough a long time ago to devise a national anthem for the Caribbean islands; that would have been good for all of us, to push our chests out and feel proud because we were one soul and one body. That is something I seriously regret when we have such brilliant songwriters and musicians in the Caribbean. If I become involved with the West Indies in the future, that is something I will push hard for, a national anthem for us all, and especially for our cricketers. Someone should arrive at something, a serious piece of West Indian music that could be sung by one of our famous singers.

★

The one-day game and the World Cup are now well established, and the next to come will be a five-day world championship. It seems inevitable, but I do not see it taking over in popularity from the one-day game which, I believe, will get bigger, stronger and more popular. Cricket at all levels is a thinking man's game and if you haven't the capacity to think quickly enough, there won't be room for you. A five-day world series around the world would be fascinating and would solve a lot of problems, not least of all those rankings which often leave me confused and bewildered, particularly when we moved up to second after suffering our worst spell for years! But it is the one-day game which, I am sure, will continue to dominate in this modern, computer-driven world where time is money and no one has the leisure to spend four or five days waiting for the outcome of a single game.

8. Sledging Can Be Fun

There is nothing I enjoy more than a cold beer with the opposition after the game and swapping stories when you are socializing between games. But on the field things are different. Cricket may sometimes seem more like a war than sport to the spectator, and there is no doubt that, over the years, the game has become increasingly competitive, as its profile has risen, thanks to the long hours of cricket shown on television. I have no problem with that. I am as competitive as the next man, probably more so! I believe in playing to the limit and doing what it takes to win – but only as long as it is left out there on the pitch and not brought in off the field. Winning, though, really is everything. Some of the exchanges, particularly out of context, seem intolerable, but it's difficult to convey the intensity at the centre of a test match. And, despite appearances, the aggression this belief generates is usually nothing personal.

The infamous art of sledging comes in many varieties, ranging from the vile and abusive in certain parts of Australia to clever repartee which can have everyone within earshot rolling on the ground with laughter. I didn't often partake, relying instead on my glare which often, I am told, spoke louder than words. But I couldn't resist a dig at Glamorgan's Greg Thomas when I played against him at Taunton in 1986.

Thomas was supposed to be the new find, the quickie who could shake you up. He was a big strong guy and when he got it right he was as good and as rapid as anyone about. We had our confrontation on our tight little ground and, when I played and missed a few times early on (as you are entitled to do), he began to get a little hot under the collar. After another ball had whistled past the edge, Greg followed through into my face and said with great cynicism, 'Viv, you seem to be having a little trouble negotiating the seed today. For your information, it is red, it's round and it weighs five and a half ounces.'

I could hear Hugh Morris in the slips saying, 'Oh, no. What have you done, my son?'

David 'Bumble' Lloyd, umpiring one of his first games, couldn't keep the grin off his face as he knew what was coming – and, indeed, he went on to use the story in his after-dinner speeches.

The next ball was perfectly in my zone, allowing me a free swing of the arms, and I put the ball straight past Greg and into the river.

While spectators hung over the stand to see if they could see it floating in the water, I turned to Greg and said, 'As you know what it fucking looks like, you had better go and find it.' I think I went on to score around 130 in about 70 minutes and Greg limped out of the attack, much chastened. It was certainly the fastest century of that season – and all thanks to Greg telling me what I should be looking for and what I should be hitting. I don't know whether the line did the trick or not, but I raced to my century in 40-something balls. I didn't hear a lot more from him that day.

One fast bowler neither I nor anyone else for that matter could shut up was the Aussie, Lenny Pascoe, who bowled me four bumpers in a row at Adelaide in the Australian series in 1982. Lenny is renowned for being pretty fiery and a bit crazy, and features regularly in any conversation on the circuit about wild on-the-field behaviour. He is a Yugoslav/Australian with an extremely fragile temperament, which is summed up by his nickname, 'Loosehead'. From my own experience I know that he is a big strong guy with a big chest and he can be very slippery and very quick.

This particular innings he decided he was going to pepper me and give me the full treatment. He began with a bouncer for his first delivery, and I ducked. His second delivery was another bouncer, which I got under again, as I did the third bouncer. I couldn't believe he would bowl a fourth one in a row – but he did. This time I was somewhat less than graceful and, as I ducked, I twisted awkwardly and my cap fell off as I lost my balance. It must have looked more alarming than it was.

Lenny was quick to see how uncomfortable I was as I made a grab for my cap, with my bat at an awkward angle and my body twisted about so as not to disturb the stumps. He came right up to my face and snarled, 'The next one you fucking miss will make you a fucking hospital case, mate.'

His captain, Ian Chappell, had set him four slips and a gully and wasn't best pleased to see his fast bowler wasting the new ball. But none of this mattered to Lenny as you could see the fumes coming out of his nose and ears. Ian tried to tell him to pitch the ball up more and I added to it by shouting, 'Ian, please don't stop him from bowling like that because you will stop me from scoring some runs.' I knew it would wind Lenny up further, but I didn't care. I was pumped up, facing a guy who was trying to put me in hospital or kill me.

Lenny heard my comment and had enough about him to try the three-card trick as he bowled a much fuller ball, hoping to catch me on the back foot again. It was the right thing to do from his point of view, but he was a little bit off line and the length wasn't right, and I got the meat of the bat behind the ball and smacked it back past him. Whenever I played this particular shot, fast bowlers somehow forgot to get in my face and, sure enough, Lenny turned round and started hustling back to his mark. Suddenly there was no confrontation any more. I thought to myself that I should keep this particular bush fire burning. I knew that the ball was going to the boundary, but I ran anyway in order to get to his end of the wicket because I wanted to look in his eyes and see what was there now.

His eyes were wild and I gave him a scare when I put my face into his. He screeched back, 'The next ball I bowl will put you in fucking hospital, you . . .' But they are never the same after a taste of their own medicine.

Pascoe just melted away after a few fours and his captain took him out of the attack.

Those who can take it are exceptional. Confront Dennis Lillee, for instance, and he is such a competitor that he just seems to grow bigger. In those fierce battles of the Packer era, Dennis Lillee was always in my face. It became too much and when he roared for a leg before wicket, I ran the single – straight through him. He didn't like that too much and even whinged to the umpire, saying I was trying to knock him over. I was.

There was bad blood between us in Perth when he kicked Javed Miandad. I deliberately tried to work Dennis up to try and make him make the same mistake again, but this time with me. But, sadly, he never bit. Had it been me, I would not have needed the bat. I would love to have taken him on in front of his home crowd and see how much fight he really had. These Australian fast bowlers are so aggressive it was as though they wanted to fight, and I honestly wanted to fight him.

There were others I would gladly have fought, for example Craig McDermott and people like him because of their foul mouths. I had a burning desire to shut them. I was becoming increasingly frustrated at the things that were being said, but I began to realize that, while a few of the Aussies were genuinely tough, those with the dirtiest mouths and who behaved in the most aggressive fashion were not always what they seemed. If you want tough, look at the Australian rugby and Aussie Rules players, they are the guys who really walk the walk down under. Some Australian cricketers try to follow that machismo line when they are not really that hard. Talking filth made them feel tough.

Being charitable, it could be said that the worst sledging was often brought about by frustration. That was certainly true of Jeff Thomson, who was really fiery and feisty. Jeff was one of the nicest guys I know and when he cursed and shouted it was more often than not at himself.

The worst I came across was the 1975–6 Australian team, who were a quality side and were aggressive with it. I was just a young pup, learning my way in test cricket. I had only toured India before that. It was difficult because I had never experienced this sort of thing before, where even third man and fine leg would shout abuse at you. Australian cricketers hunted in aggressive packs. It was only when the quality of their cricket slipped, however, that some of them seemed to concentrate on sledging rather than playing. This is when it became rampant.

By the time I played in Sheffield Shield cricket I was used to it; it was not so much racial, more the Aussie way of sounding brash. I was playing for Queensland against New South Wales with Lenny Pascoe et al.

In my experience and in my view Craig McDermott was one of the very worst. Whenever he had the ball in his hand he was trying to portray how tough he was, but when Australia needed a few runs from the tailenders he was fearful and his batting suffered. When it was time for him to be on the receiving end he became a real 'Billy', as he was called. He screamed like a pig when the ball got above chest level and he ran away from the crease. He was the perfect example of someone trying to be tough when he wasn't built that way. You must be well rounded when you are trying to be a hard man, not only when the ball is in your hands but also when you are facing someone hell-bent on revenge. Man, he was a pussycat in those circumstances. He allowed his enthusiasm to run away with him. What came out of his mouth made him appear tough, but I always looked on him as a little pussycat, someone you wouldn't look to squeeze but who needed to be treated with tender loving care.

He was one of those Aussies who, because of his competitive nature, wanted to blast you verbally; but when the bat was in his hand all you could hear was 'Meow, meow.' There was a lot of screeching and not a lot of real manliness. To me there was something missing, a little hole in his heart somewhere which said that Craig McDermott wasn't as tough as he made out. I realized that and started to give him back some of the rubbish he was throwing our way. We were playing against him in Antigua; the series was won and we drifted mentally and lost. Rather than playing cricket we confronted each other, and it was one of those series when a lot happened.

When he came in I deliberately moved myself from first slip to silly point and loudly instructed Curtly Ambrose to give him a few chest-high balls to see whether he had the stomach to handle it. I made sure he had heard me and then went back to my position and stared into his eyes. I had Gus Logie at bat/pad and I swear I could hear Craig's heart pounding, there was so much feedback emanating from him. Every now and then I would stoop down, look into his eyes and give him a few verbals just to let him have some of his own back. He was trying to be all cool and taking deep breaths, a sure sign when you are breathing out of control that something is wrong.

I said to Gus, 'Stand back a little bit, Gus, you are in Craig's path there and the way he is running like a thief he is going to trample on you soon.'

He backed off and Craig said, 'I love it, Viv.'

I said, 'I know, I can smell your do-do already.'

He lost it then and cried out, 'Umpire, I am trying to bat here.'

Curtly fired one in at him and he started running again, a real coward. I turned and said to him, 'You can fuck off, you piece of Queensland shit.' He made a statement in his book that during that exchange I called him a honkey. At that time I didn't even know what honkey meant; it is not a word I have used or would use. He can interpret what I said however he wants, but I don't know which bit of it he didn't understand. Craig is a nice enough guy off the pitch but on it he is pretty intense, and on occasions he'd lose it.

Someone I've never played against but who seems to be cut from the same cloth is Glenn McGrath. I saw him in Antigua when he did what managers do in American baseball, kicking the dust at umpires, spitting in the vicinity of an opponent and trying to impede the batsman when they were trying to take a quick single. He is undoubtedly a great bowler for his era but if he doesn't curb these silly little antics and control himself and his attitude, one day he will meet up with the wrong individual. He ought to remember what momma used to say, 'Beware of who is out there because you don't know who is who.' One day he may confront someone who is bigger and badder than him. I would love to have played against him. We would most certainly have squared up and it would have been nice to test his mettle; it would have been interesting to know whether he still had the same stomach for spitting and the rest of that stuff with someone in his face. McGrath is beautiful to watch and undoubtedly is the pick of today's fast bowlers. He bowls with sustained, consistent pace. But if he carries on like that, someone may break his wrist and that will stop him bowling.

When you run across a batsman taking a single, you can get yourself hurt. I, for one, would be like a desperate rat and I would trample all over him. I wouldn't have to use the bat, but he would do well to remember that the batsmen are carrying a piece of wood and wearing protection. He isn't.

The authorities must do something about it before this aspect of the game turns into rollerball. To be honest, we became involved, but that was because we were bitten and we bit back. We had to become a lot tougher, but not in the same way. I don't remember, for example, Andy Roberts swearing at anyone. The truth was, he did not need to because the ball did far more damage. In fact he hurt more batsmen than any other person I have ever seen, and he used to hurt them seriously. I can recall numerous faces he has disfigured. He was renowned as a hit man in that category. Yet he was a very quiet man on and off the pitch. Another was Michael Holding, who also let the ball do it for him. 'Whispering Death' used to frighten them, but I never heard him or Joel Garner say anything.

Malcolm Marshall was the only one who would get involved. When he had the ball in his hand he would breathe fire, and if he beat the edge he would mutter and curse and ask the batsman if that was a baseball bat he was using. Malcolm and Alan Border were always at daggers drawn. Malcolm had a long memory and he never forgot anything that had been said to him. Whenever he bowled at the Australian captain he would be right in his face, and most times he won. He bowled Border some of the most lethal deliveries I have ever seen. All you had to do when AB came in was to give Malcolm Marshall the ball. Much of it was born out of respect by one great cricketer for another. He admired Border's grit and his ability to fight and wear down the bowlers. He was going to get up his nose any way he could – and he usually did.

I certainly had a much lower boiling-point than any of our fast bowlers. Perhaps it was a good thing I was a gentle off-spinner and not a paceman!

But have you ever seen a fast bowler cry? I did in the 1975–6 series against the Aussies when Michael Holding found out for the first time how tough they were, not just physically but mentally as well. They would do anything to win.

Ian Chappell, whom I liked and respected, would often say, 'Why, when you nick a ball, walk? That only makes the umpire's job easier. He is there to make a decision, he is paid to make a bloody decision.'

I can accept and see that, but it still did not go down well when he made thick contact to a good ball from Michael and was caught behind by Deryck Murray. The Australian umpire stood his ground, shook his head and said no. Some of the umpires in that series were notoriously partial in their verdicts. Ian Chappell stood there as though nothing had happened. This was the final straw for Michael. He had bowled well without luck and had had a succession of very good appeals turned down. He was totally frustrated and this time when the umpire shook his head for such an obvious decision, Michael laughed in a sick way and said in his distinctive Jamaican accent, 'This man can't be real.' He took his long slow walk back to his mark. I could see him shaking his head and then he squatted down on his haunches to get his thoughts together and accept the fact that the guy had hit the cover off the ball and had not been given out.

Suddenly and without warning he started sobbing. Lance Gibbs, Clive Lloyd and I ran up to him and tried to console him. It just underlines how passionate these guys were. Success meant everything and, with nothing going our way in the series, the frustration just became too much to bear.

We had been warned and given the advice that when you play in the other man's backyard you have to play to his rules and fight fire with fire; in other words, play it as tough as him. Michael was still learning and maybe that was the day he became a true fast bowler because it was the last time he cried in public and it was the batsmen who suffered after that.

★

Perhaps the best way to handle sledging was shown by little Gus
Logie. We were batting together and facing a very hostile spell
from Rodney Hogg, who had hit me on the jaw. Gus, despite his
diminutive stature, stood to his full height and kept dispatching
him to the boundary. Hogg, becoming increasingly irate, decided
to rough him up with a few short balls and a few neatly chosen
swearwords, like 'you little, short-arsed bastard' and 'you little piece
of shit'. Gus's response was to be increasingly nice, and this got
right up their noses, especially when he replied, 'Thank you,' to
everything that was said. He was a very funny man and he rattled
Rodney with his response. He and Jeff Dujon completely unsettled
the bowler and eventually he lost his rag. Once a fast bowler loses
it, he is easy meat and they took him to pieces and won the match
from what had been a difficult position.

Lillee was always pretty accurate with his line and if you missed
his bouncer you were hit. It was as simple as that. Watching Dennis
run up, you could see the seam all the way. Whenever he bowled
the bouncer it was basically over off stump and moving away, so
you had to be in a good position to hook that away. What is more,
he never bowled a short ball without a reason. He was the most
dangerous fast bowler I have ever faced.

Not that he or anyone else discouraged me from hooking. I took
the Ian Chappell stance on the subject: if a shot has brought you a
lot of runs you cannot abandon it. Sure it will get you out now
and again; but if, on the majority of occasions, you have won most
of the battles, then stick with it. I felt that when I was batting
against a notorious fast bowler and hit the ball sweetly for six, it
was a special shot. It was one way of taming that bully. It was a
temporary victory admittedly, putting you one up and making you
feel good. There was no better sight for me. It is a myth that has
grown over the years that I used to shout 'shit ball' *every* time I hit
a ball to the boundary off a fast bowler. But it certainly happened
for a while in Australia against people like Lenny Pascoe or any
bowler who wanted to get in my face. I would ask out loud, 'More
of that, please.' It was done with a purpose, and because of my
aggressive attitude sometimes they would lose it and bowl in my

zone. When they did that, all the slips, gullies, point, leg gully and mid on were redundant because I'd won the mental battle. They left a lot of vacant space and it was my time to take a toll. My favourite spot was the sight-screen – which always took some wind out of their sails.

If I'm hit for six when I am bowling spin, I feel ratty, so I can imagine what a fast, aggressive man feels like when I hit him against or over the sight-screen. That is a magnificent feeling for the batsman.

Needless to say, I didn't win them all and it wasn't always the obvious fast bowler who triumphed. When I was in Sydney with Queensland, David Colley, who had represented Australia, was a mean bowler with a reputation for scalping (hitting batsmen on the head). The problem was, that was associated with a bent elbow. He bowled a good away-swinger and the odd one that came back in, but that faster one was so very much quicker that everyone said he used to put a jerk in it.

I felt the weight of it once when he hit me straight on the head. Colley had unleashed one of the most lethal bumpers from the shortest of runs. It was then that I heard the heavenly choir from the slips, lots of chirping coming from behind the wicket, telling the bowler what to do to you just as you were about to receive. It certainly knocked a few of the cobwebs out. It was a salutary lesson because I couldn't shake my head to get rid of it, the hurt went on for a few days and it didn't help the hangover.

That wasn't quite as bad as the time when Rodney Hogg hit me on the head via my hand. I was fortunate to escape that one. The hardest knocks you suffer are when the ball catches something on the way through and picks up speed. On this occasion it clipped my glove and, maybe because I was in the position to hook, my head was to the side and it hit me only a glancing blow. It hurt like hell, but I wanted to hang tough even though when I spat I saw blood. I knew that the quicker I was back in business, the better it was for business. I read Rodney Hogg's mind: he had wounded me, and I knew what he would do next. I wanted to be ready for him, but my skipper Clive Lloyd was trying to attract my attention despite the fact that I was waving off assistance and waving away the physio who had set off from the pavilion, along with twelfth man, Malcolm Marshall. Poor Malcolm was caught in the middle. Clive was on the balcony urging him to go to me while I was telling him to go back. I saw the dilemma Malcolm was in as he hesitated, and I decided to take the count of eight. I did a bit of gargling and discovered I had busted the inside of my jaw.

There we were, Malcolm and I, in front of this massive crowd in Melbourne having a quiet chat. But Malcolm was more concerned about himself looking stupid than my cracked jaw. He said, 'Smo-key, man, I felt a real dick, man, Clive telling me to come, you telling me to go.'

The crowd had picked up on it and were being very humorous about it all. Malcolm was an unhappy man as he made his way back to the pavilion to the catcalls from the Aussies.

I eventually resumed my stance and Rodney went to bowl the same ball at me. The sight of my blood must have fired him up because, although I got in the position to hook, it came at me a bit quicker than normal and hit the top edge. God bless the bat, it flew into row six in the stand. It was perceived as the typical macho Viv Richards response, even by the commentators, and I persuaded myself I felt good – but really it was a very lucky shot. I went on to make a score in the 90s while Rodney limped out of the battle with nought for plenty.

I didn't have too many problems with the English bowlers, even though the media often tried to hype up a war between myself and Bob Willis and then Devon Malcolm. The Bob Willis business blew up in 1973 when the MCC were touring the Caribbean. I faced Bob for the first time on that tour playing for the Leeward Islands, and he bowled five successive bouncers at me. I hit four of them and I was visibly annoyed when I was out in the end to the fifth bouncer. But I enjoyed the confrontation. He had won that day so I was determined to catch him on another day, not to let him get me out and to be even more aggressive than usual.

I had a contract to play in England the next year, and every time

I played against him I tried to get the better of him. But what the critics failed to realize was that I did it because I rated him so high. People have weird opinions about Willis, but he was one of England's best and most hostile fast bowlers. Everyone thought Bob had a dodgy run-up, but you only have to look at how many wickets he took and how competitive he was to realize what an outstanding quickie he was. He was a bowler who looked to swing the ball in most often. His dot ball was the one that straightened a little bit, and I never knew when it was coming. He could also be hostile and really quick. I have seen him bounce people out, and to do that you have to have good pace; and to take over 300 test wickets he had to be a bit special. And he was. It may surprise people, but, alongside Dennis Lillee, Bob Willis was the best fast bowler I faced. The entire situation was misread as a racial confrontation, black versus white. I can't ever remember a racial comment passing between us. He wasn't a guy who would say a lot anyway, but he would give you a little sarcastic clap if you got it wrong. He is a good guy and I have never had any serious hook-ups with him. His brother Bruno looks like him and works out of the Cafe Royal, and I often meet up with him for lunch when I am in London; he is cool and laid back. Bob, by contrast, is a fairly quiet man. He has his own style.

The press also tried to create a particular rivalry between Devon Malcolm and myself. They wrote that he had claimed that he had my number and knew how to get me out. When we spoke about it afterwards he was embarrassed and told me the words were taken totally out of context. I liked the man, believed him and told him not to worry about it. I knew they were trying to create a rivalry. Sure, he had winkled me out a few times, after all he was a good bowler and on his day he could get anyone out. He had taken my wicket twice already in that series, hence the hype in the English papers, and, like all of us, he had his day. My response was that, when it was my day, Devon was going to pay.

This is what makes a good confrontation. I had just come out of hospital and was without practice, but I decided to go in and play my shots. In circumstances like those, if you become lucky it can change the entire game. I hooked the first ball he bowled to me into the scoreboard and took 18 off that first over. We had no problems with Devon after that in that particular match.

Devon was a player who always gave a lot, but famously with the ball rather than the bat. He was, in truth, a bit of a rabbit and when Courtney Walsh took him out in that 1990 series, returning a few of the bouncers on behalf of his batsmen, the press took it up on Devon's behalf. They declared that it was unsporting, claiming he could hardly hold the bat, never mind protect himself.

Devon could bowl a fast, short ball and, if he is dishing it out, when his time comes he has to take what is coming. If he doesn't like it and turns his back on someone else's bumper, then he shouldn't bowl it in the first place. Everyone would then be more sympathetic towards him. The old fast bowlers' pact not to bounce each other had disappeared among the verbals years before. Devon realized then that in international cricket he had to improve his batting in a big way. He was like a sitting duck, batting on a wing and a prayer. But he accepted the fact that this is the way the game is, and he prepared himself much better in future.

Devon is intelligent and a genuinely nice person. The only time I have ever been really annoyed with him was when I heard about his treatment at the hands of England team manager Raymond Illingworth. Devon is a big enough guy and he should have put Illingworth in his place, had him on a coat-hanger and let him know that there was no need to tolerate that rubbish. He should have put him in his bloody place. It was a disgrace, Illingworth treating Devon like a little boy. I was especially disappointed by Devon's weak reaction to Illingworth's rudeness. No one would have talked to me like that. They would have had to defend themselves with their fists. Illingworth would have had to try to spank my ass to back up his words. It was a sad incident and a very bleak time for English cricket. Here was a man who gives his heart and soul for whatever team he is playing in. It was sad, especially as he is a more open-minded and warm-spirited individual than the man who tried to bring him down.

★

For all its tradition and good manners, there is still plenty of angst in England. I came across it in a most unlikely place when I was hit between the eyes by racial abuse in the lovely town of Harrogate. In general terms I have always liked the Yorkshire public: they are seriously passionate and knowledgeable about their cricket, but there is a little group who spread the virus of racism around their grounds.

I was run out while playing for Somerset there and as I was making my slow march back this person shouted out, 'Get back to the pavilion, you black bastard.' I wasn't overjoyed at being out in the first place, but this made me really angry. As I couldn't reach the offender, I stomped back to the dressing-room and pushed the bat through the door. The press loved that and they took pictures of the battered door with headlines about 'angry Viv'.

I also smashed my favourite bat after we lost the 1978 Gillette Cup final. It was one of the nicest bats I ever had, and when you have a bat you really love it does all sorts of things for you and your confidence rises. This lovely piece of English willow still had a long way to go and I was looking forward to taking it on tour.

A more conventional, but still unexpected, confrontation came when I clashed with Imran Khan in Barbados in a test match against Pakistan. I was backing myself with my usual confidence and aggression, scoring runs, and was in the 90s when I played exaggeratedly forward to Immy.

Following through, he said to me, 'You love yourself, yeah?'

I responded, 'Yes, man, I've learned a hell of a lot from watching you.'

The gentleman who was to become a renowned name in the world of cricket and a serious politician did not like what he saw that day. Fortunately, like many of these incidents, it was soon forgotten and since then I have come to know him. I respect his views and I went to a party at his house while on tour in Pakistan. Whenever we are around we try to get together, as we did during the recent World Cup in England. We definitely didn't like one another at first, but gradually as we matured and got to know each other better we realized that the world is a lot bigger than anything we have to offer and we started to respect each other. He was one of the fiercest competitors and, no matter how well you were batting, he would always have a delivery which could come and destroy you. I respect him and his cricketing views; and if the Pakistan side had a leader they looked up to and respected like they did him, they would be a much better and more consistent team than they are now. He always managed to squeeze the best out of his team. He and Miandad are two of the most patriotic individuals I have met, and I can identify with that. I am quite certain you wouldn't be hearing stories about match-fixing and other bad things if they were at the helm. Both would die for their country.

This is how all the best players feel. It's so often the passion involved in playing for your country that leads to the raw aggression which can sometimes surprise spectators. There is a place for sledging within the game, providing it stays within the bounds of reasonableness. A clever, funny exchange can lift the game, but there is no room for overtly racist remarks, for comments when the bowler is into his run-up or when the sledging descends to the level of foul personal abuse or physical contact.

Basically, these quickies are bullies who always act so big with the little guy whom they can pick up with one finger and push around. I know a few guys in the West Indies who would have loved that confrontation. It's one of the things I've missed most since retiring.

I watched Glen McGrath mess Brian Lara around. He was just being a bully and displayed a lack of class. I look at these things and get very angry. I think the guy is too good a cricketer to become involved in all that. To spit on a cricket field shows what is in his mind. If he had done it near me, there would have been war. I have had good experience of fighting wars and I have never been hung up on whether these people wear a big moustache or show fierce looks. It's not how they look; it's what is in their heart!

The sport has become naturally aggressive and is all the better for it. But when it starts to become physical, that is when it is dangerous. My advice is not to start what you cannot finish. There is always someone tougher, as almost every heavyweight boxer in history has discovered. I don't go looking for physical contact on the cricket field, but I've never shrunk from it. Sometimes you're faced with the choice of physical confrontation or backing down. And I won't back down. If I was taking a quick single and Glenn McGrath stepped in my way, all I would have seen would have been a bag of bones. One of us would have had to give way, and if he wanted to prolong his bowling career it would have had to be him. I know he would have made the right decision.

9. A Welsh Swansong

My sudden and dramatic departure from Somerset cast me into limbo. It would have been easy to quit England for the sunshine of the Caribbean and recharge my batteries, but I was not the kind of person to be forced away from something I enjoyed. The new ruling of only one overseas player meant that I was unlikely to get another county for that season with everyone already fixed up, but I wanted to play cricket in England that summer and I was given the opportunity to play League cricket for the first time. It was a case of getting back to basics.

When I first arrived, I was told not to blink in case I missed it; that was how small Rishton of the Lancashire League was. As it happens, I didn't miss the ground, since we flew there by helicopter!

This was no sabbatical. Any thoughts of a hatful of runs and a handful of easy wickets were soon tempered by the reality of the serious cricket played on damp, difficult strips against captains who knew how to make the best of the local lie of the land. They were no respecters of reputation since there had been a steady stream of top players through the League over the years. In fact cricket at Rishton was hard. The wickets weren't the same quality as those strips I had played county and test cricket on around the globe. But what I will say is that the people in that part of the world are among the nicest I have ever met. They were very warm and loving and they embraced me seriously. I loved them in return and we had a good relationship.

It was always going to be a one-off. The wickets were very damp that season and there were times when I would lie on my bed in the hotel room and watch the rain beating against the windows. I would tell myself that there was no way there could be any cricket that day, and I would turn over, have another snooze and wait for the call to tell me that the game was off. The call would come –

but more often than not to tell me that the captains were tossing up and could I get to the ground as quickly as possible. It went to show that anything could and did happen in League cricket in Lancashire.

The weather was so bad that summer that I could hardly see the colour, front or back, of my number one bat where I had struck the muddy ball or patted down the wicket after every delivery. But it was a great experience and a lot more exciting than I had expected.

I did not go there just for the money. I think I needed to be in cricket but away from the county scene, its politics and its intrigue, and to recharge my batteries. But even where the cash was concerned it was considerably better than anything I had ever been offered at Somerset; indeed the £30,000 was around twice what I had been earning.

It could have been very lonely; but I was prepared to mix, and the clubhouse at Rishton proved to be the centre of all civic activities, with a busy bar and a good snooker table. I had a wonderful time meeting the local people who, after their initial interest, treated me as one of their own. What was also important was that there were a lot of West Indians in the League and it gave me an opportunity to be with these guys, and every now and again we would all have a night out. It was like the good times back home and there was no danger of being homesick in Rishton.

Once involved, I was totally committed to Rishton. I could have played for the Rest of the World at Lord's and in a centenary match but, not having played at the highest level and on those sort of wickets, I backed off and stuck to the wet and sticky stuff. I had a good season and we were pretty successful, with Rishton coming third in the League. My biggest disappointment was that I finished the season suffering from chickenpox, which meant that I couldn't attend the traditional party for the professional. The illness wasn't as bad as it might have been, but it took me down and was very debilitating.

What I discovered about League cricket was how tense the players were when performing. The rivalry was intense to say the least, and there were times when other players and I had to step in to stop people from fighting, usually batsman against bowler. It was sometimes more like a boxing match than a cricket match. I had seen nothing like it before, not even in Australia. They play it tough and hard in that part of the world and, of course, I was considered a prize scalp. What I found irritating was that if you had these guys on a good county or test match wicket, they wouldn't survive; but what was frustrating and disappointing was that my level came down. Cricket matches on those grounds were a lottery. Imagine, just as you are about to play a shot, that a piece of mud flies into your eye. You had better believe it because sometimes we played in pouring rain. At first I would ask the umpire if we should go off. They looked at me as though I was from a different planet. You could feel them thinking, 'This is what they pay you for. They don't pay you for days off!'

It wasn't long before I became very much a part of that environment. Also part of it was our local football club, Blackburn Rovers. This was long before Jack Walker's money took them to the dizzy heights of the Carling Premiership title. Ewood Park was only a couple of miles down the road and, indeed, there were lots of sports grounds within easy reach; even Manchester and Leeds were within comfortable driving distance.

One sport I didn't get involved in was Rugby League, which was big in that region with local team Wigan the kings. We would regularly see the fans coming back from what appeared to be an annual pilgrimage to Wembley with their red-and-white flags and scarves fluttering out of the coach windows.

The standard of cricket wasn't the highest but the competitiveness was better than the cricket, and that basically made up for the lack of good pitches and quality players. A good performance by one of the players meant a collection, and I would often go round the boundary and help collect for someone like the captain, David Wells.

While Rishton represented a step down from county cricket, there was worse to come, with illness forcing me out of the game for a year and my international career coming to a bitter climax a year later, prematurely as far as I was concerned. I had officially announced during the 1991 series against Australia in the Caribbean that my last series as captain would be in England that summer. If I were going to Australia on the next tour in the winter of 1992, it would have been as a player under the new captain, Richie Richardson. I wanted to go to Australia that one last time and I guaranteed the selectors that they would have the usual 100 per cent from Viv Richards. I felt that, freed from the captaincy, I could give my country one last big season and finish my international career on a high note. I wanted to play as a free man and end my test career the way I began it. It wasn't a selfish thing. We needed some stabilizing forces in our batting in that series and in the World Cup that followed, which I saw as being my swansong. That was my glorious vision, but sometimes I was just too dumb and too personal to see what was happening.

Maybe it was the instinct I had when I scored 189 against England at Old Trafford where I felt totally unflappable and knew what I was going to achieve and how I was going to achieve it, regardless of how many wickets were falling at the other end. Sometimes this power, the power of the Almighty, acts in many different ways. These powers were calling me and telling me what needed to be done. They were telling me that I wasn't going to be at my best performing in the World Cup for my country if I was captain. It was going to be a chance for the new captain to have a revitalized Viv in his side, a Viv with a new spirit and vigour who was not chained down with the burden of captaincy. Being able to deliver for my country was uppermost in my mind when I made my decision. I am amazed that others did not see it that way and it was sad that some members of the selection panel were influential in bringing that about. Had I not resigned as captain, I do not think there was any doubt that they would have let me carry on – they would not have had much option.

It saddened me even more that the new captain, Richie Richardson, a man I knew and had a lot of time for, allowed himself to be influenced by those people who wanted to see me out of the way for good, despite my record. Maybe I had become too vocal and set in my ways for those selectors and board members who wanted to have greater control over the cricket team. But Richie of all people knew that I wasn't going to be a detrimental force and that there was no ego involved. I just wanted to represent the West Indies in the best capacity I could, and I felt that Richie was dictated to in a big way. They told him that he wouldn't have the respect of the other players and that there would be problems if I was still around. This is where I believe he should have stamped his own personality on the situation and taken proper command. They convinced him, but I am sure that Richie, a fellow Antiguan, knew me well enough to know that I was and always would be a team man and that there had never been a better in the sense of doing what was needed for the team. Richie knew my commitment.

When he first came into the team he was recognized as an opening bat, but there was no way he was going to dislodge either Haynes or Greenidge, so I dropped down the order to let him bat at number three, and there he established himself. In fact the chairman of the panel, Sir Clyde Walcott, said at the time, 'I don't like to see anyone else come in at number three.' I ignored him so as to pave the way for this talented young Antiguan because I could see his talent and the future he offered the West Indies.

I feel I could have gone on representing my country for at least another three years without the burden of captaincy because I was reasonably fit and kept my weight regular. My fighting weight was around twelve and a half stone (80 kilograms) when I started; later on, it went up to a solid thirteen stone three (84 kilograms) and stayed there.

What hastened my decision to abandon the captaincy was that I sensed some problems during the home series against Australia, one of the toughest teams and one that was challenging our number one position in world cricket. Relations between the board and the players were in disarray, judging by a few incidents that took place during that series against Australia in the Caribbean. For me the writing was on the wall when I attended a selection meeting in Guyana and the selectors were telling me that there should be changes, putting question marks against the names of certain senior players.

We had lost the one-day series but had done reasonably well in the first test, having drawn in Jamaica without ever looking like losing. But in the days before the second test in Guyana, some of the selectors had on their agenda dropping opening bat Gordon Greenidge, wicket-keeper Jeff Dujon and fast bowler Malcolm Marshall. I simply could not understand what they were trying to do, getting rid of these experienced, world-class guys in the middle of a highly charged series. I felt then that it must be something personal. Admittedly Malcolm had put on a little weight but he was working on it, and there were no other obvious reasons. These three guys had played a massive part in helping to develop a team that was undefeated under me in any test series. I couldn't see the cricketing logic in what the selectors wanted to do. I felt it had gone beyond the selection of the West Indies team and I felt totally let down. But I wasn't going to let it happen as long as I was captain and had a say in the selection meetings. I stood up for what I believed in, which every captain should do, and was going to insist that we kept them in.

The meeting began and I automatically put a tick against Gordon Greenidge; someone put a question mark. Against Desmond Haynes a tick, Richie Richardson tick, Viv Richards tick, then suddenly Jeffrey Dujon question mark and Malcolm Marshall question mark. I stopped them there and then and said, 'Hold on! I want some reasons why this is being done.' I told them that it had to be discussed. I was not going to fall in line because some Tom, Dick or Harry said so. I wanted good reasons and I told them that I insisted they must be professional rather than personal. Holding on to my temper, I said, 'Let's start with Gordon Greenidge.'

One of the selectors responded, 'He has been hit on the head.'

What nonsense. I answered that we had been picking guys who have been hit on the head on a regular basis for as long as I had been playing – including me!

They were persistent. 'He is not picking up the ball.' . . . 'He's finished,' said one . . . 'He's lost it,' said another.

I was firm and said no. I wanted to stick with him and the others, especially against a tough, seasoned team like Australia. I couldn't see the sense in throwing in young, untried players who could have been scarred for life.

These selectors were looking to dismantle a successful team. These were people who bore grudges and had their own personal interests at heart. I told them that I wasn't going to have any of it, not with Greenidge, not with Marshall and not with Dujon.

They carried on. 'Dujon is not moving well,' I was told. 'He cannot move for the ball, he cannot take the ball the way he used to.'

Then, 'This man Marshall, he has gone. He has put on weight.'

I said no. We had drawn the first test, with Greenidge scoring 27 and 35; Dujon weighed in with 59 in his one innings and three catches in Australia's sole innings; while Malcolm Marshall took one for 57 in 22 overs.

There is no doubt that I made enemies for the future at that meeting. I had proved that I was not malleable. I didn't care. My country came first and I wanted the best players. We played the match at Georgetown, Guyana, with my team and won by ten wickets with 'fat' Marshall taking three wickets in each innings and Dujon seven catches in all. Then, after a drawn game in Trinidad, we went to Barbados and the same man who was finished, this blind man Gordon Greenidge, scored a double-century and Marshall bowled particularly well to take another six wickets. I rest my case.

But I won only a battle. The war was not yet over and, with my career at the international level drawing to a close, I was not going to win in the end. After the England series I was happy to stand down as captain but to offer Richie Richardson and my country my full support on the tour to Australia for the series and for the World Cup. But they did not want me. Those same selectors I had battled against over the senior players had their revenge on me. Highly respected on their own islands, in my view they let their personal views cloud their judgement and get in the way of common-sense selection. That is very dangerous. Everything they know about cricket is worthless with that attitude. These are the sort of people we have had making our selections, and they are still making them.

When I confronted Richie about touring Australia, he gave me his word that the selectors had jumped on him and said that this was his team, he should have his players around him and that the respect factor for Viv with some of the older players would confuse the issue. It goes to show the way in which the selectors were thinking. This was such a slap in the face to me because I have always been more of a team man than that. I was there not for me and not to undermine Richie but for the West Indies, as I have always been. I felt I could have gone and done a job without the burden of captaincy in my last season. If they were going to leave me out, it should, perhaps, have been after the Australian series in the West Indies in 1991, when I passed 50 only once, but in England that summer I averaged over 50 and was batting well.

Some of these cricket dunces who pretend to know so much about the game hadn't really been great achievers themselves, but they were now revelling in their power. Their intentions were obvious and, if they were looking to dismantle a team that was undefeated, then I could watch out for myself as captain as well! I didn't know what their agenda was and so I decided there and then that this would be my last series as captain because I wasn't going to drop top players for non-cricketing reasons. I felt totally happy that I was able to maintain the side which had done so well for me and had given me its full support, and I was satisfied that I could accomplish the mission against the challenge of Australia.

Maybe I lost three years from my career, but being undefeated almost certainly added to my reputation and stature. Judging by what was being said in that last series in England, I just wanted to walk away rather than be carried away. What was important was that everyone connected with cricket in that region was looking for an encore with me at the helm. But I said no more.

My final curtain-call should have been the World Cup. I made the decision to relinquish the captaincy but made myself available to go on tour as one of the troops, with a promise not to interfere unless asked to do so. It left me in a quandary, but former England international Tony Lewis came in with a masterstroke. Glamorgan needed an experienced individual to help them gain some impetus with their results and Tony, previously a fine player himself and then a cricket pundit who knew the ropes, thought I might have something to offer. They made a call, asking me if I was interested. Interested? I couldn't wait. I had loved the experience of League cricket, but now I was thirsting to get back to good wickets and good bowlers. Tony's timing was perfect for me because I was feeling so hungry to be back. I wanted to prove to the doubters that Viv Richards was not finished and that maybe all I had needed was that sabbatical, a break away from the atmosphere of intrigue at Somerset.

I would have loved to stay and finish my career at Taunton but it was not to happen with things the way they were. What is more, the money had improved dramatically since my Somerset days. Glamorgan were offering a salary of around £50,000 – and to think that Colin Atkinson had turned his nose up at me when I asked for an increase to £12,500 a few years earlier!

I enjoyed three great years in Wales. I enjoyed my cricket and scored ten centuries in the Championship matches, a couple of one-day 100s and amassed over three thousand runs. I was hitting the ball sweetly again and suddenly Glamorgan were showing a bit of potential, and it was not long before we were thinking that we could pick up some silverware, maybe one of the one-day trophies. There was a growing confidence about the side, emphasized by the improvement in fielding. There were guys in the side when I arrived who used to play on certain occasions and quit on others, especially when it became tight. I persuaded them that if teams could do it to us, we could do it to them in those clench moments.

It was a good team, with some good young players. Robert Croft was on his way up. He could be a little cocky with that cheeky face, but he was a nice individual. Every now and again he would get carried away and his concentration would lapse. To reach his true potential he needed to work hard all the time, and he wasn't always prepared to do that. I felt that he could be a better bowler than batter, but as his bowling came along in leaps and bounds his batting deteriorated. He concentrated more on his off-spin, but with work he could have improved on both and become a genuine all-rounder. There were a number of occasions when he came in at crucial stages of the game, scored runs and hit the ball cleanly. I believe that if he had worked a bit harder at his batting, he could have become a permanent fixture in the England side.

Matthew Maynard was a good bat, while Steve Watkins carried a lot of the bowling burden. I also liked Adrian Dale and the funny little Tony Cottee. He was very gutsy and was determined to do well, whatever the circumstances. Maybe his style was not as pretty or flamboyant as the rest, but he had strong commitment. He was also a more than useful footballer and was on Swansea's books for a while. At the time he was engaged to be married, and I was guilty of winding him up during our game against Sussex at Hove. The bar in the hotel was busy with some of our players and a couple of air-hostesses, while I was talking to the *News of the World* cricket writer, David Norrie. I introduced David to Tony and the two girls he and others were talking to. The next morning I informed Tony that one of the air-hostesses had sold her story of a sordid night of sex with Tony to David, to appear in the *News of the World* on the following Sunday. It was, of course, a load of rubbish, a big wind-up. But he was in an instant state of panic and he knew it would just be his word against hers. His head was down and he was telling all the guys in the dressing-room what had happened and how much trouble he was in. Tongue in cheek and trying hard not to laugh, I told him that I would try my best to speak to David Norrie to see whether he could intervene in any way, at the same time letting one or two of the boys know that it was a wind-up.

Later that day I took a call in the dressing-room and pretended it was the journalist. I could see Tony straining to listen as I said things like, 'So, you can't help,' and 'There's no way we can stop this story, then.' When Cottee overheard this, he was thrown into a further panic while the other guys patted him on the shoulder and sympathized with his increasing predicament. I played up to the situation and told him that I had been in the paper a few weeks earlier and that I hoped I wasn't going to be tied in with his problems, as I had also been drinking with him in the bar with the two pretty air-hostesses.

He was getting in a right state and pleading with me to do something to help, adding that his girlfriend would kill him when she read it, whether it was true or not. He added, 'Her parents always thought I was dubious!'

By this time I was beginning to feel sorry for him and finally I admitted that I had been having him on all day. He didn't know whether to hit me or buy me a bottle of champagne.

Even then I didn't let it drop totally and on Sunday I walked into the dressing-room with a copy of the *News of the World* tucked under my arm and briefly threw him into a panic when I told him that somehow it had got in anyway.

There was a good spirit in the Glamorgan dressing-room. Croft was quite a singer – like me, having been a choirboy in his youth – I doubt whether many county teams at the time could boast two choristers. All the Welsh are musical and we had tremendous singalongs in the pubs after the games.

We had a lot of fun and some good wins. Most notable for me was the one against Hampshire at Southampton when, chasing an improbable 363, we crumbled to 139 for five but recovered as I shared partnerships with Cowley and Metson, leaving us needing a dozen runs off the last over, which was to be bowled by one of the world's best bowlers, the late Malcolm Marshall. I drove him for two fours and then finished off the match by hooking the great man for six. Over a beer after the game Malcolm confided that it was the biggest six ever hit off his bowling.

I scored a lot of sixes at Glamorgan, even winning an award one season for the number hit. One very satisfying six was against Warwickshire when off-spinner Adrian Pierson made some remarks about my batting as I struggled on an unpredictable wicket. You would think they would have learnt, talking to me like that. He made a gesture, showing how I should play the ball. I didn't need to say a word, I just hit the next ball on to the pavilion roof at Swansea and then asked, 'Like that?' All these stories get expanded and exaggerated on the after-dinner-speech circuit. Sometimes I don't even recognize that they are supposed to be about me.

My second year with Glamorgan I suffered a lot with back spasms, and at the end of the third season I was playing with a broken finger for the last month. It was coming up to the Equity and Law final game and some seriously important Championship matches. I wanted to play because I felt that this was to be my last showing in the international arena, so why worry about a broken finger on my left hand? I strapped it up and played.

In July I was involved in a truly remarkable match at Sophia Gardens in Cardiff when we lost any chance of taking the Championship. The visitors were the eventual winners, Middlesex, but we looked to be in a wonderful position when Adrian Dale and I put on an unbroken stand of 425 for the fourth wicket as we both scored double-centuries to raise the total to 562 for three. I managed 224 from 357 balls and hit 4 sixes and 28 fours – not bad for someone who was supposed to be over the hill! But the innings meant nothing, as Middlesex took a first-innings lead, bowled us out for 109 and then won by 10 wickets, to put themselves 30 points clear in the Championship.

There was no doubt about the lowest point during my time at Glamorgan. And, strangely, it was prompted by events in the West Indies. At the time I was suffering with an ailment called fistula, which is a painful little boil on the backside. My eating habits were in disarray as a result and I wasn't taking in enough fibre. I had to have an operation and I missed a game against England in Trinidad when Graham Gooch had his hand broken. Feeling uncomfortable and irritable, I lost my head and laid siege to the press box and one particular journalist, James Lawton. Ian Botham came to see me and told me that there were rumours among the English journalists that I had cancer and that two of the reporters, James Lawton and Paul Weaver, were seeking to verify this false information.

By this time England were on top, and this was a series I relished winning more than any other. They had won the first test in Kingston and only the weather saved us from going two down in Trinidad while I was in hospital. I was ill and frustrated and unable to represent my country, and I was watching my team struggle on TV.

We won the next game in Barbados, where there must have been 80 members of the English media following us, looking for stories not always connected with cricket, and I seemed to be the prime target. I was attacked for doing a jig when I caught Alec Stewart, with some of the press claiming I was putting pressure on the umpire to obtain a verdict in my favour.

The next game was in my native Antigua and, although we continued to get on well with the English players, my relationship with some of the media deteriorated considerably. I was annoyed again by James Lawton when he approached me on the rest day and asked why I had given a V-sign to Allan Lamb the previous day. The irritation was intense, especially as Lamby is one of my pals, but Lawton persisted, winding me up until I flipped and told him what I would do to him if he didn't leave me alone. I had had enough. I had allowed my temper to get the better of me, and suddenly Lawton had what he wanted and he told me there and then that my threats would be headlines in his paper the next day. I answered that if they were I would come looking for him.

They were. And I did.

I was in the outfield, warming up, when I was shown the paper, and I went straight up to Lawton in the press box and confronted him, face to face. That was the right thing to do, but I had the timing all wrong. My team was in the field and I was in the press box. It was like a huge, unofficial press conference as all the media men gathered round us to see and hear what was going on. It was a stupid thing to do, especially as I should have been leading the team out, and as a result I was late on to the field of play and had to apologize to the West Indies Board. That's me: what you see is what you get. I am spontaneous, and if I feel that way I have to do something about it. Fortunately, once it has happened I move on. I have no problem with Lawton and we recently exchanged pleasantries in Langan's Brasserie in London.

The consequences, however, were disastrous. Another journalist, riding on the back of the story, wrote that I should be banned from playing in England and that my contract with Glamorgan should be terminated.

When I returned to Britain, it was to a flood of openly racist letters, telling me to get back to the trees, only not so politely. I couldn't understand why I needed a police escort when I arrived at Heathrow, but when I checked in at Glamorgan I discovered that there had been death threats as well as the racist letters and they were forced to monitor my mail. There was even a direct telephone line wired into my house from the police station. The story fed on itself and became so bloated that it was rumoured that I had gone crazy because of the medication I was on for my illness, and all sorts of other ridiculous statements. Even Glamorgan must have been thinking that I was mentally ill after all the publicity. As you can imagine, the problem I had was not the sort of thing I wanted to talk publicly about. It was far too delicate. Glamorgan handled the entire thing very coolly and very well. The secretary, trying not to alarm me, told me casually to be careful, beware and be vigilant.

Nothing happened, apart from a few more letters, but clearly the police were concerned for my safety. The vitriol in those letters had to be read to be believed. 'You fucking bastard, why don't you go back to the trees' . . . 'You're coming here and taking our money' . . . 'You're stopping our young players progressing' . . . 'Why don't you go back amongst your fucking animal friends' – and those were the more repeatable ones. Strangely, however, none of them carried an address for me to write back to, but what do you expect from pea brains!

It was all such a contrast to the warmth with which I was treated while in Glamorgan. The Welsh people embraced me and I felt totally at home, and there was no way that I could have left that place without helping put something in the trophy room. When I finally left, I felt that all was in place for the future and that I had helped them and Tony Lewis. I could not let him or them down after the faith they had shown in me and the chance they had offered me to finish my career on a high note.

There was no test match cricket in 1993, so I was able to channel all my energies into winning a trophy with Glamorgan. But even on the day it looked unlikely. Kent had rolled us over on the Saturday in Canterbury, where we were heading for a heavy defeat in the Championship match, and everyone in the Glamorgan camp was down on the eve of the important final game in the Equity and Law League game against the same opponents at the same venue. Realistically, there looked to be no way that we could turn the tables. Tony Cottey told me later, 'You gave the rest and me a big lift before that game. You were talking at the top of your voice, saying that what had happened in the Championship match could not happen again and you sounded as though you really meant it.' I knew what I was doing. I was talking loudly and positively, not just for our own players but so that the Kent players in the next dressing-room could hear as well. They were the big favourites and we were the underdogs. We needed a swift injection of confidence if we were going to win.

In the end we played to our limits and what was so wonderful was that it was just like those old happy days with Somerset, as the Welsh supporters came by the coachload with their flags and banners and created a great atmosphere. Winning the Equity and Law trophy was the highlight of my final season at Glamorgan. It was a joy to be at the wicket, unbeaten, when we took that title in my last one-day match, sharing an unbroken stand with the darting Tony Cottey to win that last piece of silver. I scored 46 not out and the two of us steered the ship home after there had been something of a stumble following the fine start given us by Hugh Morris. I felt that the experience factor which Tony Lewis had brought me in for had paid off. It was a magnificent feeling. I jumped for joy and celebrated as much as I had ever done when winning any trophy. People like Steve Barwick and others who had been there for years without winning any silver were delirious, and I was as happy for them as I was for myself. It was a celebration we will never forget. The corks popped long into the night and the singing went on and on. Those Welsh boys could sing! I felt thoroughly at home.

How we partied on that Sunday night, regardless of the fact that we still had a game to finish against Kent on the Monday. Yet, incredibly, I might well have finished my professional career with a century to go with that trophy. We had been set a massive total to win, but the captain had warned us that no one was allowed to block, anyone who did was to be fined. I just went out and hit my way to 83 before I holed out to Carl Hooper of all people. I could have been selfish and fiddled my way through those last few final runs, but I was under orders to hit everything and that was what I did. I was well aware of the fact that this was my last meaningful match as a professional cricketer, but I wasn't bothered, I was still on too big a high from winning that trophy on the Sunday. It was a beautiful feeling, it had been such an evening and most of us were still high when we turned out on the Monday. To be honest, we could have done without having to play and would have loved to go straight back to our fans in Glamorgan. I felt that I had repaid Tony Lewis for the faith he had in me. After being given the sack at Somerset I wanted to give that faith to Glamorgan and let the younger players see what Viv Richards was all about.

There were no regrets about retiring after the final game. I had a good season, but too many people play that song one more time and finish with a sad ending. This was a perfect way to finish with the perfect side. I loved that time in Wales and there are still happy memories and good feelings, and a great many of those Welsh fans seem to come and take pictures of my house in Antigua when they are on holiday there or stop off on a cruise. After the bitterness of my departure from Somerset this was entirely different.

There was still one remaining Championship match, against Derbyshire in Cardiff, but this was an anticlimax in cricketing terms and there is nothing I can recall about the game at all, how many runs I scored or anything else. The one thing it was worth remembering for was the way the people of Glamorgan came out to say thank you and goodbye. They were some of the best supporters I ever came across. I would see the same faces everywhere the length and breadth of the country. Whenever I stepped out of my house they greeted me and asked me how I was and made me feel completely at home. The warmth made me feel like a little kid again back home in Antigua. I felt that I was an adopted Welshman and they discovered that when I am with you, I am with you all the way, whether it was with Robert Croft when he led the singing in the bar or out there in the middle where it really counted.

10. Bush Tea

Every Englishman knows the pleasure and value of a nice cup of tea, but I seriously doubt whether high tea at the Ritz would be served with the sort of brew which saved me an eye operation at the height of my career.

I suffered from pterygium, a complaint shared by Brian Lara. The medical men told me it was a small growth on the eye itself, right in the sensitive area near the pupil. The eyes become very inflamed through dust, feeling gritty and very irritable, making life uncomfortable and seriously affecting my batting.

I also used to suffer a lot through hay fever, and a good day in England could be a bad day for Viv Richards. I used to check the pollen count on a daily basis and when the count was high I knew that the chances were that I was going to suffer. Although I was in agony with numb hands and feet in the cold weather, in many ways I was better off then than when the sun blazed down on new-mown grass. It was a no-win situation.

The problems with my eyes, I understand, can be aggravated by strong, bright sunlight and also by standing in the slips so much where, quite often, I would be looking into the sun and squinting. There were times when I became so accustomed to squinting that I carried on doing it long after I had finished the day's play. But while it was bad in the slips, it was much worse when I was batting. There were times when I desperately wanted to scratch the itch, difficult when Dennis Lillee is roaring in at you. The feeling was as though someone had suddenly tried to push a feather up my nose. I wanted to jump out of my skin when it happened.

I was prescribed tablets that I took once a day to try and help, but it was only later in my career that they diagnosed the real problem. The condition wasn't bad enough to threaten my career, but I was reluctant to have anything done because of an experience

I had when touring Australia. I was suffering from conjunctivitis and a tremendous fuss was made in the media because I missed a few matches. The press began to blow it up as something more than a simple eye infection. The speculation about an eye operation would have been even more intense while I was playing and would have become a big issue. I didn't want to have to handle that and my career at the same time. The advice I had was that it was not threatening; and the physiological problems of having an operation on such a sensitive organ and then returning to test or county cricket would have been very difficult to cope with. I decided to put the whole thing on the back shelf.

It was on a trip to Jamaica when I was explaining to some friends about my problems with my eyes that I discovered a natural remedy without the need for surgery. They told me that there was a herbalist on the island who had various solutions for a variety of ailments, including mine. The regular treatment for my problem, according to the herbalist, was a drink called bush tea or green tea; to put it simply and bluntly, it was a hot-water infusion of the fresh green leaves of the marijuana plant! Whenever I drank the tea I felt sure it was going to do wonders.

I had long heard from the people of Jamaica about the medicinal properties of the soft drug. This was long before the debates on television and in the newspapers about its healing powers for unfortunate people with illnesses like multiple sclerosis. As far as the locals were concerned, it had long helped people who were asthmatic, and a regular cup of green tea would provide relief for all sorts of illnesses, both real and imagined. There are older people both in Jamaica and in Antigua who have used the tea all their adult lives, with seventy-year-olds looking 20 years younger and leaving you in no doubt as to the reason. It was all around; I even had a neighbour who swore by marijuana and its medicinal properties.

Having experimented with smoking marijuana myself as a youngster, and then trying the tea after hearing what it could do, I became convinced that perhaps this weed had been seriously misunderstood. The herbalist explained to me what it was and said

Did you hear the one about … ?
– swapping stories with Both in the slips
for Somerset against Worcestershire at
Weston-super-Mare

Plumb – I run towards Malcolm Marshall to celebrate the lbw decision against Mike
Gatting at the third Cornhill test at Old Trafford in 1988

At home – chilling out at the non-striker's end in a one-day game against the Aussies in December 1988 in Melbourne

League of Friends – The notice on the gate welcomes me for my first game in the Lancashire League for Rishton

Fashion parade – David Gower and myself brighten up a rainy day in Jamaica in 1990 while Jeffrey Dujon prefers the traditional white

Jake the Peg – wondering where that extra leg came from or, more likely, contemplating my future during my last test series. This one was against England at Trent Bridge in 1991

Over and out – my last test appearance, against England at the Oval in 1991

Final curtain – I bid my farewells in that fifth test

Undefeated – I finish my reign as West Indies captain on a winning note with the Wisden Trophy and my record of being undefeated in any series intact

In memory – with the late Malcolm Marshall at Edgbaston in 1991

The last hurrah – signing off in the AXA Equity and Law League in the final game for Glamorgan against Kent at Canterbury in 1993

It's done – I race for the sanctuary of the Canterbury pavilion with Tony Cottey after the winning run

It's won – my face says it all. One of the most satisfying wins of my career as Glamorgan take the AXA Equity and Law title. A perfect way to end my first-class career

Well done, skip – with captain Hugh Morris at Canterbury shortly
before the singing started

Just resting – and enjoying the Antiguan sun
during England's tour in 1994

Respect – with one of the world's great football managers, Bobby Robson, at the Caribbean Cricket Centre in Antigua

From the other side of the fence – commentating with the BBC's Jonathan Agnew in the sixth test against England at the Recreation Ground in St John's in 1998

Chillin' out – a rare stogie at the
Commonwealth Games in Kuala Lumpur
in 1998

It must be Manchester – standing in the rain at Old Trafford
in the 1999 World Cup match against Australia

that some people were afraid to try it; but he asked me to give it a chance to see whether it would work. The leaves are best when they are fresh and green, and you make the tea just like any other tea, infusing the leaves in hot water.

I tried it and my eye problem responded well. There was no hallucination or anything like that, just a great relief to my problem. It remained but was definitely not as bad when I had access to the green tea; when I didn't, it was worse. It was no miracle drug. There was no immediate effect; like any medicine, it needed time to work.

Knowing how conservative people are in England, I was fascinated to hear and read the debate concerning the medicinal properties of something which has always been perceived as a dangerous drug that inevitably leads on to harder drugs. When we were kids in Antigua, pretty well every kid in the region would take the risk and flirt with the danger this easily acquired drug offered. We would ask, 'Why is it that people say this is bad? Why is it that we cannot do this or that?' As kids, it was a new era when, in the late 1960s and early '70s, the Beatles were singing about drugs, there was flower power and soft drugs were high on our agenda. As kids, you hear about the dangers, but I suppose that made us even keener to test it out. We would sneak away and find a little space, leave someone to look out and smoke the occasional spliff. There was always one of the older children who knew somebody who could get their hands on marijuana. The adults as well as the youngsters would use him for their supply. No one ever forced me to try it; I did it of my own free will. When you first venture into it, the experience is a shock to the system as you cough and splutter over your first one. It was an adventure, just like your first drink of rum, your first cigarette or your first fumble with a girl behind the rum shop or in the park.

I must admit that I never used to feel comfortable smoking anything. My father did not smoke and I never really fancied it. I've come to enjoy the odd cigar though, the first being at Somerset after we won our first trophy. Someone had a few stogies and I was in such a great mood and, with champagne, it just felt right, associating a cigar with victory, like Winston Churchill. I never really think of it as smoking, it's more like a prop. And, like President Clinton, I don't inhale. As a much younger man though, I was aware that smoking and drinking did not go hand-in-hand with a hoped-for career in sport.

I am lucky that I have never been addicted to anything. I have tried things and I have enough of my wits about me not to let any of them become a habit; I was far too focused on sport. Anything taken too heavily, whether it be aspirins or green tea, is not good for you. But, in my view, the green tea was good for my condition and for me. I was of the opinion that God put these plants on our earth for some reason. I wondered how it is that something so natural and non-toxic could be considered so dangerous. Nature has its poisons, but in this case it is man who has abused it by developing its dark side. We've all heard about the menace of cocaine. In some parts of the world people happily chew coca leaves because of the enjoyment this gives. The problem arises when evil individuals come along and develop a refined product which costs lives. Hard drugs like heroin, cocaine and crack are truly evil and need to be controlled, and the people who peddle them illegally should be punished. Yet even cocaine and heroin – or at least derivatives of them – are invaluable to the medical profession.

Marijuana, despite its medicinal qualities, is sometimes put into an even higher category, especially in the Caribbean. A guy caught with a little spliff in Antigua is liable to be fined $EC5,000 or, if he hasn't the money, he has to go to jail. What really angers me is the influx of drugs being brought into my country from abroad, the hard drugs that destroy lives and families. I know that a massive trade is building up through people who come, unchallenged, into Antigua in their boats and then sell drugs to the dealers at a massive profit. These are the people who should be stopped, not the local man who enjoys an occasional spliff or the sick woman who uses marijuana to relieve her pain and help her to enjoy a more normal life. I am not advocating the free-and-easy recreational use of marijuana, but we should start considering the whole matter more seriously. I am not recommending that soft drugs should be sold freely in the shops or be allowed unrestricted widespread use, but I do believe that if a thing is medically beneficial then it should be licensed and made available in a controlled way. Children must be protected from it, just as they are from alcohol and cigarettes, but those who need it should have access to it. Why should anyone have to suffer because the medicine they need would make criminals of them?

If marijuana were available in a licensed, legal way, this would seriously damage the illegal trade in drugs and drug-running, a particular benefit of this being that people buying marijuana would not be exposed to dangerous and destructive hard drugs through contact with criminal dealers.

Much medical evidence points towards the beneficial effects of marijuana, and there are influential voices supporting its controlled decriminalization. I recently watched a television programme in which a Lord Chief Justice in Scotland was doing this very thing. When you have people like him, people who are in control of others' lives, voicing these opinions, then it is time to listen.

I also understand that research initiatives are underway to establish the facts concerning the medicinal properties of marijuana, one series of tests being conducted by the Royal Pharmaceutical Society in the United Kingdom. I applaud that initiative as a step in the right direction. We are not yet that enlightened in Antigua. If you are a drinker and go from beer to rum, it doesn't mean you are going to be an alcoholic any more than going from a cigarette to a spliff is going to make you a drug addict.

Having tried smoking the drug when I was young, I quit because I didn't think it would be good for my cricket – it's hardly performance-enhancing – and I didn't want to do anything illegal, something you think about seriously when your father is a strict prison officer. In all my time in English cricket I never saw what I would call a drug culture. There was the odd cannabis smoker, but I rarely if ever saw the hard stuff being used. In any cross-section of society there will always be the odd one or two who indulge in various practices, and Warwickshire and England fast bowler Ed Giddins had to pay the penalty for being caught out in a drug test.

A potentially far bigger problem for cricket, and one that needs watching carefully, is the use of steroids which, I believe, could be very beneficial to the modern fast bowler. There is a drug-testing procedure in cricket but it does need stepping up, both during competition and out of competition. There is no proof that this particular drug is being used and abused on the circuit, but as it is prevalent in so many other sports around the world it would be naïve to think that it has never been tried by an ambitious young quickie who wants to bowl faster for longer. Someone who is really quick to start with could become completely lethal in such circumstances. Without mentioning names or the location, I have been very suspicious of certain cricketers who have suddenly developed considerable upper-body strength and become much quicker over longer periods.

While I believe that the use of steroids is completely wrong, I can well understand the desire to build up strength, as I worked hard on it for my own game. When I was young I was a little whippy figure and started using a bat of around two pounds five or six ounces. Then gradually, as I became a little stronger, I found it a little light and moved to 2.8 and then to 2.9 or 2.10 and stayed there. I had the weight in the bat but needed to be confident that it picked up light but still had a bit of meat in the middle.

Even when I was young I always had good body-definition. My shoulders were square and my waist small. I was physically in shape without having to do any specific training, keeping fit through playing cricket and football and running. Then I saw a mate doing sit-ups so I started to do that; then others told me about various other exercises, for the back, to make the buttocks tight, and the rest. We did a whole lot of sit-ups to strengthen the back, pull-ups on the bar and, of course, we swam a lot in the sea. Maybe having that definition from an early age, exercising and then the supplements, proteins, all started to help me bulk out a little power. I had some energizing powder to mix in a glass of water and milk or a chocolate shake, adding the protein my body needed.

I really started filling out when Dennis Waite came along and not only increased the running, mainly up and down steps, but also the sit-ups and everything else. It was no longer 20 or 30 sit-ups but 200 or 300. As I was doing them in the middle of a group, no one wanted to be the one who was the wimp or the weak link. You couldn't pass out. The bodybuilding was gradual, starting locally on my own, then with friends, and on to group training with the Leeward Islands cricketers. Then it was on to Somerset, using gyms when it rained, to strengthen the legs and knees, West Indies and Queensland. As I developed muscles and built up my strength, so the weight of the bat changed, but once you have a good pick-up and hit a few in the meat you begin to feel confident about the carefully crafted piece of wood in your hands.

When I went to Glamorgan, drug tests had just come in and I was tested. It was, of course, negative as no green tea was served in the pavilions at Swansea or Cardiff. Personally, I used a lot of vitamin supplements, C, B and E, and other things from the health shops I frequented. There was a certain protein powder that I used to take for my breakfast and all the little vitamins that go with the product. My body naturally needed them, particularly because of how much I perspired when I was playing; I needed to put a lot back. There was always the nagging concern that there could be something in the powder that I didn't know about, but I was careful to study the label and the list of ingredients. Athletes all over the world use a cocktail of vitamins and supplements with substances like creatine becoming increasingly popular and, maybe, the cause of problems in other areas.

I never tried any of those sorts of things, but I was concerned when one day I was asked to give a random sample when Somerset were playing Gloucestershire. Normally I would have had no problem with this, but the way it was conducted this time aroused deep suspicions within me. As a rule, you are supposed to see the names of those to be tested come out of a cap; these are supposed to be random tests, and even cricketers have certain rights. It was the year when I felt that things weren't all they might have been. If I was going to be tested I wanted to see my name go into the hat with all the others. This did not happen and I was just informed that I had been selected for testing. In the circumstances I refused to do it. Maybe I was feeling paranoid but, at the time, Martin Crowe was rumoured to be coming to Somerset and I felt they were looking to get rid of Viv Richards. I was there until nine o'clock, when I told them I was going home to my bed.

I was hauled before the disciplinary committee at Lord's, with my defence being that it was a Somerset player, Nigel Felton, who had informed me that I was to take a drug test. This wasn't right in my book. There was something fishy about the entire episode. The powers that be gave me just a reprimand because they also knew it was all wrong. I told them I did not trust the system and that I was worried by what was happening at Somerset and that I thought that they wanted to push me out through the door. Stranger things have happened. I could have been fed anything during the course of the day, in my tea, in my food, whatever. It may sound like a conspiracy theory, but at the time I was feeling insecure about my position at the county. I take my career seriously and I cannot think of anything more stupid than swallowing a drug before going out to bat. It is hard enough facing these fast bowlers without dulling your senses or feeling you are Superman.

The use of cocaine, heroin or any of those hard drugs should be actively discouraged. They are not good in any way for the sports-man or for the image of the sport. If you are caught, you have made your own bed and you have to lie on it. I also believe that, once you have done your time, you have erased your black mark. Every individual needs a chance and Ed Giddins has shown that. His rehabilitation was complete when he was called up for England. But if anyone errs for a second time, then the punishment must be increased and, as far as I am concerned, it's three strikes and you are out.

The only place in the world where I have ever been tested is England, where I was called upon three times. Testing should be made compulsory in all sports in all parts of the world, but I fear that this is not the case. What is good for one should go for all. Personally, I am totally anti hard drugs. I have a less absolute opinion about marijuana. I am not suggesting that every kid should go out and smoke a spliff or drink bush tea, but I do believe in its medicinal benefits. What I'd like to see are more open minds about this side of it, once science has the proof to support it. For a sufferer of MS it is inhuman to deny him or her the relief it can give, and only grown-up, sensible debate can lead to the present situation changing.

Injury and illness are always the biggest fear for any sportsman, especially for the professional, who relies on his body for his livelihood and to support his family. I have had my fair share of knocks, bumps, breaks and bruises over the years, although there are those who say that I deliberately flirted with serious injury by not wearing a helmet.

When I was in Australia, touring in 1979–80, I had some back problems and I couldn't bat or field in the way I would have liked. As in many other sports, it needed pain-killing injections just to get me out there. It was a bad time for me and I was in a lot of pain. My entire right side felt numb and all the would-be medics in the team told me it was a pinched nerve. Rudi Webster, who is now the team therapist, discovered that there was a slight crack in a bone in the lower part of my back. It certainly served to concentrate my mind wonderfully for, despite the presence of Dennis Lillee, Jeff Thomson, Lenny Pascoe, Rodney Hogg and Geoff Dymock in that series, I scored 140, 96, 76 and 74 in my four innings as we won the truncated three-test series 2–0.

We were due to go straight on to New Zealand afterwards and I had to miss all three tests there as the doctors gave me six weeks away to get strong and recuperate. The cure was to rest on the beach and swim as much as I could. It sounds fine, but I was annoyed to miss out against the Kiwis, especially as we lost the series 1–0 after a one-wicket defeat in Dunedin, when Richard Hadlee took 11 wickets, and drawn matches in Christchurch and Auckland.

Injuries and pain-killing injections have played their part throughout my career but, strangely, not always in a negative fashion. There was my favourite innings, scoring 61 with a broken thumb when we were chasing at Sabina Park against India, and my hip was damaged in Melbourne when I scored 153. These were two significant innings when I had to stand and deliver, and I'm sure that the injuries somehow helped me concentrate.

On the whole, I guess I have been pretty lucky over the years. I missed a game against England with my acute fistula and another against Pakistan in Guyana. Most of the injuries have been broken fingers, including all four fingers on the left hand and my thumb on my right hand. I picked these up mainly through fielding in the slips, trying to take return catches and also trying to take a return from the field to run someone out. In fact, I can't remember anything worse than bruising while batting – apart from a little crack in my jaw! However, there's bruising and there's bruising. A helmet I could do without, a box was essential. If I ever needed convincing – and I didn't – there was an incident when I was playing for Queensland versus New South Wales, and the un-predictable Lenny 'Loosehead' Pascoe nipped one back and hit me in that sensitive area. The ball, travelling at around 100 miles an hour, hit me flush on the metal box, which immediately dented, trapping a certain part of me. I don't know what dying feels like, but that was the closest I have come. I have never known such pain, looking up at all those people in white gazing down at me, and a million stars exploding in the sky like a private showing of *Star Wars*. As if the pain isn't enough, you then have some lunatic like physiotherapist Dennis Waite, a man with an odd sense of humour, bringing out the ice-pack. I suppose it is better than after-shave, but only marginally. I soon realized that you *can* feel even worse than when you are first hit. For days afterwards, because of the swelling I was walking around like someone with a carrot stuck up his backside. It was a real Monty Python silly walk that saw me flick out one leg to the right every other step to give me a little freedom. I am sure a lot of people who saw me must have wondered what I had been up to the night before.

On the whole my injuries have been irritating ones because, even though small, they forced me to be put out to grass while they repaired. I was particularly upset at breaking my finger in my last season at Glamorgan, as it was my last hurrah. It would have been pretty sad for me to finish like that, especially as we had had such a good thing going. I knew there was no more international cricket left for me, so I made a calculated decision to continue playing with my broken finger until the very end of the season. I played in all the major matches, including the final of the Equity and Law that we won against Kent at Canterbury. It was one of Glamorgan's best years, as we finished second in the Championship as well. It was a great reward for me, especially as I was not in the best of health. Physio Dean Conway's job was to patch me up and shove me out on to the field every morning. He would fix the finger and I would take my place in the unusual role of the outfielder.

Sod's law decrees that the ball follows the injured player or the guy who is having a bad hair day – and, sure enough, I still took my share of catches. There was no question of hiding. It has always been my instinct to take the catch or dive around first and think about the consequences afterwards. I felt I owed it to my team mates and myself. This is sometimes what sport is about: beating the odds and overcoming difficulties. It is easy to go out and do it when the odds are stacked in your favour, but quality and courage come through when your back is to the wall. Despite the broken finger, I felt secure because I was so committed. This was a challenge I came to relish.

Injury can definitely focus the mind. Batting with it didn't worry me. It was the top hand and, although I found it hard to get my hand around the grip, I could manage most shots even though it sometimes meant that I would have to pull my hand away. I was proud of the fact that I scored 46 not out in the final game of the AXA Equity and Law League at Canterbury against Kent and into the 80s in the Championship match on the Monday. Maybe I could have gone out scoring a century if I had pushed the ball around, but the captain told us that as it was the last match he didn't want to see anyone blocking and anyone who did would be fined. We were chasing an impossible 400 and something to win, and we blazed away in a glorious do-or-die charge. A positive stroke was played at every ball and I eventually holed out in the deep at 83.

It was great fun, but we wanted to get back to Glamorgan to begin the celebration. Injury hadn't spoilt the last first-class game of my career, and it certainly wasn't going to spoil the party.

11. Over and Out

One of the biggest changes in the game to have taken place during my playing career was the increasing influence of television. It's brought money into the game as well as introducing it to a much wider audience. More cricket can be seen by more people than ever before, but this has brought with it huge extra pressures. Perhaps those who've suffered most, though, are the umpires whose every decision is put under a microscope. Every decision is reviewed and any mistake mercilessly exposed.

Like every player, I've had my disagreements with umpires all over the world; but one of my great inspirations in cricket was the English umpire, Dickie Bird. I have always found the little Yorkshireman to be one of the most amusing characters in the game. From time to time cricket can seem boring, but just walking out to the middle and seeing Dickie with all his quirky mannerisms used to cheer me up no end. He could make me laugh even if I wasn't in the mood. What is more, most of the times when he has stood in a game in which I was playing I seemed to do rather well. He was at the Oval in 1976 for my 291 against England; at Harrogate when I scored over 200 for Somerset against Yorkshire; at Old Trafford for the 189 not out against England in a one-day international; and at Lord's for the 145 and the 138 not out – among many others. He has certainly witnessed more of my better innings than any other umpire and, as he was the best there was, it was a privilege having him standing there.

When we bumped into each other, he would say, 'Master, everywhere I turn out, master, you get some runs. What have you got in store for me today?' At the end of the day he would say, 'I have seen the best of them, master, they can't touch you, master.' It used to make me feel so good, whether he meant it or not. In his long career he would have seen the very best there was, on the county circuit and around the globe, standing in a privileged position, as close as you can be to the action without wearing a helmet!

One thing he did not like about me was my straight driving. Not that he had anything against the shot or the way I played it, but just the fact that he was paranoid about the ball hitting him. At the Oval one day he must have been thinking about it more than ever, for he pleaded with me, 'Master, don't hit it back at me today.' Whenever I batted, he was like a cat on a hot tin roof, always on the move and ready to duck at the first sign of trouble. He was unlucky because the straight drive was one of my favourite shots. The closest I came to fulfilling his worst nightmare was when I hit Derek Underwood straight back. It came sweetly off the meat of my number one bat, and when Derek tried to catch it the ball hit his hand and ricocheted away towards the umpire, who of course was Dickie Bird. I wasn't worried about Underwood, he could look after himself; however, I was worried about Dickie, who contorted himself into all sorts of shapes in an attempt to avoid the ball, accompanied by a high-pitched scream, followed by a big sigh as it whistled past him and went to the boundary. Still shaking, he said, 'Master, oh master, if that had hit me, that would have been the end of Dickie. Poor Dickie.'

He is a good man and he was a good umpire. He was what I called a batting umpire: he appreciated seeing good batsmen. Maybe that was why I lasted so long when he umpired! Bowlers would moan a bit that Dickie's mind was made up before the appeal for leg before wicket if the batsman was coming forward. He would always give the batsman the benefit of the doubt, which is as it should be. As he grew older he lost some of his quality, but that happens to all of us, whether we are players or officials. Just before he quit he seemed to lose a little of his concentration, something you would never have associated with Dickie in his prime when he was up for every ball.

Another Englishman who also sees the funny side of umpiring is David Shepherd, a most humorous man. I also enjoyed playing for Somerset against him when he played for Gloucestershire.

You could never take umbrage when he was standing because he represented the funny side of the job. He is another with a lot of mannerisms and superstitions that the commentators soon got to know about and passed on to the cricket fans. So when a batsman was on Nelson, 111, he would hop around on one foot, a superstition he carried on from the time when he was a player, when he would make sure his feet were off the ground whenever one of his team mates was on the dreaded figure. Shep has created the same sort of image as Dickie Bird whereby the people love him and players look forward to him being on duty. An umpire can receive no greater praise than that.

I have always believed that the English umpires were the most honest. They may not have always given the right decision, but they would always try to be fair and administer the game in the way it should be administered.

This wasn't always the case around the world: Australia was notorious for 'home' decisions, and there were problems in Pakistan, in India and even at home in the Caribbean. This is what brought about the change to neutral umpires. Imran Khan was maybe the first to demand neutral umpires, and when we toured Pakistan we had two Indian umpires.

Gradually things improved and, with the advent of the international panel with Dickie and our own FIFA football referee and test umpire, Steve Bucknor, they reached the fairly satisfactory state they are in now. Steve is acknowledged to be one of the best and we are very proud of him in the Caribbean.

I had more problems with umpires in Australia than anywhere else. They were too lenient to the players from the country of their birth. I was always worried whenever the ball hit the pads. I had some problems as the captain of the West Indies when I was asked to mark the Australian umpires out of ten. I would say to them, 'How can I mark you out of anything if you don't make a decision, especially when we are fielding? If you gave a decision, then I might be able to give you two or three out of ten.'

I was fined for abusive behaviour towards R. J. Evans of Queensland, as was Malcolm Marshall in Adelaide. It is totally wrong to dispute an umpire's decision, but in the high-tension arena of test cricket it is bound to happen from time to time when a player honestly feels that he has been cheated by a rank bad decision.

My little local difficulty came when, bowling my off-breaks, I hit Dean Jones on the back foot with a little, slow, straight one. There was no doubt that he was out but the umpire told me that I was in his way and that he couldn't see to make the decision. That was it, I had had enough. I blew my top and told him, 'I didn't know you could see. Thanks for telling me. You're not blind, then. You have eyes to see me but nothing else.' It was becoming embarrassing and I took the leash off my players and told them to express themselves. It was wrong of me to do that, but you can only take so much.

One other, rather more unusual incident was the famous occasion when umpire Barry Meyer apologized for giving me out lbw at Lord's against Ian Botham as I went to clip the wide ball down the leg side. The hardest bit was to accept his apology – but I was still out and nothing had changed in the scorebook. It was decent of him and nice to hear, but it did me no good.

Another difficult decision for the umpire is the catch behind from a thin edge. Sometimes it may seem as though the slips are going up for a dubious catch behind, but this can be misread. When I fielded in the slips I was concentrating on what might be my catch, but when it slides past a shout is almost an automatic reaction because you don't always know whether there is contact or not.

I remember an incident when Rob Bailey of England clipped one down the leg side and was taken by our wicket-keeper, Jeffrey Dujon. As far as I was concerned he had nicked it; but when I looked at the television slow-motion replay he had clearly missed it. My angle and my position told me that he had hit it. I appealed loud and long and he was given out. It was interpreted by the media as unnecessary pressure on the umpire, Lloyd Barker. But it was up to him to retain his composure and make his decision. It is my job to appeal and his job to make a decision. It created a big row in the Caribbean as radio broadcaster Christopher Martin-Jenkins had hinted that I had cheated by putting Barker under undue pressure with a prolonged appeal and forced him to change his mind. Even with hindsight I have to say that, if the same incident happened tomorrow, I would do the same thing. At the same time I am sorry for Rob Bailey as it was an appeal that might have shortened his international career.

On the practice of a batsman walking when he knows he has given a thin edge, I have always felt that it is up to the individual. I must admit that I wasn't consistent at walking; it would often depend upon the state of the game. If it was for my country and the situation was critical, I would stand there if I thought I could get away with it and leave it to the umpire. No one can call you a cheat for standing when you have someone there to make a decision. It is swings and roundabouts.

There was a time against Yorkshire in a NatWest Cup match at Headingley when I nicked it and stood my ground, whereas on other occasions the bat would have been under my arm and I would have been off to the pavilion. The reason why I didn't walk in this instance was because of the abuse I was receiving from the crowd and I had made up my mind that if I had an opportunity to take two knocks, then why not? It was a personal thing. At the end of play the Yorkshire cricketing public were really annoyed and were flocking around my car, calling me an effing cheat and worse. But, at that ground, it was no different from normal, they had often abused me. This was a case of Viv Richards' revenge. It wasn't just the fans who were cross, David Bairstow and the entire Yorkshire team were annoyed with me, but I didn't care. It is called human nature. They would have had to break my stumps into pieces for me to walk before the umpire lifted his finger. I went on to score 80 not out, and we won an important match. If I am playing against hard-nosed individuals, they have to shoot me; but if I am playing against people who hold the game in high esteem, then I will do everything I can to maintain that dignity and do the right thing. But if you are as die-hard as I am, I can play hard ball with the rest of them. It doesn't worry me.

When I was fielding and the batsman nicked the ball, my attitude was to ask them why they were hanging about. We are all hypocrites

in a situation like that and everyone is looking for the extra advantage
in order to win. There are plenty of English batsmen who don't
walk; ask Alec Stewart about that! You have to splinter his stumps
into hundreds of pieces before he'll go. They, like the rest of us,
walk when it suits them. I have seen Mike Atherton rubbing the
crease with his toecap, ready to go again, when he could have
walked; and I have even seen the gentlemanly Colin Cowdrey do
it. When he has a ton and he nicks it, the gloves come off and off
he goes. What a good guy! But if his back is against the wall and
the situation is critical, he will take his chances with the rest of
them.

You have to see both sides of it.

Despite all the disputes, I am still not an advocate of modern
technology for decisions like lbw. I feel that it's still best left to the
umpire's judgement, since changing this could undermine the
umpire's overall authority over the game. Mistakes will sometimes
be made, but in the long run these tend not to favour one side over
another.

For disputed catches taken low down, though, the television
replays could help as much as they have for run-outs. A classic
example where this would have been the case is the controversial
catch Steve Waugh took to dismiss Brian Lara in Barbados. Steve
knew in his heart of hearts that he had not taken a clean catch. It
wasn't as if it was the normal contentious bump ball. The video
showed what was happening under his body as he realized that the
catch wasn't there, then you could see him scoop it up and put it
in the right place. The cameras saw that Lara was not out and
exposed the action for what it was. Sometimes you can understand
a wicket-keeper being unsure about whether or not a catch is clean
because his hands don't have the same sensitivity as those of a man
in the field. But every player knows whether it is a bump ball. In
the case just mentioned, Steve claimed the catch that had been
shielded by his body from the officials, and it played a huge role in
how they were doing in the series. It doesn't just affect an innings
or a match but an entire series, as who knows what it did for Brian

and the rest of the team's confidence? Steve was a bit naughty and it reinforced my belief that some of the Aussies would do anything to win. It would have helped so much to have had television take the pressure off the umpires for a crucial decision like that one. One decision can turn a match and play a vital role in the result; it can make the difference between winning and losing and, in some cases, even worse – as in Jamaica, when my dismissal nearly led to a riot.

Of course, usually the Caribbean crowd becomes excited for more positive reasons, such as when one of their favourites achieves a landmark. Often some run on to the pitch. Viewers who are watching on television must wonder what is going on when members of the public press up close to you; what they are doing, in fact, is pressing money on you. It happens not just in the Caribbean but also on the subcontinent in India and Pakistan. I suppose the equivalent in England is the professional in League cricket having the hat taken round for him. But even that can be spoilt. You are caught up in the excitement, with people patting you on the back and putting bucks in your pocket. There was one individual whom I knew by reputation, fortunately; when he came up to say well done and began patting my pocket, I knew it was not so much to put something in as to take something out. I cottoned on pretty sharply and, as I felt the hand coming out, I gave it a little tap and saw that he had a handful of notes. There is always the odd one who wants to take advantage and take you to the cleaners. I doubt whether he managed to get out of the Recreation Ground in one piece once people around him had realized what he had been up to.

Sometimes the amount could be quite generous; $EC20 (£5) was normal, but those who had come home from their new lives in America, St Croix or St Thomas, where they earned good wages, would give as much as $US100. It could add up to a lot of money. Before the game someone would be telling you, 'Score a hundred today and I will give you a hundred bucks.' Or they might even have it announced over the tannoy. And they meant it. But it doesn't happen as much as it used to because players earn more and money has become tighter for the average spectator.

One area that does worry me is the pitch invasion. Sadly, it seems to be the way of the world and the current trend; there are some lunatics out there who don't have the game's best interests at heart and use any occasion for their own selfish ends. I was disappointed and ashamed when certain things happened over here in the Caribbean. Guyana was different, that wasn't a violent act; but in Barbados it was bad and, when a bottle went past Steve Waugh's face, it made me very ashamed. If the bottle had hit him we would all have suffered for the rest of our lives. I was totally ashamed to be a West Indian on that day – and, as anyone who knows me will testify, that is not something I say lightly.

I can understand current players expressing their fear at what may happen, especially after what happened to Monica Seles, when she was stabbed in the back by a crazy spectator. Who says that cannot happen in cricket? I had scored a ton playing for Somerset against Surrey at Lord's and when we won the game easily I ran for the cover of the pavilion as the crowds poured over the boundary. As I left, one of them tried to snatch my cap; he did it rather clumsily and pushed a finger into my eye. It blurred my vision and I was so furious that I chased him. There was such a big crowd tumbling over the ropes that he was able to avoid me by dodging behind groups. He thought he had rid himself of me, but I kept after him, found him and rugby-tackled him to the ground. He was in a state of absolute panic as I showed him the damage he had done to my eye and told him that if he had taken my cap cleanly I would have left him alone, but because he did such a clumsy job he had to give me my cap back. He did so, with some relief that I wasn't seeking further retribution.

There is a new breed of cricketers who recognize the danger of a stampeding crowd. I agree with them; it is too dangerous and the risk is not worth taking. We saw an ugly incident at Hove during the 1999 World Cup, when a spectator jostled Azharuddin. I felt it came to a head in England during the World Cup and, although no one was hurt, it could easily have happened. The problem is that the idiots see it happen on television and they want to copy it. Where does it end? What we must not do is wait until someone is seriously hurt or even killed.

The over-exuberant appeal, not walking or even Steve Waugh's 'catch' off Brian Lara may not be quite within the spirit of the game, but at least they're not premeditated. One debate in professional cricket that has run and run is that on ball-tampering. It is illegal and, if you are caught, you serve your time; but, like not walking, I'm afraid it is all part of the modern game. It is something that has been going on for years as the bowler has sought for supremacy over the batsman. Scuffing the ball, raising the seam with a bottle-cap or a nail, rubbing lip salve or old-fashioned Brylcreem into the flannels and from there on to the ball to give it an extra shine has been going on for ever. As a batsman, I say good luck to you if you can get away with it; but remember, if you are caught you will be severely punished.

As a captain I wouldn't, however, say to my fast bowler, 'Come on, try and get your seam up.' That is up to him, but if he is doing it and getting wickets and putting us on top and he has not been spotted by the umpires, then who am I to tell him to stop doing it? However, I would certainly have said something sharp if he were using an implement like a bottle-top rather than nature's gift to him of a long fingernail or thumbnail. No one can tell a bowler to cut his nails. There are certain individuals who use all sorts of lotions, especially sun cream these days. Just look at how many bowlers use sun-tan cream even when it is cold and overcast; that is a real give-away. Sun-tan cream was no use to me, so I used to put a little Vaseline on my face. That was my sun-screen.

They talk of reverse swing as something new, but when I first toured Pakistan in 1975 we saw Imran Khan and Safran Nawaz do it on a regular basis with the old ball. The South African, Clive Rice, was another who could do it at will with an old ball, suddenly finding new life in it, making the ball duck back on you very late just when you thought it was gift time. All we have now is a different phrase, and 'reverse swing' is a sexy expression for the commentators to use.

★

The rules and regulations are set, but there is always someone looking for an idea to beat them, and they deserve the credit, especially in India and Pakistan where the wickets are so flat and true. Don't be kidded that this happens just on the subcontinent. Sometimes in England the seam would be lifted so much that when it went past your nose it sounded like an angry wasp, and when you took a catch in the slips it would sometimes bust your hand open because the seam stood out like a razor blade.

As for Mike Atherton and the infamous dirt-in-his-pocket incident, well, it just made me laugh because I couldn't work out what it was supposed to do. Why take dirt and put it in your pocket when it is all around you on the field? Whatever was in this intelligent man's mind at the time is equally baffling. Ball-tampering was big news at the time and it was suddenly considered to be a serious breach of the rules. Knowing, as he must have, that such is the coverage by TV these days, whatever you do, whether it is picking the seam or picking your nose, it is going to be recorded by one of the many cameras, what on earth made him do it? I think it is a good idea that the ball now goes back to the umpire in between overs, just as they do in baseball when a ball hits the ground.

I suppose we were fortunate with our seam attack in the West Indies that there was never any need to get involved in the worst excesses of gamesmanship. Our methods were more direct: we would simply try to bowl as well as we could. In any case, we had a special weapon of our own in the softening-up process – it was called the bouncer! We had bowlers of such quality and such ability, they needed nothing more than the sweat of their brow or the Vaseline on their skin. Michael Holding, Malcolm Marshall and Andy Roberts were all natural athletes who needed no unnatural help in taking wickets.

As far as I was concerned, there was nothing wrong with helping to keep the ball clean and keeping the shine on it as long as possible. I could always spot within minutes those who were taking advantage with the sun-screen or the lip salve.

Picking the seam with your fingers is a skill, but using a metal bottle-top or nail is out of order and dangerous. I would have put a stop to that if it had happened in any of my teams. There were, however, captains who were less scrupulous – or perhaps they suffered from a temporary loss of vision. Perhaps the sun-screen ran into their eyes!

As well as deciding whether a man is leg before wicket, has given a catch behind the stumps and all the rest, the poor umpire also has to look for the illegal delivery, the throw. There have been accusations and suspicions ever since overarm bowling began that certain bowlers threw – and nothing has changed. The latest to come under suspicion are the Sri Lankan off-spinner, Muttiah Muralitharan, and Shoaib Akhtar, currently the world's fastest bowler, who both had the finger pointed at them while touring in Australia. Muralitharan is one of the game's outstanding talents, who suffered humiliation at the hands of the Australian umpires despite being cleared by the international panel. He is double-jointed, in much the same way as Geoff Green, the South African who was no-balled out of the game in 1960. He, like Muralitharan, could not extend his arm fully. Maybe because of all the problems he has gone through, the Sri Lankan has become stronger. His mental strength is very good. When your livelihood is under question and under attack with accusations of chucking, it must play havoc with your mind. He was never deterred by what was said or written about him, he kept his head held high and walked away; and he can go on to greater things, judging by what he achieved in his brief first spell in English cricket at Lancashire. He is a world-class spinner and what he has done in the face of all his problems is phenomenal.

When I first looked at his action, the first thing that comes to mind is that it looks jerky and not like the normal off-spin action. He is different and he is special. There was suspicion for some time and the authorities have cleared him twice, so what is all the fuss about now? They are the body who rule, and they have made their decision; now we should all relax and agree that we have something rather special and unusual to enjoy. If I had played against him I would have played down the wrong line because to me he looks like he is bowling leg-breaks. Maybe it is something to do with his loose wrists, with the final flick so flexible that he is very hard to read.

Akhtar was just the latest victim when it was decided that his action needed sorting out because it was alleged that he threw certain balls. I must say the decision took me by surprise. I have never really had problems with any bowler for consistent throwing, but I do believe that there were, and still are, certain bowlers who, every now and again, chuck one or two. Neil Radford of Worcestershire, when he wanted to be mean and nasty, would hurl one down that would be quicker than anything he could normally bowl. It came at you completely unexpectedly because you had got used to his action and thought you knew what pace to expect. As a batsman, it is not something you stand at the crease and worry about because if you did, at the pace they bowl, you would be dead. Charlie Griffith, Ian Meckiff and Tony Lock were all accused of throwing, but they all carried on playing for many years. I suspect that it is mainly the fast bowler who, looking for extra pace, throws the odd one or two but, providing it doesn't become a habit, then I suppose we can live with it.

Much more serious have been some of the murkier stories to have emerged from the subcontinent. I don't believe that any one individual could throw a match on his own; it needs much more of a collective conspiracy. Judging by the stories coming out of Pakistan, the investigations and the accusations (plus my own experiences) indicate that there is a problem. It became a lot more serious when Shane Warne alleged that Salim Malik had offered him a bribe to bowl badly on the final day of a test match between Australia and Pakistan.

Malik, Wasim Akram and Ijaz Ahmed were all eventually cleared of match-rigging, but it left a bad taste in the mouth to see one international cricketer accuse another. But what I found dreadful about this entire affair was that, while the Australians were making these accusations, they did so in the knowledge that both Warne and Mark Waugh had sold information to an Indian bookmaker on the 1994 tour! Both men were fined at the time, although it was kept secret by the Australian Cricket Board in order to save embarrassment. I felt that Warne and Waugh were lucky to walk away from that with such a small punishment. To my mind it was a much more serious incident than the way it was presented. The ICC knew about it and they gave the Australian Board the go-ahead to sort it out themselves. It would have been so much better if it had been nipped in the bud and the investigation carried out publicly. Indeed, a public inquiry would have been interesting. As it was, the board accepted the players' arguments.

Concerns, however, rumble on, with accusations in Pakistan over throwing the World Cup final against Australia in England in 1999, and Adam Hollioake claiming to have been twice offered huge sums of money to divulge team plans and tactics in 1997, and, most recently and ridiculously, Chris Lewis, Alec Stewart and Alan Mullally being offered money to lose the last test against New Zealand in a series when England always had their backs against the wall. It's all very murky water, but from my limited experience I suspect it does go on. Happily, I have never been aware of playing in a game that had been fixed. What I do know – and it can't have gone unnoticed by the authorities and the fans alike – is that Pakistan have been a team too talented to have enjoyed such indifferent performances over the years. They should have been far more consistent, especially remembering the meagre totals they were bowled out for in certain games. It should have led to more inquiries, both internal and external.

We always heard lots of talk about match-fixing whenever we were in Pakistan and India. There was always talk about who was and who wasn't involved. Even talking about it is not good for the game – never mind doing it. But it has been swept under the carpet, and as a consequence the rumours grew worse and worse. It has gone on for so long, and people I respect both in India and in Pakistan assure me that the rumours are, sadly, true; and the 1983–4 tour to India gave me pause for thought.

On the eve of the opening day I received an anonymous telephone call in my hotel room, with the warning to be careful as bookmakers were involved in the test and that one of the umpires had been 'bought' and was on the take. I dismissed the conversation from my mind, but those words came flooding back when I tried to turn a ball from Kapil Dev down the leg side and took it, well outside the leg stump, on the pads. I couldn't believe that Kapil Dev even appealed, but I was even more staggered when I was given out. To say that I was annoyed would be an understatement. By the time I reached the pavilion I was incandescent, following my bat into the dressing-room a fraction of a second after I had hurled it, but not before I had up-ended the table on which the team buffet had been set. People were diving all over the place, trying to save the food and avoid my temper and me at the same time. Thumping through my temple and the purple mist that had enveloped me was that telephone call of the night before. I would never suggest that the umpire had actually been bought, but the knowledge of that phone call didn't help my rage.

Although I have never physically been offered a bribe, I have had a few casual suggestions of 'What if . . .' before the speaker scuttled away under a glare which I normally reserve for the most evil of the fast bowlers. People should know from my past history and my passion for the game and for my country that I will not be bought. I never did get to the bottom of that telephone call, nor did I discover who had made it despite several attempts, not only on that tour but also on subsequent visits. All I know is that it was a voice with a local accent and he clearly believed that something was going on.

If nothing is done, we will continue to have rumour, speculation and ignorant opinions. If anyone is eventually found guilty, they should be dealt with severely, harshly and very quickly. It is unfair to millions of cricket fans who support the players and their countries to allow these things to drag on without a resolution. It is my view that, whether an attempted bribe works or not, it will bring a divided dressing-room because you would never find 11 men willing to sell out their country. The half who are patriotic and ready to die for the cause would feel all wrong walking out with those who are taking backhanders, and either way the team are going to end up losers. It is not on, not at all.

I could never imagine a player like Imran Khan being involved in anything like that, because he loves his country, the way I love the West Indies and Ian Botham loves England. Imran's pride wouldn't allow him to, any more than ours would me or Ian. The problem needs to be taken more seriously and be thoroughly investigated. Anyone caught and proved beyond doubt to be involved in match-fixing should be given the maximum punishment, both within the game and under the laws of the country in which it happens. In my view, it's a kind of treason, selling your country out. At one time that would have meant being put in front of a firing squad! How can anyone sell out his or her country for a few bucks? It is beyond my comprehension.

I also firmly believe that cricketers should be banned from betting on games in which they are involved. I thought it was a very serious issue when Rod Marsh and Dennis Lillee placed winning bets with an English bookmaker that they would lose a test in which they were huge favourites. That was not the normal thing to do, whether they thought it was funny or not. I'm afraid I cannot see the joke in it.

From much of what I've written here you could be forgiven for getting the impression that I think the game is in desperate trouble. This is not the case. Very few individuals are responsible for behaviour that does any serious damage to the game's reputation, and they need to be tackled in the strongest possible way. The gamesmanship that is rife throughout the game is born out of the will to win. Providing it doesn't get out of control, it adds to the competitiveness of test cricket, and it is the continued strength of competition that will ensure the game's healthy future.

12. A Tale of Two Countries

Mickey Mouse declarations and Mickey Mouse bowling have taken the edge and the competitiveness out of the County Championship. They simply cannot get it right, even now that they have split the County Championship into two divisions. That sort of cricket breeds laziness, and too many times when they were out in the field players would look up to the balcony, watching for that declaration that the captains would have agreed over a cosy lunch. They would have calculated exactly how many runs were needed in exactly how many overs using non-bowlers to bowl those rubbish balls.

I believe that is one of the main reasons why county cricket – and therefore English cricketers – have not been as competitive as they should have been. Too many county captains would manufacture a result to please the public, declaring an innings too early or putting on a rubbish bowler to give away quick runs. It was birthday time for batsmen, who would go out and score the fastest ton in the world. It was a farce, distorting the averages and making a mockery of the batsmen who score their runs in real play against serious bowling.

County cricket has not progressed in that sense at all. It still goes on – as we saw when Hampshire and Derbyshire contrived a result that sent Warwickshire into the new Second Division in the 1999 season. I could understand Warwickshire's complaints and concern, and it was a pity that something was not done about it there and then to ensure that this kind of thing was stopped once and for all. The authorities never had a better opportunity. The argument was that it was within the rules, but that does not stop the rules being changed. The authorities fudged that when they were in a great position to alter the laws and help the game progress and improve.

It has happened before. I know, because I was involved in a

false declaration of another sort which made the headlines, when Somerset declared after one over and one run to ensure their passage into the next round of a one-day knock-out competition.

If teams are not good enough to bowl you out, then tough luck. To win a two-innings match, sides have to be prepared to bowl out the opposition twice if they are to win. It is no use if it cannot be done a second time around, and these cheap declarations have bred either laziness or, as we have seen more recently, dodgy tracks that are equally bad in producing test-playing cricketers. Test matches are so precious that you cannot afford to give your opposition an equal chance unless you are down in the series and need to gamble in order to obtain a result. You give yourself a 70–30 chance but never, ever, a 50–50 chance. The same attitude should apply on the county circuit.

Cricket, like all sports, is cyclical, but England have been down for too long now. The game has changed so much and the English, stuck in their ways, have been left behind. It may be a radical thing to say, but I believe that the coaching manuals need to be rewritten. It is not only the batting but also every aspect of cricket. Take fielding, for example. Gone are the days of the fat men fielding in the slips and hiding the worst fielders. We are now catching up with the fitness regimes of other sports so that fielders are quicker, slicker and more athletic, although I still have my doubts about the effectiveness of the sliding stops. Bowling has seen the introduction of reverse swing (or at least has recognized its existence!), and, at test level, leggies seem the only spinners capable of taking wickets. People who have been out of the game for a long time wrote the manuals and they need to be brought up to date. Batting is also stuck in a rut. You still see the young Englishmen coming through the public schools and the county colts teams with the old-fashioned stance, told exactly how they should face the bowler, where the elbow should be pointing, the direction the bat should be aimed at, what sort of grip they should have. Too much time is spent trying to persuade the unorthodox to be orthodox. Take, as an example, the leading England fast bowler, Bob Willis. His bowling action was hardly straight out of the manual. But I doubt whether he would have been the same penetrative strike bowler if the coaches had insisted that he change as they have changed so many others.

You have to wonder how much damage those coaches have done to class batsmen like Mark Ramprakash and Graham Thorpe by telling them how to approach an innings. It is up to the individual to work this thing out and whether or nor he is comfortable with it. Why can't you hit the ball off middle stump over mid-wicket? I did!

English cricket is, in a sense, too sophisticated. It's well developed, everything is in perfect order for the top players to do well, but there's no room for flexibility or flair. Often, when I whipped the ball away to leg off my middle stump, the experts would suck in their breath, shake their heads and tell me that I was hitting across the line. What is wrong with that when you consistently hit the ball for four? I considered myself an artist and it is up to me to craft my shots the best way I can for maximum effect. If a bowler bowled at my middle stump, then as far as I was concerned he was bowling into the area where I wanted him to bowl, the area I loved, the area where I was strong. Did that make me a bad batsman? I don't think so. Ask some of the bowlers who consistently bowled at my stumps. I would hit across the line and they would call me a lucky bastard. The more I did it the luckier I became!

To fulfil the potential of some of the more promising craftsmen, perhaps it is time to go against the grain and, rather than curb their aggression, they should be encouraged to follow their natural instincts. What should be drilled into every player's head, as it was into mine, is shot selection. No one can hit every ball to or over the boundary; you have to be selective and not believe you can do it off every ball. In discussing this, Andrew Flintoff is a name that comes instantly to mind.

Something else that holds back the game in England is that there are far too many ordinary cricketers in English county cricket; too many who just take and do not give. I watched them play on the county circuit myself, looking to keep their places, to play for a benefit and little more. In short, no ambition. There are those who deserve everything they receive from their benefits, but many others just sit in the background, contributing little and hoping to see out their time and take a lump sum into retirement. I have seen it so often. When that benefit comes up, guys who have been a total waste of space throughout their career want you to support their matches, play in their golf tournaments and sign their cricket bats for them. County cricket is full of these individuals who do not want to take the next step forward but who will do anything and everything to achieve that pot of gold at the end of the rainbow, living off more talented and dedicated players for one reason only. Often these selfish men are keeping out a youngster who may be more ambitious and prepared to work harder in order to attain the highest possible level as a cricketer.

No country has experimented more than England in terms of trying to beef up their cricket. So many theories have been tried: coaches, managers, this consultant and that expert; but what needs to change in a big, big way is the attitude of individuals. Too many times, selectors suffer because of players going out to the middle in a representative match and choking, failing to consolidate on what they have done in domestic cricket. There is little that can be done about this from a selector's point of view if you have picked the player out of all those provided by county cricket.

That next step up makes so many look completely out of their depth. And it is usually to do with attitude; often these players are good enough but they don't believe in themselves. In test cricket there are fewer loose balls to hit, and when you add the tension to that it makes it a totally different game.

It is crucial that the selectors try to spot a potential international when the individual is young, based not solely on ability but on character as well. Once that player has been identified, then the selectors must persevere with him. There are far too many one-test wonders in England who are picked and then discarded because of one bad performance. Look at my first two test innings: 4 and 3. What if they had said, 'Oh, this Viv Richards may be good, playing for Somerset and Antigua, but he is not good enough for test cricket.' There would have been nothing I could have done about it. Admittedly, this is not the sole preserve of English cricket. It happens too often in the Caribbean as well.

Another retrograde step England has made in recent years is picking two different teams, one for one-day cricket and one for test matches. What is that all about? England seemed to be looking for bits-and-pieces cricketers, 'bitsers' as we call them, someone who can bat a bit and bowl a bit and who is then picked at the expense of a real specialist. This policy was shown to be out of step when the 1999 World Cup in England amply displayed that teams are much better equipped if they have specialist batsmen and genuine bowlers. We saw the wrong policy come back to haunt teams like England. Sooner or later the top batsmen will sort out the Mickey Mouse bowlers and will take them to the cleaners. But let them try sorting out real bowlers like McGrath, Warne, Walsh and Donald.

I have watched with amazement and incomprehension as England have dropped their best bowlers for an important one-day match in favour of an inferior bowler who might be able to bat a bit. Why then, when county players step up to a higher level, do they fail? The reason must lie in what is happening in domestic cricket. Just because he can do it in a Sunday League match doesn't mean he will be able to reproduce it at the higher level.

I am not sure that the correct answer is to split the County Championship in two, as they decided to do to herald in the new millennium. It could even work against them, with one division having the best quick bowlers and the other the best spinners, as looked like being the case in that first season.

When county cricketers think that the fewer days they have to put in in the field, the better it will be for them, it's just laziness. This is when the bad habits start. I would be in the field and would watch fielders looking up at the balcony, complaining that the opposing captain was going to bat for another over, when the attitude should have been getting the other side out and then batting yourself.

If I were given a totally free hand to change whatever I liked in the system in order to improve the game, I would stick to the basic principles. Let the players compete in a fair environment by having groundsmen produce a wicket that is good both for pacemen and for good batting. If you can bat, you will survive; if you can bowl, you will take wickets. What is needed is the guts and determination to bowl teams out twice; once is not enough. That will give teams a greater incentive for winning and for attacking play. Treat every game as a test match, without stupid declarations. Any captain found guilty of violating the best principles should be censured. If a game is going to be a draw, let it be a draw. If we do this, then we can sort out the bad sports and make games more honest.

There can be a bit of a Catch 22 situation in trying to keep the hard edge to the cricket without losing the entertainment. The question every player should be asked at the end of a game is: have you worked hard enough to produce a genuine finish? I know the spectators are the ones who pay at the turnstiles, but do they really like to watch uncompetitive cricket? I understand that Derbyshire fans booed their own captain, Dominic Cork, off the pitch in a contentious end-of-season game against Hampshire which had a bearing on the format of the two divisions for the next season. I believe that supports my point. There is no real satisfaction for a spectator in watching that sort of unreal victory. The majority of those watching the game in England, particularly the longer game, are knowledgeable and understand it as well as most professional cricketers do. They don't want to be insulted by a contrived finished. If they did, they might as well watch a charity match. If they want results every time, they can watch the one-day games – and there are enough of those in England to satisfy everyone's appetite.

Any team that wants to kill a game dead should be dealt with severely, as should the team who indulge in deliberately slow play. There should be observers watching each game and from their reports the authorities should impose sanctions against offenders. England must weed out the bad county captains and the bad players if they are to progress in the international sphere.

★

But it doesn't end there. Management also has its part to play. They should be ensuring that life on and off the field is approached in a much more professional manner. Their players should go into games with their minds focused and not with the happy-go-lucky attitude that has too often been the case in the past and which persists today. Teams should be professional in everything they do: eating, drinking and sleeping, as well as playing. From my experience in England, I'm sure that cricketers' unhealthy diet and lifestyle contribute to the syndrome of injured fast bowlers from which England suffers more than most. Just look at them before the tour to South Africa in the winter of 1999: Dean Headley with a back injury, Alex Tudor having to prove his fitness before the tour, Darren Gough struggling and Andy Flintoff with his back and foot problems. It is no coincidence, and I believe that this is what is killing England in terms of a lack of consistency. The players they have picked and relied on in order to maintain a particular pattern on the field have not even been able to complete the training sessions all together at one particular time. Top players are wrapped in cotton wool before a match starts. It is a clear sign that something is seriously wrong.

It is amazing when you compare them to the West Indies' indestructible Courtney Walsh, who has been a soldier for a long time, going on strongly for a good number of years. Of course, he has had his share of niggles, with his ageing knees and other little injuries, but he has remained fit enough to come to the post all the time. All those who have broken down should go and ask Courtney or Allan Donald or Glenn McGrath why they have remained strong, suffering fewer injuries, particularly back problems, and why they have spent so much quality time on a cricket field.

It is not just the occasional injury with the English quickies, but all the time. I would like to know how they are being fed and trained. To be strong you have to eat the right sort of foods for your body to maintain its strength, and the training has to be geared to allow the body to endure the contortions and stress every fast bowler goes through. England takes these players on tour – and the next thing is, they are on their way home with an SOS going out for a replacement.

They should seek advice from all the top individuals for, until they do, they are going to continue suffering as the world's under-achievers. You cannot do your best job as a professional sportsman if you are unfit, boozing or living off fish and chips every night before driving to the next game. Fitness is crucial, in the modern game more than ever.

England doesn't have a monopoly on the need to change. In the Caribbean we are having similar problems as the English and have been on the back foot for far too long. However, I still believe that there is lots of hope for cricket, both in England and in the Caribbean. Our cricket will come again in the West Indies, judging by the youngsters I have seen playing. In Antigua we try to instil in players the importance of playing in representative matches, whether it be for their country, for the Leeward Islands or for the West Indies. Cricket is still vitally important in the Caribbean. There is no other sport, not even the Olympics, that we all follow as closely and that brings all the islands together to the same degree. When a test match is being played, whatever island you are on you will see people with a radio to their ear and others asking 'What is the state of play?'

Just walking down the street, you can tell when the West Indies are doing well in a test match from the messages passed on by the taxi-drivers and the honking of the horns of the other cars. Equally, when the West Indies are doing badly everyone walks around with a long face and in a bad mood. During the recent tour to South Africa, the West Indies was like a morgue. We were in seriously bad shape and there were lots of programmes on radio and TV and in the papers dissecting the reasons. It was not just the experts and the ex-cricketers who joined in the debate but also the ordinary people off the streets, with letters to the papers and telephone calls to the radio and television stations. It was good in so far as it showed how much everyone cared. They were intense about the issues and clearly were worried.

People in the Caribbean need this success; they need to know that we can compete at something out there in the big wide world.

Winning at cricket was something that made everyone proud and happy. Through cricket we made our mark on the world. Cricket is more than a sport in the West Indies. With islands so diverse and widespread, it is the thing that brings everyone together as one nation. When Andy Roberts and I became established in test cricket, it helped put Antigua on the map and eventually become a test match venue. To make the front pages of newspapers like *The Times* in England or *Time* in America is something special for the whole region. Not even our island's prime ministers have enjoyed the sort of publicity Andy, Curtly Ambrose and myself have enjoyed. In all modesty, I know it's true to say that we helped increase tourism to our country, and I am very proud of that. It has even been suggested that there should be a little monument to cricket in our capital, St John's, to celebrate what cricket has done for the country. Why not? Taxi-drivers and coachloads off cruise liners already come to our houses to take pictures. Here in Antigua, it gets almost like Gracelands sometimes! While it can be a little off-putting to wake up in the morning, draw your curtains and see tourists spilling out of a coach and taking pictures of your front door, it's also a good feeling. Antigua used not to be one of the main islands on the tourist trail. It is now.

I have always felt that we are here on earth for a certain time to accomplish certain things, and I believe that, at the time when we were having an enormous amount of success, we couldn't see beyond our noses to prepare or build for tomorrow. We have been lucky over the years during which we have had top performers not coming through the system but making the best of their own individual and special talents. In our region we seem to breed naturally tall, big, strong guys, but we didn't place any emphasis on producing a succession of fast bowlers to replace those who were already there. The hope was that we would be lucky again, when we should have had a school to bring on the young pacemen.

Our problem was that we had so many good fast bowlers coming through at the same time, bowlers like Franklyn Stephenson, Sylvester Clarke and Hartley Alleyne who would have walked into the side now but who have only a handful of caps to show for their quality. The failure to produce new talent was put down originally to young West Indians watching basketball on American TV sports channels and wanting to play in the NBA, but I don't believe that this caused the rot to set in. It was a lack of attention by the authorities. We need to have top cricketers going round the islands, preaching the gospel of cricket. Certainly encourage youngsters to play other sports, but make sure that cricket is the one closest to our hearts. It won't ever be the best-paid sport in the world, but it is a much better living than most, giving the young man the chance to be known internationally and to become a better person in life through the experiences it provides. Former players need to tell the youngsters what we have achieved in cricket as a nation in the past and what it means to represent the West Indies, something that has bound us together as one nation over the years. As I write, we are at our lowest point; now more than ever we need to spread the word about cricket.

One reason why cricket in the Caribbean has suffered is politics. I firmly believe that there is too much inter-island rivalry. There are only a few officials who can be trusted. They all have their own agenda and, after the meetings, who knows what goes on in Barbados, Antigua or Jamaica? It is a serious problem when there are so many different cooks, and the first thing to suffer is the broth. The thing that has kept West Indies cricket alive in the past was that there was no need for them to plan ahead because of the quality of the players they already had at their disposal. Now that is gone, all we have are negative views and criticism. At administrative level we need to put the horse before the cart. We are spending too much time marketing a product which isn't ready to be marketed. The emphasis should be on developing the team first. It is hard enough to attract a sponsor, but it is doubly difficult when a team is performing poorly. The sponsors will come in only if the sport looks to have a bright future.

The facilities around the islands are grim. We keep trying to tell the Ministers of Sport on the islands that we need better facilities, especially in the rural areas. Basketball does it very well at the schools and in the villages, so why shouldn't cricket? It doesn't need millions to be spent on it, just some nets and some prepared wickets or all-weather nets, so that when someone wants a knock on a Sunday morning or a player wants to coach schoolchildren, they haven't got to go and prepare a strip themselves in the nearest available field.

If we provide cricket facilities and sufficient motivation for young West Indians, we will find the next generation of young West Indian cricketers. Once we do, we need to nurture them, providing scholarships and professional coaching to bring them up to scratch. In Antigua, we can take them to the excellent Caribbean Cricket Centre at Club Antigua, where they have superb nets as well as a square that is big enough for practice matches. This is the sort of centre every island needs. I was very pleased to be involved in its conception and development, along with my co-author, Bob Harris, an Englishman; but it shouldn't take a holiday company to establish something like the CCC rather than the government.

Even some of the test grounds in the Caribbean have not been up to standard in recent years. Jamaica, renowned for having some of the best wickets, produced a really dangerous track recently for England, with the game having to be called off after a few overs were bowled at the English batsmen. There should have been guinea-pigs to try out the strip before committing professionals to risking their health in a test match. It looked dangerous to me but, supposing West Indies had been in that position, would England have taken the same stance? I like to think so, but I am not sure. I thought the gesture made by Brian Lara was rather humane, damned good and the correct one. I would have done the same thing. You don't want to see someone maimed.

For me, the best wickets are in Australia, although the wickets were consistently good in England until recent years. In India some can be too good, giving the bowler no chance, while in other parts they are no good. The wickets in the Caribbean have, without any shadow of a doubt, deteriorated. They are not as friendly to our fast bowlers as they have been over the years, and as a batsman you go out and are never quite sure; they vary from match to match. To ask some of the up-and-coming youngsters to play on these pitches is unfair. The tracks aren't what they were when I started playing and I do not believe I would have been the same batsman if I began again now.

I believe that there should be an inspector working under the West Indies Board to give advice to the groundsman and the local committee. A certain standard should be set for all test wickets. There are far too many hand-to-mouth programmes and not enough long-term thinking. If I ever have my say, I will make sure that something is done because it is no use having a good wicket in Barbados and then going to somewhere like a spinner's track in Trinidad or wherever and finding it totally different. If we want to breed good young players, we must give them suitable wickets that are not too dangerous. You cannot develop good cricketers on bad wickets. That is why school and college wickets should be the best; give them the short end of the stick and the children will run away. It is no use starting at the test team and working down, it has to start at the bottom and work its way through to the top. If we learn to deal with the smaller things first, then maybe we can learn to handle the big problems.

We are also short of role models at the moment. Brian Lara should be in that key position, but his stock needs rebuilding, especially after the problems before and during the embarrassing tour of South Africa and some subsequent poor results. Brian himself needs a strong leader and guidance. You can see him crying out for help and if he is not going to get that, as a young and inexperienced captain leading what is becoming a young and inexperienced team, there is going to be absolute chaos and further trouble for the West Indies. There is no doubting his ability; what he achieved against Australia put him back on a level with Sachin Tendulkar, currently the best batsman in the world. They were some of the greatest knocks I have seen, particularly coming in the wake of the troubles in South Africa. At other times he can look a bit inferior and maybe even casual. But greatness goes with the individual who looks lethargic one day and rips you apart the next. He does possess those qualities and I hope he realizes it and leads from the front.

When I speak with him, I find him a mature kid who can hold his own in any company. But we all make little mistakes and there are times when he is a bit casual. My advice to him would be for him to become a little more aloof and more professional, though it is hard to do when you have been one of the boys. He needs to be more forceful and he needs to make sure he is first on the bus, first to arrive for practice and he must take a genuine interest in being leader of the team. He will never have the respect of his peers if he misses aeroplanes, is late for meetings and doesn't turn up for practice, no matter how good he is out in the middle. There were signs that Brian Lara was learning from his mistakes when he returned from the troubled tour in South Africa for the home series against Australia. He did very well individually and looked a much more mature captain, but then, after that false dawn, there was another low point in the 1999 World Cup. If Brian could be as focused as he was all the time against Australia, he would reach that consistent level to make himself truly world class again. The talent is there; it just needs bringing out. Sadly, Brian decided to quit the captaincy after our traumatic tour of New Zealand, but I am sure he will come again some time in the future.

Responsibility shouldn't rest only with Brian but with everyone involved in the running of the team. I saw it at close hand for myself in England during the 1999 World Cup, first as a commentator for the BBC and then as an emergency coach when Malcolm Marshall was taken seriously ill. At that time I felt that some of the problems stemmed from the management. Clive Lloyd was a brilliant captain and a great friend, but he seemed to have lost heart a little. Senior players told me that some weak attitudes were displayed and that a lot needed to be done to make the team better, not just on the field but off it as well.

I saw for myself that things were desperately wrong and that it needed a firm hand at the tiller. When I became captain it was important for me that I had people with me like Malcolm Marshall, Courtney Walsh in his prime, Jeffrey Dujon and Desmond Haynes.

Malcolm was very knowledgeable and would come to me with certain suggestions, as would Dujon and Haynes. Sometimes a captain should have belief in himself and should make his own decisions. But when I had someone like Malcolm out there with me, I had to listen because he can only help you and the team. I listened to my senior players before making my decisions.

Brian Lara could use Jimmy Adams, Courtney Walsh and Curtly Ambrose, but it seems he did not have the same sort of support and help that I had because he was in a changing team, whereas mine was pretty steady.

Just as in England, there has been too much inconsistency in terms of selection. A classic example was when the board brought in Lincoln Roberts, from Jamaica, normally an opener, for Carl Hooper. He batted at number three, didn't do so well and never played again. Surely, if he was good enough to come into the side in that vital position in his first test, he must have been worth more than one chance. No selector could possibly think that highly of a player for one game and then think nothing of him in the next without it reflecting on his own knowledge and ability.

Cricket hasn't changed. It is still the same basics. The problem is that some don't get to grips with the basics properly before trying to move on. We have to beware of this. Cricket is the same essentially simple game and the batting and the bowling have always been the same. Providing those running the game in both England and the West Indies don't lose sight of this and make sure that all their changes to the structure of the game are made with one thing first and foremost in mind, the quality of the basics, then the time will come again for both countries.

13. Life Goes On

I was fortunate in that I wasn't left in limbo with nothing to do after I finished playing. I enjoyed doing some work for the Antiguan Tourist Board, travelling to the World Travel Market in London and other events, basically helping to promote my country. That was another eye-opener. It amazed me that so many ordinary people were doing things for their country on such a low budget, but when the people in high office who hold the purse-strings are involved, they do it in style, everything is first class, regardless of the cost. This tells me that they do not have their country at heart.

Immediately after that I became involved in Club Antigua and the development of the Caribbean Cricket Centre and the promotion of the holiday resort. Cricket still had a deep hold on me and I was enjoying putting something back that could be of benefit to the entire country. Then I had a call from Javed Miandad, who told me that there was a prince in Brunei who was a fan of mine and who would like me to go over to his country to talk to him and coach him. I already had on the table an offer to play in South Africa when I took the call from Javed about the possibility of coaching in Brunei. I was now forty and was concerned that I wouldn't be able to compete in the way I wanted to, particularly after my break from playing at the top level. South Africa was and still is very much like Australia in terms of the competitive edge, and I felt sure that in order to play over there I needed to be at my best and not on the decline. Western Province made me an offer, but the fee was nothing compared to the money that had been offered to me during the apartheid years. From being offered an open cheque by Ali Bacher, I was suddenly down to $US80,000; a lot of zeros had dropped off the end of the cheque.

★

Javed's phone-call offered a very attractive alternative, though. The figures I was quoted to coach in Brunei were considerably better than the offer to extend my career with six months of tough cricket in South Africa. I accepted the offer to travel to Brunei as the guest of Prince Hakeem and I met him and the other people involved. I must have made an impression in my first meeting, and the man who made the travel arrangements came to me and offered me a contract which ran for four years, with two weeks in Brunei and two weeks at home in Antigua each month. It was quite a tiring arrangement, but the fact that Prince Hakeem became more of a friend than an employer softened it considerably.

They looked after me superbly in Brunei and, of course, in the height of luxury. I had at my fingertips all the pleasant things in life: wonderful food, beautiful buildings and the roads full of expensive new cars. The Brunei folk were warm and friendly. In contrast to England, Australia and the West Indies where pubs and bars proliferate, Brunei is a non-drinking society. It was certainly different, not as high-profile as Singapore and Malaysia with their neon-lit bars. This place was much, much more conservative. But it was not oppressive in any way, and no one bothered me about drinking. I was allowed to bring in two bottles of spirits and I took advantage of that allowance to have a quiet drink in my own quarters when I fancied it.

The same restriction applied, of course, to the others who came out to join me. My old mate, Ian Botham, Jahangir Khan, the world number-one squash player, British Ryder Cup captain Bernard Gallagher, golfer Sam Torrance and the current England manager Kevin Keegan were just a few of the sports personalities who came to the country. Keegan was particularly popular for the work he did with underprivileged kids out there. We were involved in tennis, golf and football. The Prince was an all-round sportsman and fully into all sports, and I was happy to be working with someone like that. The people of Brunei tried hard to lift their sporting profile and compete in all the major events, especially the Asian Games. Prince Hakeem himself represented Brunei in the Olympics and qualified to compete in the Sydney Games in 2000 for he has a great deal of talent. While we became friends, one still has to respect his royal position. He is, after all, brother to the Sultan, then reckoned to be the richest man in the world.

While cricket has provided introductions to a great many stars from sport and show business, Brunei seemed to bring it all together in the most incredible way. I met several English rugby players, including Jeremy Guscott, Jason Leonard and Lawrence Dallaglio. I liked all three, but I was particularly impressed with the attitude of Dallaglio, who struck me as a truly competitive warrior. I could tell, simply by talking to him, what a strong character he was and what a good leader. What a shame it was that he allowed himself to run off at the mouth to a journalist who was posing as something else; that's the trouble with some sportsmen: when they have a drink, they can get carried away. I have to say that I really liked the Wasps captain and was also very impressed with his performances in the Rugby World Cup in 1999.

I also enjoyed a meal with the world's best Formula One driver, Michael Schumacher, the man who beat him for the world title, Mika Hakkinen, the Scot David Coulthard and the Irishman Eddie Irvine. That was an amazing dinner party. Celebrities from show business also flew in regularly. One night I was invited on stage by Sting and Bryan Adams when they were performing to celebrate Prince Hakeem's birthday; because of protocol I had to decline their invitation as I had to remember whose birthday it was. Maybe on another night I'd have joined them – which would have been an unusual spectacle. Others who came to Brunei were Michael Jackson, Tina Turner and Whitney Houston. I was quite impressed by Michael Jackson. After reading about his strange lifestyle I had totally the wrong impression of him. When I met him in Brunei he was engaged to sing at Prince Hakeem's birthday party. I expected him to be very fussy and finicky about everything he did, but he proved to be the most professional of them all. Everyone agreed that he was outstanding. I found him a very warm, friendly guy.

Among the many celebrities to visit Brunei, one of those I respected most was rock guitarist Eric Clapton, whom I had previously met through Ian and the Bunbury's charity cricket team. Since I first met him he's become a great friend of Antigua and has visited us many times. He has done marvellously well for the island, starting a drug rehabilitation clinic and pumping in lots of money, not just for our islanders but for anyone else he can help. The environment is perfect for what he is doing and it is an enormous boost for our country. I was there at Sotheby's when he auctioned off his guitars to raise money for the project, along with Beatle George Harrison, his son and percussionist Ray Cooper. They all seemed to be huge cricket fans; it was very flattering that they all knew who I was and what I used to do.

Mick Jagger, like Eric Clapton, also loves the game. I met him for the first time in Barbados and then again with Elton John in Australia when we played in the Perth Cup. Graham Fowler and I took him to the dressing-room and introduced him to all the players. Elton was also to visit Brunei.

Part of the appeal of meeting these musicians is that I have always been keen on music; I used to write poems for the local calypso singers, poems that relate to the locality and things that happen. I have never kept any but just passed them on to the singers – not that anyone would understand them if they read them. Everything is cut short, with the 't's and the 's's missing off most words. If nothing else, this has certainly extended my network of friends around the world and I still see Prince Hakeem on a regular basis when we are both in London. There seems to be a great synergy between show business and sport, and cricket has opened a good many stage doors for me.

Ian Botham and I both rose to the top of our sport at about the same time, a time when there was something of a shortage of characters, and we seemed to fill the gap. Even those who didn't watch or even like cricket would see us on television programmes; I was invited on to the 'Terry Wogan Show'. It all served to make us household names. Because we were on so often, it made people think they knew us personally. I was prepared to fall in with this because the positives far outweighed the negatives.

The most memorable of these television appearances for me was when I was on 'This is Your Life'. I genuinely didn't know anything about it until Eamonn Andrews tapped me on the shoulder and showed me the red book. I had been told by my English lawyer, Roy Kerslake, and close friend Peter McCoombe that I had to attend an awards ceremony at the Lord's Taverners Club, where Ian Botham would be presenting me with some award or other. Roy instructed me to wear something smart, and he picked me up himself on a Saturday morning and we headed to London. When we got there, the very first person I saw was Ian, and then Trevor McDonald, whom I knew fairly well. I started thinking, this must be quite a big event. It was not until Eamonn said, 'Vivian Richards, this is your life,' that I had any idea what was going on. They had to bleep out my reply – but they were ready for that, as Ian had warned them of my likely reaction. His prediction was word-perfect.

It was some day! Although my father was ill and couldn't travel, my mother flew in from Antigua, and my brother Mervyn came from the States along with my childhood friend, Terry Beckett, whom I grew up with at the Ovals and who was also now living in America. They all came, Miriam and my kids, my football team, while my father made up for his absence by saying hello via a satellite link. All the guys from Somerset were there, along with Nigel Starmer-Smith and celebrities from the world of movies and television. They even had the immigration officer who helped sort out my work permit at Heathrow airport. Here was a guy who could have finished my career in England before it started.

It left me with a lump in my throat the size of a cricket ball, but a little corner of my mind was thinking, 'I hope they don't have this person on or that person on who could tell a few secrets.' Although I had not had an inkling of what was going on behind my back, I had been suspicious that my wife, Miriam, was making various trips around the place and not telling me where she was going. I was asking, 'What are you doing this for? . . . What are you doing that for? . . . What's going on?' I did not have a clue.

★

Miriam and I are both very proud of our children. My daughter Matara who is now eighteen has been busy with her exams, gaining eight passes. The plan is for her to spend a year at college in Antigua before going to university in Canada. Having been born in Canada, she has the higher education facilities of that country available to her. She is heading for bigger and brighter things. Mali, my son, is two years younger than his sister and is seriously into tennis and cricket; he has already represented Antigua in his age group at both. My first interest is getting them fully involved in school because I have always felt that life is in stages and that school is an important experience if they are to go on to do other things. With the effort parents put in to give their children the best schooling possible, it is important that they fulfil their potential.

Mali has never been forced towards cricket, but it seems natural for him to head in that direction. Much of it is completely his own choice and when I was away he would watch my videos from an early age and totally enjoy watching his father and cricket, and it delighted me that he would ask questions about my cricketing life.

From his first school he started to take a real interest in the game, but tennis is also heavily on the agenda and he is representing the island at all levels. Gradually cricket has taken a greater hold on him and he has started to love the game more. Without pushing him, I have waited for him to make a decision and then I have given him direction.

I am not sure where his interest in tennis came from, but down the road from where we live is Vikings Tennis Club, where they give children lessons on Saturdays and they hold little tournaments. He then picked up the sport in school and then during summer holiday camps. At the moment, his interest in the two sports is fairly level. He is, however, developing well at cricket and at sixteen was captain of the Antigua Under-19 side. He understands the game and is keen to watch whenever touring sides come over, or if there is a big game he will go along to watch on his own. He has not traded on his father's name; he is determined to make it on his own. In fact he is left-handed, which makes him completely different from me and may also reduce the pressure, as I was a right-hander.

I do worry about the future and what it holds for them. It is a bit frightening to see so many kids graduating and then not having something solid to do with their qualifications, particularly after parents have sacrificed so much to give their children an education. Antigua is their homeland and one can only hope that there will be a system in place by the time they reach adulthood so that they can have access to a piece of the action at home rather than having to go abroad to seek their fortune, as so many of our bright youngsters have had to do.

As a parent, you can only give them guidance and the best sort of advice. Mali is still a long way from being a professional sportsman, and the first thing I would like to see him fulfil is his work at school, earning his certificates, which is something my father always wanted me to do. Once that is in place, then he can have a real go at sport, but with the knowledge that he has something to fall back on should he suffer a nasty injury or not come up to the mark.

I tell him about the simple things in cricket, the basics that are too often ignored: to watch the bowler's arm, to focus on what he has in his hand and play accordingly (the more you pay attention to the ball, the sooner you will be in position to play the right shot). When you see the ball, the seam, the flight and the direction it takes, then you can play the right stroke.

He is a solid batsman with a good defence, but he likes hitting the ball. He seems to be able to adapt to circumstances, but there is a long way to go and only time will tell if he does develop.

I have had a few matches since I quit the game so, along with staying in touch via satellite television, it meant for a while that I didn't really miss it. I have played some 'Legends' cricket with some other old timers, but I also played against New Zealand as a guest for the Caribbean Universities and scored 40-something, even though I had not picked up a bat in anger for a long time. The problem was the twos and threes; if you couldn't strike the ball over the boundary on a regular basis, running between wickets became very tiring. I heard that when the brilliant Scottish international footballer Dennis Law hung up his boots, he never kicked another ball. I couldn't give up my sport like that because I love playing cricket so much. The hand still gets twitchy when there is a bat nearby. I plan to carry on turning out for the Legends and in charity matches for as long as I can still enjoy a little knock. I kept only one bat, my boy Mali took the rest and he puts them to much better use. When I am coaching it will be necessary for me to hold the bat and give catches. I have my cricket pants, bigger sizes these days; my boots remain the same and my old gloves are handy in case I am called upon. Of course I kept my cap! I enjoy the fun side of the game now, especially the Legends games. I would dearly love to arrange a tournament in Antigua with England and the Australians so as to renew a few old acquaintances and swap a few rum punches instead of punches of the other sort. The trouble is, competition's in my blood and in the end I knew I needed another challenge. I wanted to test myself at coaching.

The Commonwealth Games in 1998 gave me my chance. It was a wonderful opportunity for Antigua and for myself to see what we could achieve in a one-off tournament. In the past our small island had put out top players for the West Indies, but there was scarcely ever a chance for them to come together and play for Antigua and Barbuda. This time they did, and we turned out a team that featured test stars the likes of Richie Richardson, Curtly Ambrose, Kenneth Benjamin and Winston Benjamin, as well as a group of young players who had shone at Under-21 level. Getting them all on the field together had never happened before and it gave us a great feeling of identity. The atmosphere was superb among all the competing teams, with cricket being the focal point of the old Commonwealth. Being around the guys again with the Antigua team and passing on what I knew gave me a terrific buzz. Simple things like travelling on the team coach, booking a wake-up call, the discipline of not being late for breakfast or nets, all stirred up the juices and had me shedding the years. It quickly becomes a part of you and I discovered that I had actually missed it. It was just like old times.

It was a shame that England were not there, and an even greater sadness that the event won't be taking place in Manchester, England, the home of the Commonwealth and the home of cricket.

I enjoyed going to the Commonwealth Games as coach of the
Antigua team and I realized I was hungry for my sport again. That
was stoked up when I worked for the BBC during the 1999 World
Cup in England, particularly when I was asked to help out with
the coaching when Malcolm Marshall fell seriously ill. Suddenly
my name was being mentioned in terms of the West Indies again,
but Malcolm was a good friend and the circumstances broke my
heart. My chance with the West Indies team came more quickly
than anyone had expected and the reason for it shook me up badly,
because Malcolm Marshall was someone I had so much respect for.
Malcolm, to me, was so strong, mentally and physically.

With Malcolm being younger than me, his illness gave me a
different view of life and a realization that I needed to be in touch
with God a little more because it showed me that we can have
everything today and lose it all tomorrow. It was one of the worst
moments of my life when I heard the news in Southampton, where
New Zealand were playing the West Indies. At the time I first
heard of his illness I was having a drink and relaxing happily in the
bar of the hotel with some friends from Antigua. The telephone
rang and Mr Joseph, the Vice-President of the West Indies Board,
gave me the news. I couldn't sleep that night. I lay there in bed,
remembering him when he was running up, the things he used to
do with the ball, and then of him lying on a hospital bed. I knew
then that it was serious.

It was very sad when my old friend passed away. I had known
him for many years and he was a man who had given me so much
help and support in what he had contributed to West Indies cricket,
on and off the field. It was pretty hard to take because we had lived
like a family for so many years, sharing hotel rooms, team buses
and so many different things. It was a team with a strong camaraderie
and the bond between Malcolm and myself was as strong as any
and he was a big help to me when I was captain. At forty-one he
was taken away terribly early. It was a horrible period for anyone
who was associated with him, knowing what he meant at Hampshire, in South Africa where he also played club cricket, for the
West Indies and in world cricket generally. He was a tremendous

individual who had so much to offer in terms of his knowledge of the game. It was a great pity that he was unable to fulfil his coaching dreams. He had so much to give and had only just begun to make inroads.

It was so sad to lose not only Malcolm but also Sylvester Clarke and Sir Conrad Hunte in such a short time. It makes it hard to take when you have been on a cricket field with players and have shared so much; but nothing surprises when you see so much suffering around the world. Death always has the final say. It happens.

Of course, I'd rather it had come about in any other way, but I had no hesitation at all in answering the call from my country. I have to feel a thing to really want to do it and, once I feel it, I give it my everything. I wanted to be involved. I was, of course, under contract to work with the BBC, but they knew that my country always comes first. The BBC were very good, they eased me out; I hoped this was a reward for being professional with them. I had enjoyed my time behind the mike; it brought me back close to the game at the top level. It is amazing the things that go through your mind while you sit there, watching, and the memories it evokes. It was great to meet up with some of the people I had played against who were working for other broadcasting companies or newspapers. It was just like old times – but with a bit of extra weight involved!

It is amazing, the doors that were opened to me simply because I could hit a cricket ball hard, not just the fame and the glory but all the other things that go with it. You don't think or even dream of these things when you are a youngster wanting to be a cricketer. Not having been to university or college, my diplomas are from the University of Life. There is no greater feeling than when you go to a place like South Africa and you see the esteem in which you are held because of the decisions you made when they were struggling for their own identity. Someone said to me recently that there are so many honours and letters after my name that there wasn't a big enough piece of paper to put them all down.

And not just in the accepted cricket-playing countries of the world. I was recently honoured in America, where the Mayor of

Los Angeles bestowed on me the freedom of the city. A huge number of guests attended, and I believe I am still dreaming and I don't know when reality will hit me. I am overwhelmed, grateful and thankful to the people who have had the thought of doing these things, not solely for me but for my sport and my country.

Every honour is equally important to me. I would never categorize them or put them in order. I embrace all of them equally, from the doctorate from Exeter University to the little country cricket club who award me a club tie. Exeter University was an experience to remember, not least of all wearing a mortar board and throwing it in the air at the end of proceedings. I could understand why they did so with such gusto: it was relief that it was all over. It was a long ceremony and I dozed off a bit. I dreamt I was watching Chris Tavare bat – that was how slow it was. I had to sit at the front with all the big boys, and there I was thinking, when is this going to be finished? There were more than 300 graduating, plus the speeches from all the professors. I was grateful that I didn't have to make a speech myself. The best part of it was to mix with all the students who had really earned the letters after their names – unlike me – plus, of course, the tea and cucumber sandwiches. Somerset gave me the day off and I invited a few friends to watch the ceremony. Strange but, on reflection, it was from that moment that things started to go wrong at the county. Perhaps my getting the honour upset one or two people, or perhaps I invited the wrong people to watch.

I was also proud to receive the Order of the British Empire in Antigua when the Governor-General did the duties of the Queen in Government House. That was good news, as was the knighthood I received on 7 September 1999. The knighthood surprised me big time. I had heard a little word here and there, but no one could confirm it until I was finally invited to Government House and had a meeting to discuss the possibility of receiving the honour and the protocol involved. I have always looked on myself as being a rebel and now suddenly, it seems, I am part of the establishment. It won't change me. I am still the sportsman who is reasonably fair and enjoys doing the things he does. I must admit it was pretty satisfying and fulfilling to be honoured in such a way, and I didn't hesitate in accepting. I am proud and happy to accept whatever my country chooses to bestow on me.

There are not many who have been honoured in such a way: a couple of governors, the late President, Sir Vere Bird, and myself. It is only a handful, presented by the Antiguan government and rubber-stamped by London under the new format. Our ruling Labour Government sent the recommendations to the Governor-General Sir James Carlisle, who passed them on to the crown for the Queen's approval. It is an honour to join Sir Garfield Sobers, Sir Clyde Walcott and Sir Everton Weekes, Lord Learie Constantine and Sir Frank Worrell.

Being named the *Wisden* 'Player of our Time' was an unexpected and highly satisfying award, as it was my peers who voted for it. My vote went to Ian Botham, not because he is my best friend but for what he did to turn English cricket around and the satisfaction his success gave to so many people.

I was also appointed an ambassador-at-large by our Foreign Office, along with Richie Richardson, perhaps for services to cricket and maybe for the commercial benefits we have brought to the country through increased exposure. This distinction came to me through my lawyer, Harold Lovell, and it was quite nice in a sense because of the protocol that goes with a special passport – not that I have used it on a regular basis. Because of the status of the passport, I am immune from certain regulations in my country. One of the tangible benefits when I am travelling is that there are special channels at immigration, which means that I am not hassled a lot at Customs. That is useful when you step off a long flight, when you are tired or if you are making a connection from Gatwick to Heathrow on the way to Brunei. It also means invitations to official functions, which opens doors and widens the contacts. There is even special car parking at airports!

My heritage has been important to me and I never forget that, first and foremost, I am Antiguan and Barbudan. When I see what cricket has done for the unity of the islands I am happy to have been part of that and representing the West Indies. No government has ever been able to establish that same conjunction of suffering agony and joy together. Nothing can touch that force. Cricket is still the only thing that brings everyone together. Caricom have done a good job in terms of trade in the Caribbean, but we still let ourselves down in many areas because of internal jealousies in our politics. This is why it is so important for the West Indies to do well in cricket.

When I played, it was sufficient to earn enough to pay for my house and look after my family. It was better than working from nine to five; I was doing something I thoroughly enjoyed and was being paid for it. It was not the best pay for a sportsman, but it was more than if I had been a coach or had worked in government. I am fulfilled. There are not many people who have the opportunity of representing their country and being held in such high esteem. All through my cricket it has given me a wider perspective on life; it has opened up many other doors for me. I wore my pride on my sleeve for everyone to see, and maybe in some quarters I was even hated for the intensity I brought to the game. I am proud to have represented my country, and to have a pay cheque at the end of it was a bonus.

As for myself, I have no problems. I am comfortable with myself, with what I have done in the past and with what I would like to do in the future. I am prepared to stand up and be counted, and whoever wants to come with me will be welcomed; if they don't follow me, it won't change my views. God gave me mental and physical strength and consequently I do not fear any individual, no matter how strong they may think they are. I do not walk the middle ground, I am either with you or against you. I go for it or I don't. That is how I played my cricket and that is how I live my life.

14. Burning Ambition

It was a strange feeling when I went back into a West Indies dressing-room for business again. Things had changed; here was a side who were underachieving, while my experiences were all about winning, or at least never losing a series as captain. But it was nice to be in the place again. Considering the situation, the atmosphere in the dressing-room was better than I had expected. It was jovial and happy – though, I felt, sometimes a little too happy in defeat. That is something I could never understand. Losing made me very unhappy. It is good, however, to relax during the game, both on and off the field. The important thing is to work towards consistency.

I felt that the players welcomed me, and the respect they showed me was rewarding. Of course I knew something about everyone and their reputations, while there were some familiar old faces like those of Curtly Ambrose, Courtney Walsh, Brian Lara whom I had come to know to some degree, Keith Arthurton and Stuart Williams. It was good to meet up with old friends and to be introduced to new ones.

I felt then that I had something new to offer. I wanted to try and get into the individuals' minds in order to dispel the ideas planted by critics that West Indian cricketers did not have a cricketing talent any more. I felt that, if I was going to do the job, I would do it in the same way I did the captaincy: my way, not like the Australians, the English or the South Africans. I still feel that, given time, I can do it in my own way and make them click, bring out that natural West Indian ability and athleticism and let the natural ability shine through. I want my natural instinct to take over, not to follow some set pattern decided years ago in England. I want to put on my thinking cap, draw on my experiences and bring in my own ideas.

When I was first told that there was a possibility of my being involved in West Indies cricket again, I was delighted. The problem was that Malcolm Marshall was still involved and, because of our friendship and my respect for him, the one person I did not want to upset was Malcolm. When they said I could play a part in the motivational side, he came to me and we sat and talked about how I could be involved. At the time he was having his own problems with the board, but he still found time to discuss my situation with me and I held him in high esteem for that. We came to some sort of conclusion about our respective roles, deciding that we would work together rather than me replacing him.

When the idea of my working with Malcolm was first discussed, words were coming back to me from certain board members that Clive Lloyd couldn't see how the arrangement would work and that he appeared to dismiss it. After all we'd been through together while he was captain of West Indies I felt belittled and found it difficult to understand why Clive would react like this and show such a lack of faith in me. That no one had ever said anything to my face made it even harder to take. I couldn't believe it, but it still placed an element of doubt in my mind which was hard to dispel. There are few things over the years that have upset me as much as the thought that Clive could have lobbied against my working with him and the team, particularly as I know that the success of West Indies cricket has always been his top priority.

In New Zealand he told me how much he thought I was contributing and that when he wrote his report he would give me his recommendation. Sadly, my uncertainty remained. I felt unsure about where I stood, and it made me very apprehensive, but I tried to rise above my concerns. I was there to do a professional job for the sake of West Indies cricket. I wouldn't let anything stand in my way and refused to get involved in conflicts, real or imagined. There has been too much of that over the years and it does our game no good. Clive announced halfway through the tour to New Zealand that he was to quit at the end of it. It hurt me to see at first hand the problems we faced as we comprehensively lost both the two-match test series and the one-day tournament.

But it was not just Clive. Too many of the young coaches have tried to put me down because they had their own designs on the job. They may know about coaching, but what I find amusing is that as players some of them used to run away from fast bowling and had hearts the size of peanuts. They claimed they have been around for a long time compared to my brief experience as a coach and that they should be offered the job as second string to the manager and in control of the captain.

That is one of the reasons why I became involved. I have seen these people and what they have done with the younger players who have not had their problems solved. I am prepared here and now to overcome the hypocrites and rise above those people who have their own interests at heart rather than those of the West Indies. I am an individual who is ready to put himself forward to help in whatever capacity, physically or morally, to do whatever needs to be done.

There are some quite simple things that need to be done to make our players better individuals and consequently better cricketers. First and foremost there has to be discipline, even in small matters, like turning up on time for meals and for the bus, and paying attention at team meetings. This is a team sport and you cannot hope for results unless everyone is pulling in the same direction and helping one another. I am one of those coaches who invent routines as we go along rather than drowning in set practices. There are always options open to keep players' minds alert and interested.

Things like catching practice I do a little differently from other people. I don't have everyone standing around in a circle. I just tell them, now we are having catching practice; from that moment on, wherever they are or whatever they are doing, they might suddenly get a catch. This works on their sharpness as well as their catching. By the time they get out on to the field, instead of playing around or chattering, they are ready for action. If anyone turns his back on me, he is risking injury. Even if we are talking, he may suddenly find that I have hurled the ball at him. He must be alert. It is no use saying 'I am not ready.' I need to get that instantaneous reaction.

What else do I have to offer as a coach? There is my experience, to begin with; I have been there and done it. There is hardly a situation they will go through that I haven't experienced already, not just the downs that they are suffering now, but the ups that are bound to come with hard work and application. I would try to instil pride into them, not solely individual pride and pride for their country but also pride in performance. We give our wickets away too easily for my peace of mind. It should always be your philosophy to make the opposition work hard for your wicket and not give them a soft dismissal. I believe that we should do the things we are strong at, enhancing the unorthodox, and then work even harder at the things we are weak at.

There is also a hell of a lot of work to do on confidence if the West Indies are to recover their lost pride. That was patently obvious to me during our demoralizing tour of New Zealand when all the good work we had done vanished in a puff of smoke once the two-test series began. Even the incoming batsman's walk to the crease is lacking something when the body language says to the opposition that he doesn't really fancy the battle ahead. Sometimes you have to show a little macho spirit, your manliness. Show them who is in charge, even when the odds are stacked against you and although it is eleven against two out there in the middle. If the body language or the talk between the batsmen in the middle is wrong, it can only encourage the bowler and the fielders. I believe that there is still an abundance of talent in the West Indies but it has to be developed, and the batsmen shouldn't think their job is done when they have passed 50 or even 100. It is from there that you go on to prove your quality as a test player.

It is a similar story with fielding. In the past the West Indies have been an example to the rest of the world, but we have fallen back, which suggests that we haven't been working at it properly. If we are not getting results, there must be something wrong, and the first thing to go for is hard work. It may sound simple but, if players are prepared to work hard and enjoy the practice sessions, we will enjoy playing; but if we are going to think, 'Oh no, practice again', that attitude will be transferred to the match.

It is important to create intensity, not just when you are in the middle but also when you are practising. These are just some of the things that I can see, and I am sure that I can use my experience and my motivational skills, if I am allowed to, to make the improvements needed. I cannot change everything overnight, because of what's already in place, but, given time, it can happen.

Coaching is something I honestly never thought I could go into. Me, who always scorned coaching, becoming a coach! It is a case of the poacher turned gamekeeper. But to be able to help someone who has lost his confidence or someone you can see could be a better player with a bit of help is very satisfying, and to do it for your country is something special.

I was very disappointed when I was overlooked as coach for the 2000 tour of England.

As for the selectors, there are still some of them around who are working to their own agenda and until we get rid of some of the board and some of the committee members we are not going to end the slump we are in now. Results indicate that something is drastically wrong but the selectors are not doing enough to put it right. There are some very, very good players, but one half are performing and the other half are not; you cannot expect the same people to do it over and over again. It is a team sport and everyone must contribute.

It doesn't help, either, when a professional sportsman puts in so many hours and receives so little financial return. If there is a complaint, however, it should be discussed and negotiated in private and not aired in public on the other side of the Atlantic, as happened before the abortive tour of South Africa. When the West Indies started rowing before the South African tour, it hurt me personally very badly. I hated to see us washing our dirty linen in public; it was a mockery. The entire cricket world was watching us and laughing at us. I felt that we did not need this. It was not only an insult to our history but also to the country we were about to visit. Here we had the first black South African president in Nelson Mandela and, because of our identity and our colour, we were seen as mentors to the young black Africans who may have felt that they were not being given a chance in the largely white South African cricketing fraternity. We were seen as the cricketing nation to give them a lift, in a fashion similar to Brazil's influence in soccer. We owed that to the South African people. They had obviously heard of the pre-eminence of the West Indies in the past, but there was no way we were going to represent that with a team that included people who were not able to mentally negotiate and participate. It was too heavy a burden for the others to carry.

The team manager, Clive Lloyd, had some experience of handling these affairs but both sides chose to ignore his view that discussions should have taken place in South Africa rather than in England. If the manager is ignored from the start, then the entire tour is doomed before it begins. It was never going to be a happy tour, and the results proved that the players' minds were not where they should have been. It did a lot of damage to our pride and reputation, not just to lose 5–0 but to lose without putting up a fight. It was total carnage, something we will not forget for a long, long time.

Of course, the money was an issue, but it should have been sorted out before the tour was under way, and neither the players nor the board came out of the shambles with any credit. We have had problems with the board over wages in the past, but it was never allowed to escalate or become public debate, with meetings at airport hotels. I have some sympathy with the players, having had my own problems with the board, and I understand that it was probably a whole back-log of issues, not just the finances, which finally brought the circus to town. Please God nothing like that ever happens again. Let us hope we learnt from our public disgrace.

When I was appointed coach for the West Indies tour to New Zealand, I was delighted to have the opportunity to be working with Brian Lara again. Brian probably felt I had been a bit harsh with him when he was first making his way into the team. There were many who thought he should have been in the team a lot earlier, but I did not select him as often as he would have liked because I was one of those captains who were very faithful to their players, the players who had helped to take us places and with whom we were still winning. It was in my thoughts to bring him into the team every now and again, include him in the squad and gradually work him in, but there were many others who wanted to rush him. It wasn't that he was not ready, but he needed to see how we operated, to see what was going on within the squad and to witness the discipline and other aspects of the team.

A lot happened to Brian very fast and he learnt some hard lessons. I don't know the circumstances as I wasn't there but, obviously, if he took a mobile phone on to the field, clearly that was wrong. Admittedly, over the years I have seen players run off the field to take calls, but this is one step further on; he must have known that it was not cricket and not professional. I tried to be a father figure to him because I could see a wonderful talent in him and I felt that after I retired he could be the one to take over and help keep West Indies cricket at the top. I believed that as captain I had to play my part in laying out the discipline and certain guidelines, and to this end I used to invite him to join me in my car when we were touring England and talk to him about the responsibilities, passing on my own experiences. I often let him drive and, being young and vibrant, he would wait until he thought I was asleep and then put his foot on the accelerator to go faster. I would open one eye when I felt the surge of speed and say, 'Hey, man, you want the authorities to put me in prison?' Those early days clearly made an impression on him, for Brian was very supportive when he became captain, telling the board that he wanted me to work with him in some capacity.

I was reminded of all this when we travelled to New Zealand. When we were driving to the nets, he walked to the back of the bus to talk to the younger players and I heard him tell them how aware I was of the young players' problems and of the advice I had passed on to him. He also told them how he would be fidgeting while watching the cricket, awaiting his turn to bat. Someone might come up and suggest that he went with them to do this or that; and I would turn to him and say, 'Where you going, man? Just sit your backside down there.'

There was another incident when we were on our way to a game in Kent and he told me that he could bowl leg-breaks and that he would like the opportunity to show me what he could do in a match with three or four overs. When we were out on the field he kept looking at me with those big, pleading eyes until I eventually threw him the ball and let him bowl, and bowl, and bowl, until he looked at me pleadingly again and this time he said, 'Cappy, I am getting a little tired.'

I looked at him and said, 'You asked me to bowl – so bowl!'

It was good fun. I liked him, but I felt that sometimes he could be led the wrong way and that it was my duty as captain to help him. We would talk for hours during those car rides and I would tell him about the facts of the sporting life, explaining that you could have everything today and it could all be gone by tomorrow. He was clearly going to be one of the game's big earners, and I explained how he should channel his earnings and put the money to the best use.

I was pleased when I heard Brian relating these stories to the youngsters, telling them that they should have been around when I was captain, mimicking my voice and the expressions I had used all those years ago to point the new breed in the right direction.

At one stage I was afraid that he had lost his way a little, but he has shown the character to overcome any problems he has had. Working with him as the coach, I have been seriously impressed. We have a good rapport. I like his attitude and he is seriously concerned about the future of West Indies cricket. He desperately wanted to turn things around as captain. I have been impressed by his work ethic and his knowledge. People may think because of his comparative lack of success that he is wanting in this department, but that is not true. He is very willing to learn and in New Zealand we had a dialogue every day during which he was totally responsive.

The others also responded and despite the reverses on the field when our batting collapsed twice, I felt that a good working relationship could solve most of the problems without the coach becoming totally commanding and a bully. I tried to gradually ease my way through and add my own little ideas rather than take away the things they had learnt from Malcolm Marshall. Malcolm was a wonderful individual with lots of knowledge, but sadly he did not live long enough to fulfil the things he wanted to do. He had a wonderful cricketing brain, and I wanted to help them realize some of the things he had taught them and to drill into them what Malcolm would have loved. If my opportunity comes again I will dedicate my work to Malcolm and hope to fulfil some of his ambitions for the team.

I have learnt as an individual that in the past I may have been too harsh because of this competitive attitude I have which causes my whole character to change. With growing experience and the maturity I've gained since I quit playing I hoped that I could have helped them achieve their goals with a smile on my face instead of a scowl. If there are times when I need to be hard or serious, that is when the professionalism will show and I will not shirk from it. The years I had out of the game probably did me a lot of good.

One of the major problems the current team have is that they keep hearing that their team is no good compared with the teams of the past; that can have a negative effect on the players when it is constantly being rammed down their throats. We don't want to have to play the role of reliving the past; we must work with what we have now to make it the best it can be. I am looking forward in the hope that we can achieve the goals of today and tomorrow, not those of yesterday. What we achieved in the past should not be forgotten, but it should be an inspiration not a yardstick. I tried to eradicate that and let the guys know that they have some responsibilities going into the new century and that, among us all, we must make of it what we can.

I gained a lot of satisfaction from the job. It was great to be around the guys again. After my seven years out of the game I came back fresh and, having looked at it from the outside, it has been a good place to be. When you are in the middle of it you are never quite sure, especially when you have just retired. I added my own little input and my own ideas, putting in a few personal factors in order to try and help them enjoy what they were doing and make

them smile, rather than waking up with a shudder at the prospect
of what lay ahead.

I have rested my body and my mind since my retirement from
professional cricket and now, having recharged the batteries, I am
ready to throw my hat in the ring, both in cricket and in politics
– if the two can be separated in the West Indies. Being selected as
coach to travel to New Zealand at the turn of the millennium was
just the first step in my ambitions and make no mistake, I am as
fiercely ambitious as a person as I was as a cricketer. Cricket, as
always, will come first and I desperately want to see the West Indies
restored to their proper place in the world game, but this time
with a structure beneath to bring on the young talent and ensure
continuity.

This drive could be helped in other ways. I would also love to
see a combined West Indies football team. You only have to look
at the input from the Caribbean all around the world in the sport
to see what sort of team we could send out. I don't believe that
Trinidad, Jamaica, Barbados and all the other islands can survive
alone in this. The World Cup is getting bigger and tougher and,
while Jamaica did well in reaching the World Cup finals in France,
we are not going to do it on a regular basis if our resources
continue to be split. Why not have a Caribbean team? Imagine if
the governments and everyone from the region were all involved
so that it becomes totally professional, with the sole aim for the
team of qualifying for the World Cup and the Americas Cup.
Trinidad and Tobago have made a start by forming the Caribbean's
first professional league, marketing and promoting it properly and
even taking games around the other islands. It can work, and I
believe that we have got to work together. The players would love
it but the problem would be the administration because everyone
would want to be chief or king, they would want the power; and
they will break apart in their fight to attain it. It would not be a
pretty sight. The footballers would work together – but would the
officials? In cricket, all too often we have seen officials protecting
their status and basing too many of their decisions on whichever
island they are from. Initially there was reluctance to give me the

West Indies captaincy because I was the little boy from Antigua. Let's stop this partiality for certain islands like Barbados and Trinidad and think instead of the West Indies in its entirety.

Now that we have people like the great manager Bobby Robson and Graham Kelly, ex-Chief Executive of the English FA, taking an active interest in our region, it can only increase our potential and our chances. There is no better organized league in the world than the Premiership in England, and we can learn from them. Manchester United striker Dwight Yorke sets a great example, and I believe there are a lot more like him out here in the Caribbean. I was pleased to hear Dwight say in an interview that he believed top players could be found over here. They could be tigers, given the backing. Sadly, as with cricket, there is a lack of facilities in the region. Trinidad has good facilities; Odyssey International in St Lucia has started to develop a facility similar to the cricket centre in Antigua, and St Kitts has initiated an international tournament. All this can only help, and anything that brings the islands closer together and helps build confidence and pride in the region can only be a good thing.

While sport is one way of achieving this, there also needs to be a broader political approach, and I'm becoming serious about going into politics. If I am convinced that I have the backing of the people of Antigua and Barbuda, I shall be ready to serve them in whatever capacity they deem suitable. I am ready to go as far as they want in order to help the people. I love this country of Antigua and Barbuda passionately. Just being a local and having participated in a high-profile sport with which people of the region are in touch means that what I have achieved is well documented. It places me in a privileged position in our society and it is a position I will not misuse or abuse, the way so many have done.

I don't believe one's political views should ever stop one from making an input, but you have to have some party affiliation if you are going to try to make radical changes. The problem is that in a small island community such as ours, if you have an opinion about the way things are run, someone is always ready to try and get back at you because of what you have said or written in the past. That in itself is out of time and belongs in the past. When someone is persecuted because of their political views, it only increases division.

The native people should be reaping some of the rewards that tourism and other businesses have brought to the island, and sadly this is not the case. I have great concerns about that and over exactly where we are going in the future. I went to my daughter's graduation where there were lots of intelligent kids leaving school, but what were the plans for their future? There didn't seem to be much in place for them.

Some of us seem to have lost sight of the values that are the foundation of our country, while others have neglected their love for the country in the name of greed. There are intelligent people who should know when wrong is wrong, but, maybe because they are filling their own pockets and doing well personally, they don't see the problems in front of them. These are the people who are seriously dangerous and the ones who will run Antigua into the ground if we let them.

Tourism is now far and away our biggest dollar-earner but what has troubled me is: where are those dollars going, into whose pockets? I look at some of the people who are advising in this region, notably in the area of the construction of hotels, golf courses and luxury housing, which are being built without using local labour. Contractors and workers are being brought in ahead of Antiguans.

I worry about my country and its future and I am concerned that certain paths I want to walk on or roads I want to drive on won't be available to me or to others in the not-too-distant future. Antigua's future should belong to the people of Antigua. The 'buddy' system seems rife and a nice tight family has been formed. Because of this clique, investors can come to Antigua, spend their money, purchase the best property and the best land and gradually swallow up the country. It does seem that a handful of people are gaining too much of a stranglehold, which isn't good news. A small country like Antigua would benefit much more from a greater variety of investment, not solely in tourism and the building of hotels. But it seems that there are those who have friends in influential positions who have themselves become very powerful and have created their own little empire, which cannot be good for the rest of us. I believe investment can be made without selling your soul. But, from what I have observed, in future the land will be exchanged between an elite group who have the money to do it, taking it out of the reach of the hard-working individual. That is dangerous.

I have a lot of concerns for this country, and seriously so. We can only hope that we come to our senses collectively; more Antiguans and Barbudans need to play an active role in local politics. The late Papa Bird, the father of our country, held the view that, when you give your land away and it is wasted, then you become nothing. We become sitting ducks and we are heading for those swamps. I have been asked on numerous occasions to become involved. I have sat and talked about it seriously and collectively, but when I am ready to go I don't want people around who say 'Yes' today and 'No' tomorrow. This is a cause I want to champion. We must get Antigua back on track and spread the wealth more widely rather than treating it as an exclusive catalogue from which only a few can order. We want every Antiguan to have access and to know what is going on. Our people need inspiration, and that I can give to them if and when I am called on.

I sense that people are ready for change. They are concerned about the future and for Antigua and Barbuda. I share their concerns and I'm ready to do whatever I can. If the chance arises to be part of a system which can run things properly, then I would like to be part of it. I like to think that I am pretty straightforward and down to earth. As in my cricket, I would like to bring some discipline to the way the system is run. Without discipline everything falls down, whether in sport or politics. I believe I can help because of my no-nonsense approach and my refusal to settle for second best. By making sure I have the right people with me, the country can be run properly and honestly for a long time. I want to work with a team that always puts the country first and that wants to put things back into Antigua and Barbuda. Our people need to have the confidence that they will be given the opportunity to achieve whatever they want. Some of us have been given the chance, but others have not been so lucky.

As a cricketer I was always a team player and never knowingly sought personal glory. I have probably become a little selfish over recent years, notably in my personal life. Part of that is because, as your profile increases, it becomes harder to know whom you can trust. But dealing with people on a collective basis, the voting population, things are different. There can be no excuses. This means, for me, that you must always do the correct and proper thing. I am now in Antigua far more than I ever was since I was a very young man. I walk around and see our people no longer holding their heads up high; it is as though they are tiptoeing in their own country because of their low level of confidence and lack of self-esteem. Witnessing this fuels my appetite for getting involved. What is really needed is the backing. Throughout my life, both on and off the cricket field, I have been a proud Antiguan first and foremost. If the people feel that Viv Richards can do a job, they must back me, safe in the knowledge that I will back them in return. I will always fight on their behalf in any way I can.

Appendix: Career Statistics

Test Career Breakdown

Date	Opposition	Venue	Result	Batting 1st Inns	Batting 2nd Inns	Bowling 1st Inns	Bowling 2nd Inns
1974							
22 Nov	India	Bangalore	West Indies beat India by 267 Runs	4	3	0	0
11 Dec	India	Delhi	West Indies beat India by an innings & 17 Runs	192*	–	0	0
27 Dec	India	Calcutta	India beat West Indies by 85 Runs	15	47	0	0
1975							
11 Jan	India	Madras	India beat West Indies by 100 Runs	50	2	0	0
23 Jan	India	Bombay	West Indies beat India by 201 Runs	1	39*	0-10	0
15 Feb	Pakistan	Lahore	West Indies vs Pakistan – No Result	7	0	0	0
01 Mar	Pakistan	Karachi	West Indies vs Pakistan – No Result	10	–	0	1-17
28 Nov	Australia	Brisbane	Australia beat West Indies by 8 Wickets	0	12	0	0
12 Dec	Australia	Perth	West Indies beat Australia by an innings & 87 Runs	12	–	0	0
26 Dec	Australia	Melbourne	Australia beat West Indies by 8 Wickets	41	36	0-2	0
1976							
03 Jan	Australia	Sydney	Australia beat West Indies by 7 Wickets	44	2	0	0-4
23 Jan	Australia	Adelaide	Australia beat West Indies by 190 Runs	30	101	0	0
31 Jan	Australia	Melbourne	Australia beat West Indies by 165 Runs	50	98	0	0-38
10 Mar	India	Bridgetown	West Indies beat India by an innings & 97 Runs	142	–	0	0
24 Mar	India	Port of Spain	West Indies vs India – No Result	130	20	0-17	0
07 Apr	India	Port of Spain	India beat West Indies by 6 Wickets	177	23	0	0
21 Apr	India	Kingston	West Indies beat India by 10 Wickets	64	–	0	0

Date	Opposition	Venue	Result	Batting 1st Inns	Batting 2nd Inns	Bowling 1st Inns	Bowling 2nd Inns
1976 cont.							
03 June	England	Trent Bridge	West Indies vs England – No Result	232	63	0-8	0-7
08 July	England	Old Trafford	West Indies beat England by 425 Runs	4	135	0	0
22 July	England	Headingley	West Indies beat England by 55 Runs	66	38	0	0
12 Aug	England	The Oval	West Indies beat England by 231 Runs	291	–	0-30	1-11
1977							
18 Feb	Pakistan	Bridgetown	West Indies vs Pakistan – No Result	32	92	0-3	0-16
04 Mar	Pakistan	Port of Spain	West Indies beat Pakistan by 6 Wickets	4	30	0	0-27
18 Mar	Pakistan	Georgetown	West Indies vs Pakistan – No Result	50	–	0	0-11
01 Apr	Pakistan	Port of Spain	Pakistan beat West Indies by 266 Runs	4	33	2-34	0
15 Apr	Pakistan	Kingston	West Indies beat Pakistan by 140 Runs	5	7	0	0
1978							
03 Mar	Australia	Port of Spain	West Indies beat Australia by an innings & 106 Runs	39	–	0	0
17 Mar	Australia	Bridgetown	West Indies beat Australia by 9 Wickets	23	–	0	0
1979							
01 Dec	Australia	Brisbane	West Indies vs Australia – No Result	140	–	0	0
29 Dec	Australia	Melbourne	West Indies beat Australia by 10 Wickets	96	–	0	0
1980							
26 Jan	Australia	Adelaide	West Indies beat Australia by 408 Runs	76	74	0-7	0
05 June	England	Trent Bridge	West Indies beat England by 2 Wickets	64	48	0-9	0

| | | | | Batting | | Bowling | |
Date	Opposition	Venue	Result	1st Inns	2nd Inns	1st Inns	2nd Inns
1980 cont.							
19 June	England	Lord's	West Indies vs England – No Result	145	—	0-24	0-1
10 July	England	Old Trafford	West Indies vs England – No Result	65	—	0	0-31
24 July	England	The Oval	West Indies vs England – No Result	26	—	0-5	0-15
07 Aug	England	Headingley	West Indies vs England – No Result	31	—	0	0-0
24 Nov	Pakistan	Lahore	West Indies vs Pakistan – No Result	75	—	1-31	2-20
08 Dec	Pakistan	Faisalabad	West Indies beat Pakistan by 156 Runs	72	67	1-0	0
22 Dec	Pakistan	Karachi	West Indies vs Pakistan – No Result	18	—	0	0-10
30 Dec	Pakistan	Multan	West Indies vs Pakistan – No Result	120*	12	0	0
1981							
13 Feb	England	Port of Spain	West Indies beat England by an innings & 79 Runs	29	—	0-16	1-9
13 Mar	England	Bridgetown	West Indies beat England by 298 Runs	0	182*	0	2-24
27 Mar	England	St John's	West Indies vs England – No Result	114	—	0-26	1-54
10 Apr	England	Kingston	West Indies vs England – No Result	15	—	0-29	1-48
26 Dec	Australia	Melbourne	Australia beat West Indies by 58 Runs	2	0	0	0-17
1982							
02 Jan	Australia	Sydney	West Indies vs Australia – No Result	44	22	0-21	0-33
30 Jan	Australia	Adelaide	West Indies beat Australia by 5 Wickets	42	50	0	0-38
1983							
23 Feb	India	Kingston	West Indies beat India by 4 Wickets	29	61	0-0	0
11 Mar	India	Port of Spain	West Indies vs India – No Result	1	—	0	1-14

Date	Opposition	Venue	Result	Batting 1st Inns	Batting 2nd Inns	Bowling 1st Inns	Bowling 2nd Inns
1983 *cont.*							
31 Mar	India	Georgetown	West Indies vs India – No Result	109	–	0-24	0
15 Apr	India	Bridgetown	West Indies beat India by 10 Wickets	80	–	0	0
28 Apr	India	St John's	West Indies vs India – No Result	2	–	0-13	0-36
21 Oct	India	Kanpur	West Indies beat India by an innings & 83 Runs	24	–	0	0
29 Oct	India	Delhi	West Indies vs India – No Result	67	22	0-8	0
12 Nov	India	Ahmedabad	West Indies beat India by 138 Runs	8	20	0	0
24 Nov	India	Bombay	West Indies vs India – No Result	120	4	0	0
10 Dec	India	Calcutta	West Indies beat India by an innings & 46 Runs	9	–	0	0
24 Dec	India	Madras	West Indies vs India – No Result	32	–	0	0
1984							
02 Mar	Australia	Georgetown	West Indies vs Australia – No Result	8	–	0-3	0-8
16 Mar	Australia	Port of Spain	West Indies vs Australia – No Result	76	–	1-15	2-65
30 Mar	Australia	Bridgetown	West Indies beat Australia by 10 Wickets	6	–	0	0
07 Apr	Australia	St John's	West Indies beat Australia by an innings & 36 Runs	178	–	0-7	0
28 Apr	Australia	Kingston	West Indies beat Australia by 10 Wickets	2	–	0	0-4
14 June	England	Edgbaston	West Indies beat England by an innings & 180 Runs	117	–	0	0
28 June	England	Lord's	West Indies beat England by 9 Wickets	72	–	0	0
12 July	England	Headingley	West Indies beat England by 8 Wickets	15	22*	0	0
26 July	England	Old Trafford	West Indies beat England by an innings & 64 Runs	1	–	0	0-2
09 Aug	England	The Oval	West Indies beat England by 172 Runs	8	15	0	0

| | | | | Batting | | Bowling | |
Date	Opposition	Venue	Result	1st Inns	2nd Inns	1st Inns	2nd Inns
1984 *cont.*							
09 Nov	Australia	Perth	West Indies beat Australia by an innings & 112 Runs	10	–	0	0-4
23 Nov	Australia	Brisbane	West Indies beat Australia by 8 Wickets	6	3*	0	0-1
07 Dec	Australia	Adelaide	West Indies beat Australia by 191 Runs	0	42	0	0
22 Dec	Australia	Melbourne	West Indies vs Australia – No Result	208	0	0-9	1-7
30 Dec	Australia	Sydney	Australia beat West Indies by an innings & 55 Runs	15	58	0-11	0
1985							
29 Mar	New Zealand	Port of Spain	West Indies vs New Zealand – No Result	57	78	0-7	0-1
06 Apr	New Zealand	Georgetown	West Indies vs New Zealand – No Result	40	7*	0-22	0
26 Apr	New Zealand	Bridgetown	West Indies beat New Zealand by 10 Wickets	105	–	0	0-25
04 May	New Zealand	Kingston	West Indies beat New Zealand by 10 Wickets	23	–	0	1-34
1986							
21 Feb	England	Kingston	West Indies beat England by 10 Wickets	23	–	0-0	0
07 Mar	England	Port of Spain	West Indies beat England by 7 Wickets	34	–	0	0-7
21 Mar	England	Bridgetown	West Indies beat England by an innings & 30 Runs	51	–	0-9	0-7
03 Apr	England	Port of Spain	West Indies beat England by 10 Wickets	87	–	0	0
11 Apr	England	St John's	West Indies beat England by 240 Runs	26	110*	0-3	0-3
24 Oct	Pakistan	Faisalabad	Pakistan beat West Indies by 186 Runs	33	0	0	0
07 Nov	Pakistan	Lahore	West Indies beat Pakistan by an innings & 10 Runs	44	–	0	1-9
20 Nov	Pakistan	Karachi	West Indies vs Pakistan – No Result	70	28	0	0

Date	Opposition	Venue	Result	Batting 1st Inns	Batting 2nd Inns	Bowling 1st Inns	Bowling 2nd Inns
1987							
20 Feb	New Zealand	Wellington	West Indies vs New Zealand – No Result	24	–	1-32	1-86
27 Feb	New Zealand	Auckland	West Indies beat New Zealand by 10 Wickets	14	0	0	0
12 Mar	New Zealand	Christchurch	New Zealand beat West Indies by 5 Wickets	1	38	0-29	0
25 Nov	India	Delhi	West Indies beat India by 5 Wickets	9	109*	0	0
11 Dec	India	Bombay	West Indies vs India – No Result	37	–	0	0
26 Dec	India	Calcutta	West Indies vs India – No Result	68	–	1-39	0
1988							
11 Jan	India	Madras	India beat West Indies by 255 Runs	68	4	1-36	1-28
14 Apr	Pakistan	Port of Spain	West Indies vs Pakistan – No Result	49	123	0	2-17
22 Apr	Pakistan	Bridgetown	West Indies beat Pakistan by 2 Wickets	67	39	0-19	1-8
02 June	England	Trent Bridge	West Indies vs England – No Result	80	–	0-2	0-26
16 June	England	Lord's	West Indies beat England by 134 Runs	6	72	0	0
30 June	England	Old Trafford	West Indies beat England by an innings & 156 Runs	47	–	0	0
21 July	England	Headingley	West Indies beat England by 10 Wickets	18	–	0	0
04 Aug	England	The Oval	West Indies beat England by 8 Wickets	0	–	0	0
18 Nov	Australia	Brisbane	West Indies beat Australia by 9 Wickets	68	–	0-1	0-26
02 Dec	Australia	Perth	West Indies beat Australia by 169 Runs	146	5	0-43	0
24 Dec	Australia	Melbourne	West Indies beat Australia by 285 Runs	12	63	0	0-12
1989							
26 Jan	Australia	Sydney	Australia beat West Indies by 7 Wickets	11	4	1-68	1-12

Date	Opposition	Venue	Result	Batting 1st Inns	Batting 2nd Inns	Bowling 1st Inns	Bowling 2nd Inns
1989 cont.							
03 Feb	Australia	Adelaide	West Indies vs Australia – No Result	69	68*	0-73	1-64
25 Mar	India	Georgetown	West Indies vs India – No Result	5	–	0-17	0
07 Apr	India	Bridgetown	West Indies beat India by 8 Wickets	1	–	0-18	0-16
15 Apr	India	Port of Spain	West Indies beat India by 217 Runs	19	0	1-28	0-13
28 Apr	India	Kingston	West Indies beat India by 7 Wickets	110	–	0-36	0
1990							
24 Feb	England	Kingston	England beat West Indies by 9 Wickets	21	37	0-22	0
05 Apr	England	Bridgetown	West Indies beat England by 164 Runs	70	12	0-14	0-11
12 Apr	England	St John's	West Indies beat England by an innings & 32 Runs	1	–	0	0
1991							
01 Mar	Australia	Kingston	West Indies vs Australia – No Result	11	52*	0	0
23 Mar	Australia	Georgetown	West Indies beat Australia by 10 Wickets	50	–	0-5	0-13
05 Apr	Australia	Port of Spain	West Indies vs Australia – No Result	2	–	0	0
19 Apr	Australia	Bridgetown	West Indies beat Australia by 343 Runs	32	25	0	0-8
27 Apr	Australia	St John's	Australia beat West Indies by 157 Runs	0	2	0-46	0-29
06 June	England	Headingley	England beat West Indies by 115 Runs	73	3	0	0-5
20 June	England	Lord's	West Indies vs England – No Result	63	–	0	0
04 July	England	Trent Bridge	West Indies beat England by 9 Wickets	80	–	0-1	0
25 July	England	Edgbaston	West Indies beat England by 7 Wickets	22	73*	0	0
08 Aug	England	The Oval	England beat West Indies by 5 Wickets	2	60	0	0

One-Day International Career Breakdown

Date	Opposition	Venue	Result	Batting Runs	Bowling Overs	Runs	Wkts
1975							
07 June	Sri Lanka	Old Trafford	West Indies beat Sri Lanka by 9 Wickets	–	0	0	0
11 June	Pakistan	Edgbaston	West Indies beat Pakistan by 1 Wicket	13	4.0	21	1
14 June	Australia	The Oval	West Indies beat Australia by 7 Wickets	15*	6.0	18	2
18 June	New Zealand	The Oval	West Indies beat New Zealand by 5 Wickets	5	0	0	0
21 June	Australia	Lord's	West Indies beat Australia by 17 Runs	5	0	0	0
20 Dec	Australia	Lord's	Australia beat West Indies by 5 Wickets	74	2.0	10	0
1976							
26 Aug	England	Scarborough	West Indies beat England by 6 Wickets	119*	0	0	0
28 Aug	England	Lord's	West Indies beat England by 36 Runs	97	0	0	0
31 Aug	England	Edgbaston	West Indies beat England by 50 Runs	0	1.0	4	1
1977							
16 Mar	Pakistan	Berbice	West Indies beat Pakistan by 4 Wickets	20	0	0	0
1978							
22 Feb	Australia	St John's	West Indies beat Australia by Faster scoring rate	9	1.0	12	0
1979							
09 June	India	Edgbaston	West Indies beat India by 9 Wickets	28*	0	0	0
16 June	New Zealand	Trent Bridge	West Indies beat New Zealand by 32 Runs	9	0	0	0
20 June	Pakistan	The Oval	West Indies beat Pakistan by 43 Runs	42	8.0	52	3

Date	Opposition	Venue	Result	Batting Runs	Bowling Overs	Runs	Wkts
1979 cont.							
23 June	England	Lord's	West Indies beat England by 92 Runs	138*	10.0	35	0
27 Nov	Australia	Sydney	Australia beat West Indies by 5 Wickets	9	10.0	47	2
09 Dec	Australia	Melbourne	West Indies beat Australia by 80 Runs	153*	0	0	0
21 Dec	Australia	Sydney	Australia beat West Indies by 7 Runs	62	8.0	35	1
23 Dec	England	Brisbane	West Indies beat England by 9 Wickets	85*	10.0	44	0
1980							
16 Jan	England	Adelaide	West Indies beat England by 107 Runs	88	7.0	46	0
20 Jan	England	Melbourne	West Indies beat England by 2 Runs	23	6.0	34	0
22 Jan	England	Sydney	West Indies beat England by 8 Wickets	65	3.0	19	0
28 May	England	Headingley	West Indies beat England by 24 Runs	7	7.0	50	1
30 May	England	Lord's	England beat West Indies by 3 Wickets	26	5.0	28	0
19 Dec	Pakistan	Lahore	West Indies beat Pakistan by 7 Runs	0	3.0	18	0
21 Nov	Pakistan	Karachi	West Indies beat Pakistan by 4 Wickets	36	8.0	24	2
05 Dec	Pakistan	Sialkot	West Indies beat Pakistan by 7 Wickets	83	8.0	53	2
1981							
26 Feb	England	Berbice	West Indies beat England by 6 Wickets	3	10.0	26	1
21 Nov	Pakistan	Melbourne	West Indies beat Pakistan by 18 Runs	17	10.0	52	0
24 Nov	Australia	Sydney	Australia beat West Indies by 7 Wickets	47	0	0	0
05 Dec	Pakistan	Adelaide	Pakistan beat West Indies by 8 Runs	9	10.0	35	1
19 Dec	Pakistan	Perth	West Indies beat Pakistan by 7 Wickets	8	10.0	52	3

Date	Opposition	Venue	Result	Batting Runs	Bowling Overs	Runs	Wkts
1981 cont.							
20 Dec	Australia	Perth	West Indies beat Australia by 8 Wickets	72*	10.0	43	1
1982							
10 Jan	Australia	Melbourne	West Indies beat Australia by 5 Wickets	32	10.0	31	0
12 Jan	Pakistan	Sydney	West Indies beat Pakistan by 7 Wickets	41	10.0	41	0
16 Jan	Pakistan	Brisbane	West Indies beat Pakistan by 1 Wicket	0	10.0	52	1
17 Jan	Australia	Brisbane	West Indies beat Australia by 5 Wickets	34	7.0	36	2
19 Jan	Australia	Sydney	Australia beat West Indies by Faster scoring rate	64	0	0	0
23 Jan	Australia	Melbourne	West Indies beat Australia by 86 Runs	78	5.0	29	1
24 Jan	Australia	Melbourne	West Indies beat Australia by 128 Runs	60	0	0	0
26 Jan	Australia	Sydney	Australia beat West Indies by 46 Runs	4	0	0	0
27 Jan	Australia	Sydney	West Indies beat Australia by 18 Runs	70	10.0	48	2
1983							
09 Mar	India	Port of Spain	West Indies beat India by 52 Runs	32	0	0	0
29 Mar	India	Berbice	India beat West Indies by 27 Runs	64	6.0	44	1
07 Apr	India	St George's	West Indies beat India by 7 Wickets	28	0	0	0
09 June	India	Old Trafford	India beat West Indies by 34 Runs	17	2.0	13	0
11 June	Australia	Headingley	West Indies beat Australia by 101 Runs	7	0	0	0
13 June	Zimbabwe	Worcester	West Indies beat Zimbabwe by 8 Wickets	16	4.0	13	0
15 June	India	The Oval	West Indies beat India by 66 Runs	119	0	0	0
18 June	Australia	Lord's	West Indies beat Australia by 7 Wickets	95*	0	0	0

Date	Opposition	Venue	Result	Batting Runs	Bowling Overs	Runs	Wkts
1983 cont.							
20 June	Zimbabwe	Edgbaston	West Indies beat Zimbabwe by 10 Wickets	–	12.0	41	3
22 June	Pakistan	The Oval	West Indies beat Pakistan by 8 Wickets	80*	5.0	18	0
25 June	India	Lord's	India beat West Indies by 43 Runs	33	1.0	8	0
13 Oct	India	Srinagar	West Indies beat India by Faster scoring rate	–	0	0	0
09 Nov	India	Baroda	West Indies beat India by 4 Wickets	18	0	0	0
01 Dec	India	Indore	West Indies beat India by 8 Wickets	49*	0	0	0
07 Dec	India	Jamshedpur	West Indies beat India by 104 Runs	149	1.0	8	0
17 Dec	India	Gauhati	West Indies beat India by 6 Wickets	23	8.0	33	2
1984							
08 Jan	Australia	Melbourne	West Indies beat Australia by 27 Runs	53	6.0	24	1
12 Jan	Pakistan	Melbourne	Pakistan beat West Indies by 97 Runs	7	6.0	26	0
14 Jan	Pakistan	Brisbane	West Indies beat Pakistan by 5 Wickets	37	10.0	37	2
17 Jan	Australia	Sydney	West Indies beat Australia by 28 Runs	19	10.0	41	1
19 Jan	Pakistan	Sydney	West Indies beat Pakistan by 5 Wickets	2	5.0	24	0
22 Jan	Australia	Melbourne	West Indies beat Australia by 26 Runs	106	10.0	51	2
28 Jan	Pakistan	Adelaide	West Indies beat Pakistan by 1 Wicket	18	6.0	30	0
29 Jan	Australia	Adelaide	West Indies beat Australia by 6 Wickets	0	10.0	28	2
04 Feb	Pakistan	Perth	West Indies beat Pakistan by 7 Wickets	40	5.0	24	0
05 Feb	Australia	Perth	Australia beat West Indies by 14 Runs	7	10.0	47	1
08 Feb	Australia	Sydney	West Indies beat Australia by 9 Wickets	–	5.0	29	0

| | | | | Batting | Bowling | | |
Date	Opposition	Venue	Result	Runs	Overs	Runs	Wkts
1984 *cont.*							
11 Feb	Australia	Melbourne	West Indies vs Australia – Tie	59	3.0	26	0
29 Feb	Australia	Berbice	West Indies beat Australia by 8 Wickets	4*	10.0	38	1
14 Mar	Australia	Port of Spain	Australia beat West Indies by 4 Wickets	67	0	0	0
26 Apr	Australia	Kingston	West Indies beat Australia by 9 Wickets	–	7.0	25	0
31 May	England	Old Trafford	West Indies beat England by 104 Runs	189*	11.0	45	2
02 June	England	Trent Bridge	England beat West Indies by 3 Wickets	3	5.0	23	0
04 June	England	Lord's	West Indies beat England by 8 Wickets	84*	0	0	0
1985							
06 Jan	Australia	Melbourne	West Indies beat Australia by 7 Wickets	47	10.0	37	0
10 Jan	Sri Lanka	Hobart	West Indies beat Sri Lanka by 8 Wickets	–	10.0	47	2
12 Jan	Sri Lanka	Brisbane	West Indies beat Sri Lanka by 90 Runs	98	10.0	45	2
13 Jan	Australia	Brisbane	West Indies beat Australia by 5 Wickets	49	10.0	38	3
15 Jan	Australia	Sydney	West Indies beat Australia by 5 Wickets	103*	10.0	41	1
17 Jan	Sri Lanka	Sydney	West Indies beat Sri Lanka by 65 Runs	30	0	0	0
20 Jan	Australia	Melbourne	West Indies beat Australia by 65 Runs	74	10.0	43	2
26 Jan	Sri Lanka	Adelaide	West Indies beat Sri Lanka by 8 Wickets	–	10.0	45	0
27 Jan	Australia	Adelaide	West Indies beat Australia by 6 Wickets	51	10.0	39	0
02 Feb	Sri Lanka	Perth	West Indies beat Sri Lanka by 82 Runs	46	10.0	47	2
06 Feb	Australia	Sydney	Australia beat West Indies by 26 Runs	68	10.0	58	0
10 Feb	Australia	Melbourne	West Indies beat Australia by 4 Wickets	9	10.0	51	0

Date	Opposition	Venue	Result	Batting Runs	Bowling Overs	Runs	Wkts
1985 *cont.*							
12 Feb	Australia	Sydney	West Indies beat Australia by 7 Wickets	76	10.0	52	1
21 Feb	New Zealand	Sydney	West Indies vs New Zealand – No Result	–	0	0	0
27 Feb	Sri Lanka	Melbourne	West Indies beat Sri Lanka by 8 Wickets	12	9.0	27	3
06 Mar	Pakistan	Melbourne	Pakistan beat West Indies by 7 Wickets	1	4.0	14	0
09 Mar	New Zealand	Sydney	West Indies beat New Zealand by 6 Wickets	51	0	0	0
20 Mar	New Zealand	St John's	West Indies beat New Zealand by 23 Runs	70	0	0	0
27 Mar	New Zealand	Port of Spain	West Indies beat New Zealand by 6 Wickets	27	0	0	0
14 Apr	New Zealand	Berbice	West Indies beat New Zealand by 130 Runs	51	10.0	23	0
17 Apr	New Zealand	Port of Spain	West Indies beat New Zealand by 10 Wickets	–	8.0	20	1
23 Apr	New Zealand	Bridgetown	West Indies beat New Zealand by 112 Runs	33*	8.0	31	0
15 Nov	Pakistan	Sharjah	West Indies beat Pakistan by 7 Wickets	51	6.0	25	0
22 Nov	India	Sharjah	West Indies beat India by 8 Wickets	24*	0	0	0
27 Nov	Pakistan	Gujranwala	West Indies beat Pakistan by 8 Wickets	80*	2.0	16	0
29 Nov	Pakistan	Lahore	Pakistan beat West Indies by 6 Wickets	53	0	0	0
02 Dec	Pakistan	Peshawar	West Indies beat Pakistan by 40 Runs	66	0	0	0
04 Dec	Pakistan	Rawalpindi	Pakistan beat West Indies by 5 Wickets	21	2.0	6	1
06 Dec	Pakistan	Karachi	West Indies beat Pakistan by 8 Wickets	40*	2.0	9	0
1986							
18 Feb	England	Kingston	West Indies beat England by 6 Wickets	–	0	0	0
04 Mar	England	Port of Spain	England beat West Indies by 5 Wickets	82	0	0	0

Date	Opposition	Venue	Result	Batting Runs	Bowling Overs	Runs	Wkts
1986 *cont.*							
19 Mar	England	Bridgetown	West Indies beat England by 135 Runs	62	0	0	0
31 Mar	England	Port of Spain	West Indies beat England by 8 Wickets	50*	0	0	0
17 Oct	Pakistan	Peshawar	West Indies beat Pakistan by 4 Wickets	7	0	0	0
04 Nov	Pakistan	Gujranwala	West Indies beat Pakistan by Faster scoring rate	17	0	0	0
14 Nov	Pakistan	Sialkot	West Indies beat Pakistan by 4 Wickets	0	0	0	0
17 Nov	Pakistan	Multan	West Indies beat Pakistan by 89 Runs	4	1.0	3	0
18 Nov	Pakistan	Hyderabad	Pakistan beat West Indies by 11 Runs	0	9.0	24	1
28 Nov	Pakistan	Sharjah	West Indies beat Pakistan by 9 Wickets	–	0	0	0
30 Nov	India	Sharjah	West Indies beat India by 33 Runs	62	0	0	0
03 Dec	Sri Lanka	Sharjah	West Indies beat Sri Lanka by 193 Runs	39	0	0	0
30 Dec	Pakistan	Perth	Pakistan beat West Indies by 34 Runs	10	0	0	0
1987							
03 Jan	England	Perth	England beat West Indies by 19 Runs	45	1.0	5	0
04 Jan	Australia	Perth	West Indies beat Australia by 164 Runs	13	0	0	0
17 Jan	England	Brisbane	England beat West Indies by 6 Wickets	0	10.0	27	1
20 Jan	Australia	Melbourne	West Indies beat Australia by 7 Wickets	–	2.0	7	0
24 Jan	England	Adelaide	England beat West Indies by 89 Runs	43	3.0	21	1
25 Jan	Australia	Adelaide	West Indies beat Australia by 16 Runs	69	0	0	0
28 Jan	Australia	Sydney	Australia beat West Indies by 36 Runs	70	0	0	0
30 Jan	England	Melbourne	West Indies beat England by 6 Wickets	58	6.3	16	0

| | | | | Batting | Bowling | | |
Date	Opposition	Venue	Result	Runs	Overs	Runs	Wkts
1987 cont.							
03 Feb	England	Devonport	England beat West Indies by 29 Runs	1	0	0	0
06 Feb	Australia	Sydney	Australia beat West Indies by 2 Wickets	25	7.0	29	3
18 Mar	New Zealand	Dunedin	West Indies beat New Zealand by 95 Runs	119	10.0	41	5
22 Mar	New Zealand	Auckland	West Indies beat New Zealand by 6 Wickets	14*	10.0	34	3
29 Mar	New Zealand	Christchurch	West Indies beat New Zealand by 10 Wickets	–	8.0	37	0
09 Oct	England	Gujranwala	England beat West Indies by 2 Wickets	27	0	0	0
13 Oct	Sri Lanka	Karachi	West Indies beat Sri Lanka by 191 Runs	181	8.0	22	0
16 Oct	Pakistan	Lahore	Pakistan beat West Indies by 1 Wicket	51	2.0	10	0
21 Oct	Sri Lanka	Kanpur	West Indies beat Sri Lanka by 25 Runs	14	3.0	17	0
26 Oct	England	Jaipur	England beat West Indies by 34 Runs	51	8.0	32	1
30 Oct	Pakistan	Karachi	West Indies beat Pakistan by 28 Runs	67	10.0	45	0
08 Dec	India	Nagpur	West Indies beat India by 10 Runs	1	9.0	39	1
23 Dec	India	Gauhati	West Indies beat India by 52 Runs	41	8.0	37	1
1988							
02 Jan	India	Calcutta	India beat West Indies by 56 Runs	3	9.0	48	2
05 Jan	India	Rajkot	West Indies beat India by 6 Wickets	110*	8.0	42	3
07 Jan	India	Ahmedabad	West Indies beat India by 2 Runs	17	10.0	43	1
19 Jan	India	Faridabad	West Indies beat India by 4 Wickets	9	8.0	31	0
22 Jan	India	Gwalior	West Indies beat India by 73 Runs	33	9.0	34	2
25 Jan	India	Trivandrum	West Indies beat India by 9 Wickets	–	8.0	40	2

Date	Opposition	Venue	Result	Batting Runs	Bowling Overs	Runs	Wkts
1988 *cont.*							
12 Mar	Pakistan	Kingston	West Indies beat Pakistan by 47 Runs	15	5.0	30	0
19 May	England	Edgbaston	England beat West Indies by 6 Wickets	13	7.0	29	0
21 May	England	Headingley	England beat West Indies by 47 Runs	31	8.0	33	0
23 May	England	Lord's	England beat West Indies by 7 Wickets	9	0	0	0
10 Dec	Pakistan	Adelaide	West Indies beat Pakistan by 89 Runs	1	9.0	43	0
13 Dec	Australia	Sydney	West Indies beat Australia by 1 Run	12	10.0	46	0
15 Dec	Australia	Melbourne	West Indies beat Australia by 34 Runs	58	10.0	55	1
17 Dec	Pakistan	Hobart	West Indies beat Pakistan by 17 Runs	10	6.0	48	2
1989							
01 Jan	Pakistan	Perth	West Indies beat Pakistan by 7 Wickets	–	5.0	21	0
05 Jan	Australia	Melbourne	Australia beat West Indies by 8 Runs	48	5.0	29	1
07 Jan	Pakistan	Brisbane	Pakistan beat West Indies by 55 Runs	18	5.0	21	0
12 Jan	Australia	Sydney	Australia beat West Indies by 61 Runs	3	1.0	6	0
14 Jan	Australia	Melbourne	Australia beat West Indies by 2 Runs	14	10.0	48	0
16 Jan	Australia	Sydney	West Indies beat Australia by 92 Runs	53	0	0	0
18 Jan	Australia	Sydney	West Indies beat Australia by Faster scoring rate	60*	3.0	12	1
07 Mar	India	Bridgetown	West Indies beat India by 50 Runs	40	10.0	47	3
09 Mar	India	Port of Spain	West Indies beat India by 6 Wickets	11*	10.0	42	4
11 Mar	India	Port of Spain	West Indies beat India by 6 Wickets	3	10.0	47	2
18 Mar	India	St John's	West Indies beat India by 8 Wickets	–	10.0	48	1

Date	Opposition	Venue	Result	Batting Runs	Bowling Overs	Runs	Wkts
1989 *cont.*							
21 Mar	India	Georgetown	West Indies beat India by 101 Runs	–	10.0	41	3
13 Oct	India	Sharjah	West Indies beat India by 5 Wickets	34	10.0	44	2
14 Oct	Pakistan	Sharjah	Pakistan beat West Indies by 11 Runs	46	10.0	48	1
16 Oct	India	Sharjah	India beat West Indies by 37 Runs	5	10.0	40	0
19 Oct	Sri Lanka	Rajkot	Sri Lanka beat West Indies by 4 Wickets	24	6.0	23	1
21 Oct	Australia	Madras	Australia beat West Indies by 99 Runs	5	6.0	36	0
23 Oct	India	Delhi	West Indies beat India by 20 Runs	44	9.4	41	6
25 Oct	Pakistan	Jullundur	West Indies beat Pakistan by 6 Wickets	47*	7.0	38	0
27 Oct	England	Gwalior	West Indies beat England by 26 Runs	16	5.0	44	0
30 Oct	India	Bombay	West Indies beat India by 8 Wickets	–	4.0	21	0
01 Nov	Pakistan	Calcutta	Pakistan beat West Indies by 4 Wickets	21	6.5	42	0
1990							
14 Feb	England	Port of Spain	West Indies vs England – No Result	32	0	0	0
17 Feb	England	Port of Spain	West Indies vs England – No Result	–	0	0	0
03 Mar	England	Kingston	West Indies beat England by 3 Wickets	25	9.0	32	0
07 Mar	England	Georgetown	West Indies beat England by 6 Wickets	2	0	0	0
1991							
26 Feb	Australia	Kingston	Australia beat West Indies by 35 Runs	18	8.0	37	0
09 Mar	Australia	Port of Spain	Australia beat West Indies by 45 Runs	27	1.0	4	0
10 Mar	Australia	Port of Spain	West Indies beat Australia by Faster scoring rate	–	0	0	0

Date	Opposition	Venue	Result	Batting Runs	Bowling Overs	Runs	Wkts
1991 *cont.*							
13 Mar	Australia	Bridgetown	Australia beat West Indies by 37 Runs	20	4.0	29	0
20 Mar	Australia	Georgetown	Australia beat West Indies by 6 Wickets	10	4.0	14	0
23 May	England	Edgbaston	England beat West Indies by 1 Wicket	30	0	0	0
25 May	England	Old Trafford	England beat West Indies by 9 Runs	78	0	0	0
27 May	England	Lord's	England beat West Indies by 7 Wickets	37	0	0	0

Career Summaries

TEST RECORD

Batting

M	I	NO	Runs	HS	Ave	100	50	Ct	St
121	182	12	8540	291	50.23	24	45	122	–

Bowling

Balls	M	R	W	Ave	Best	5w	10w	SR	Econ
5170	203	1964	32	61.37	2-17	–	–	161.5	2.27

ONE-DAY INTERNATIONAL RECORD

Batting

M	I	NO	Runs	HS	Ave	100	50	Ct	St
187	167	24	6721	189*	47.00	11	45	101	–

Bowling

Balls	M	R	W	Ave	Best	5w	SR	Econ
5644	26	4228	118	35.83	6-41	2	47.8	4.49

SOMERSET RECORD

Batting

	Career	M	I	NO	Runs	HS	Ave	50	100	Ct
First Class cricket	1974–86	182	300	17	14275	322	50.95	56	46	160
Gillette/NatWest Trophy	1974–86	34	34	4	1410	139*	47.00	7	4	16
Benson & Hedges	1974–86	48	44	6	1499	132*	39.44	10	1	21
John Player League/ Refuge Assurance League	1974–86	158	153	17	5235	126*	38.49	35	7	70

Bowling

	Career	Balls	M	R	W	Ave	Best	5w
First Class cricket	1974–86	8562	352	4013	89	45.25	4-36	–
Gillette/NatWest Trophy	1974–86	967	–	592	20	29.6	3-15	–
Benson & Hedges	1974–86	712	–	425	12	35.41	3-38	–
John Player League/ Refuge Assurance League	1974–86	2741	–	2189	84	26.06	6-24	1

GLAMORGAN RECORD

Batting

	Career	M	I	NO	Runs	HS	Ave	100	50	Ct
First Class cricket	1990–93	49	83	11	3382	224*	46.97	10	14	43
Sunday League	1990–93	40	38	7	1244	109	40.13	1	8	18
Benson & Hedges	1990–93	10	10	0	192	48	19.20	–	–	6
NatWest Trophy	1990–93	10	10	3	485	162*	69.29	1	2	3

Bowling

	Career	Balls	M	R	W	Ave
First Class cricket	1990–93	1398	46	695	9	77.33
Sunday League	1990–93	942	5	809	37	21.86
Benson & Hedges	1990–93	438	6	263	9	29.22
NatWest Trophy	1990–93	482	4	343	7	49.00

QUEENSLAND RECORD

Batting

	Career	M	I	NO	Runs	HS	Ave	100	50	Ct
Sheffield Shield	1976–7	4	6	0	181	73	30.16	–	2	2

Index